GRANNY

THE STORY OF JOHN GLOVER

KILLER

GRANNY

THE STORY OF JOHN GLOVER

KILLER

Les Kennedy and Mark Whittaker

Angus&Robertson

An imprint of HarperCollins*Publishers*

To our parents Alice and Bill Whittaker and Merle and John Kennedy for keeping us out of trouble, and for their encouragement in life and sustenance.

To my wife Trish for her love, patience and support, and daughter Isabella for making us aware of how precious life is — Leslie.

It is with great appreciation and gratitude that the authors thank the following: members of the NSW Northern Region Major Crime Squad and the "Granny Killer" task force, especially Dennis O'Toole and Paul Mayger; Dawn; Anthony Schofield the computer whizz for keeping our machines talking; the staff of the Sydney News Limited library, in particular Lurline Campbell, John Knight and Clyde Powell; the *Wolverhampton Express and Star*, in particular Nicky Brigg and Sarah-Jane Smith; the archives staff of the Wolverhampton City and New South Wales Libraries; Joy Dobbs and Phil Booth at the *Lincolnshire Echo*; John Newnham, Tim Stott, Miranda Devine, Steve Gibbs, Brad Forest, Mal Holland, Mark Jones, Lisa Green, Marcus Casey, Graham and Mary Zanelli, Jack Darmody, the late Harold Cumming, Bridget Donovan, Justine O'Donnell and Harry Azidis.

The authors wish to thank the following photographers for providing the photographs reproduced in this book: Ross Schultz, Geoff Henderson, Barry McKinnon, Ian Gillespie, Andrew Darby, Anthony Moran, Jane Russell, Warwick Lawson, Robert Doran, Anthony Weate, Paul Hutton and Bob Finlayson.

AN ANGUS & ROBERTSON BOOK
An imprint of HarperCollinsPublishers

First published in Australia in 1992 by
CollinsAngus&Robertson Publishers Pty Limited (ACN 009 913 517)
A division of HarperCollins Publishers (Australia) Pty Limited
25–31 Ryde Road, Pymble NSW 2073, Australia

HarperCollinsPublishers (New Zealand) Limited
31 View Road, Glenfield, Auckland 10, New Zealand

HarperCollinsPublishers Limited
77–85 Fulham Palace Road, London W6 8JB, United Kingdom

Copyright © Les Kennedy and Mark Whittaker 1992

National Library of Australia
Cataloguing-in-Publication data:

Kennedy, Leslie, 1958–   .
Granny killer.

ISBN 0 207 17766 X.

1. Glover, John Wayne. 2. Murderers — New South Wales — Sydney —
Biography. 3. Serial murders — New South Wales — Sydney — Biography.
I. Whittaker, Mark. II. Title.

364.1523

Cover concept by Justine O'Donnell
Printed in Australia by Griffin Paperbacks

5 4 3 2 1
96 95 94 93 92

CONTENTS

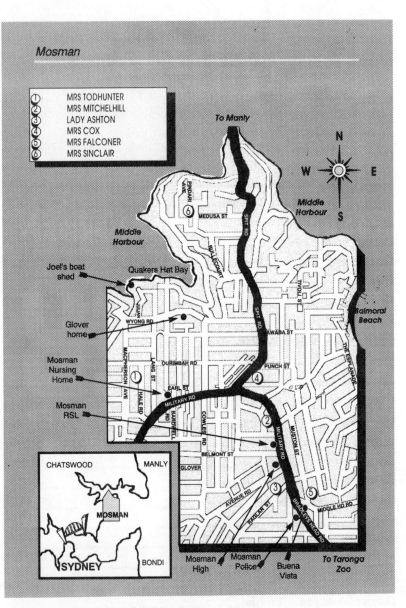

Map showing the locations of John Glover's assaults
and landmarks in the Mosman area.

CHAPTER ONE

MEETINGS

The radio alarm blares and the talkback DJ says it's half past the hour, time for sleepyheads to be up and about on this grey autumn Monday.

Normally he is the first out of bed and into the shower but today John Glover is slow. The problem has not gone away — as though it ever would. But he feels good.

Each morning for the last year, maybe longer, has thrown up the same two questions but this morning he tells himself he has the answer. There is a calm about him.

Yesterday, storms raged across Sydney, ripping roofs off nearby houses and causing flooding in the far-off western suburbs. He could not see across the street for the rain. But as he looks out the window now, it is serene and he can see for miles.

He rolls his rotund figure out of bed and towards the shower. He is later than usual. That doesn't matter, he's in no rush today.

It's been difficult with the kids lately. Since the operation and his depression they seem to be drifting away. What does it matter, he thinks, they'll have an answer soon enough.

Out of the shower, John Glover, family man and sales rep, lingers in front of the bathroom mirror, perhaps a second too long. The comb arranges each white hair into its place. He is proud of his looks to which he finds women are still attracted, despite his 57 years and slowly widening paunch.

He pulls on his black and white striped shirt, his grey trousers and black shoes as he gets his mind on to the busy day ahead. Then he goes to the phone.

"Morris, John here. Listen, I won't be able to make it in today — I've had some problems and I've got to see a solicitor for some legal advice."

Morris Grant, his boss at Four'N Twenty Pies, acquiesces. What can he do? John has been having all these troubles. For all he knows, it could be divorce on the cards. It would not surprise anybody, the way John's been acting.

John Glover has a quick bite of breakfast before he puts on his tie. The girls leave and he casually wishes them well.

"Joan, John. What would you say to a bite of lunch? I've taken the day off. Maybe a movie or something. Whatever you say."

Joan Sinclair, 61-year-old grandmother and divorcée, agrees. She is a bit hesitant, though.

She had told him months earlier that it was over, but then, she has no plans and this sounds rather innocent. She knows about John's troubles too and doesn't want to upset him.

"Just as long as I'm back by three to pick up Adam and Sam from school," she tells him. She is minding her two grandsons.

That's it then. He is all set. He goes out to the garden shed, gets his claw hammer and puts it into his briefcase.

9.10 a.m.: John Glover eases his immaculately polished blue Ford station wagon out of the garage at Wyong Road, Mosman. The normally blue-green water of the harbour below is unusually brown, the autumn sky a cold grey. Mosman is out of kilter this day, as it has been throughout the past year.

As John Glover turns out of the street, the waters of Quakers Hat Bay lie below. The hammer is in the briefcase on the passenger seat beside him and he feels strangely calm.

He can never get over how calm he does feel; how nonchalant he can be at this point. Even here at the end.

The blue station wagon proceeds up the hill towards the shops. John Glover's driving is anything but calm. His direction is wobbly, his pace unsteady.

His eyes, hidden behind sunglasses, are turning from side to side, perusing the surrounds. Maybe he will not have to see Joan after all. The car turns and turns again, sometimes slowing to a crawl, then picking up to run with the flow on Military Road, the busy thoroughfare which shatters the peace of Mosman.

The Ford veers right at Spit Junction. It follows Military Road south, through areas where Mosman is split again and again by the streets and shady avenues that follow ridges out on to the headlands reaching into Sydney Harbour.

John Glover just dawdles around these backwaters, always looking but thinking more, trance-like.

Joan is not expecting him until 11.30 but what's the point in delaying things any more? He is not going to find anyone else at this time. He heads back to Spit Junction where Military Road veers left into Spit Road, and where 20 years earlier John Glover had been impressed by the understated shops which quietly managed to convey the real opulence of his new domain.

He pulls up at the Liquorland and dashes in to buy a bottle of Scotch whiskey. Returning to the car he opens the briefcase and puts the bottle wrapped in its yellow and blue Liquorland paper beside the hammer.

10.10 a.m.: John Glover leaves Mosman and heads down Spit Road to Beauty Point, a quiet little suburb on the north side of the Mosman peninsula. He turns into Medusa Street, following it to the intersection with Pindari Avenue, where he parks the car.

It is 10.26 a.m. He gets out of the car carrying the black leather attaché case. He combs his hair and adjusts his tie then walks through the gate to Mrs Sinclair's house and closes it behind him.

John Glover and Joan Sinclair had met 18 months previously at the Mosman Returned Serviceman's Club. He gave her a lift home one night.

Of the relationship, he said: "We were just bloody good friends. A bit of sex play and some initial attempts at sex but we just gave up. The friendship remained. She liked to drink, she liked to have lunch, she liked to go to the club and play machines."

Joan Sinclair comes to the door in a slip.

"Sorry I'm early, I had to get out of the house," John Glover explains.

She ushers him in. He puts the briefcase down by the phone and they chat for a while.

"Hang on while I get changed," she tells him. She goes into her room and they talk through the double doors about maybe having lunch at home as she pulls on a black and white striped dress and comfortable white slip-on shoes.

"Do you mind if I make a call?" he asks, picking up the phone and eyeing the briefcase. He hits a few buttons at random. The line is silent but he starts talking into it. Joan goes into the back of the house and calls out for him to come down when he's finished.

He puts the phone down and opens the briefcase, withdrawing the hammer.

"Come and have a look at the leak in this ceiling — what do you think I should do?"

John Glover follows her down a small flight of stairs as she points to the water stains above.

He is right behind her, the hammer in his hand. She turns and John turns with her as she leads the way back up the steps and around into a living room area. He raises the hammer to shoulder height and brings it down on her head.

She falls. He strikes her again as she lies on a mat, smashing her skull between the weight of the hammer and the hardness of the floor. Then he strikes again, the impact sending blood flying out in a spray to all corners of the room, splattering the television set and the walls. He strikes again and again.

Blood is streaming from a massive wound to the back and side of Joan Sinclair's head as Glover pulls her dress up and removes her pink panties (he would later say, "for no sexual reason") and her pantyhose.

He goes to her bedroom and finds another pair of pantyhose, then ties the two pairs together with a basic knot and loops the ligature around her neck three times, pulling it tight and strangling her.

Mrs Sinclair's shattered body is dragged from the room, leaving a smeared trail of blood the length of the floor. Her genitals are damaged but Glover would deny sexually interfering with her.

He leaves her body face down on the landing leading to the back door where the leak had been. One leg is out to the side, pushing her naked buttocks into the air. It is the ultimate humiliation in death. Whoever finds her will see her for the last time looking like this.

Glover goes to the bathroom and finds four towels which he wraps around her head. He turns over the bloodied mat against which the hammer has just crushed her head. It is as though he is trying to cover the blood to hide from his own unspeakable actions.

He is hiding from the fact he has killed Joan and not his mother, as he might have wished.

Glover checks through Joan's handbag to see what is there. It is almost habit really. He knows he is not going to take anything. The second part of the plan will see to that.

He re-enters the bedroom and begins to undress, first removing his black shoes and dark blue socks. They are discarded in an orderly fashion on the pink carpet near her bed. He takes off his trousers and places them neatly across the end of the bed, its white quilt cover decorated with pink roses and poppies.

He returns to the body and continues stripping. First his tie and shirt, then his blue underpants. They are dropped on the floor near the body. He turns and walks towards the bathroom.

The bath taps are turned on — hot — and as the steam begins to rise he starts rummaging through the bathroom cabinet, pulling out bottles of pills with names he does not understand except for the Tryptanol. That is what he has been taking for his depression. The bottle of Scotch is pulled from the briefcase and he takes a hearty swill as he searches the cabinet for more pills.

A small collection of plastic bottles is building in front of him on the sink, next to his silver digital watch. He opens one bottle, takes a small handful of pills and puts them in his mouth, flushing the lot down with whiskey. He repeats the process — Panamax, Panadol, Vitaplex, brown pills, white pills — getting more cavalier in his selection. The handfuls are getting bigger and the swills longer.

With a few pills still rattling inside the bottles, he decides he has had enough. His head spinning, he sees a razor blade. He picks it up and makes a few token slashes at his left wrist. The bottle of Scotch is placed beside the tub as he lowers himself tentatively into the steaming bath. The room swims around him as he swigs the last of the Scotch and waits to die, fully expecting that the waves of nausea overcoming him are taking him on the final spiral to death.

It is about 11.30 a.m.

Police have the house surrounded.

It had been two years and two days since John Glover got into that bath. He was sitting passively in his white overalls, his back to the wall as he had learned to keep it for the last two years. Families moved in and out of the visitors room at the Long Bay Remand Centre. Tattooed arms lifted children into the air as the neat grey-haired man sat in the corner, an oddity. For a man of 59, his face — despite the added weight under his chin — sported an almost boyish look, made all the more innocent by his striking light greyish blue eyes.

"So what can I do for you now that you've all ganged up on me?" he asked cheerily, first looking at his girlfriend, Dawn, and then at the two journalists seated before him. A few seconds earlier he had shaken their hands in a firm business-like grasp, a habit built up from years of salesmanship. It was a manly grip used as the measure of the person.

He made light of the moment, commenting about the mutton-chop sideburns he had started to cultivate. "I thought they would help hide these," he said, pointing to the broken pink capillaries which had led most people to assume he was an alcoholic. Without being asked, he proffered that the pinkness was caused by his shaving and he demonstrated how it matched the line of his facial hair. He has always bitterly denied being a heavy drinker.

He chatted and charmed his way along without giving much away. He constantly joked and punned. "What happened to the Knight of the Round Table who went into the desert? He got his camel 'ot. Boom boom! I'm sorry, I can't help myself." He was having a good time. But it was humour, he explained later, that helped to keep him from going crazy as a prisoner of the Crown.

He was curious about the interest in him and about the idea of a journey back into his past, his English roots.

He was told that his boyhood home was now the site of a retirement village. "I knew I should have stayed in Wolverhampton," he joked.

"Tell us about your early days, John. A lot of people seem to think this whole business began back then ... Were they good times, John?"

John Glover's face lost expression briefly. He was silent and he began to reflect, as if his mind had begun opening doors long locked. He raised his right hand to his chin and cast his eyes to the floor. Tears appeared around his lashes and he began to take little gulps of air, trying to contain his emotions. It was a horribly awkward minute ... Was he angry? Was he putting on a front? Was he about to throw us out? Dawn rose to buy him a soft drink to break the tension. He sipped, composed himself and then answered.

"What has happened has put up a barrier to my past. I can't seem to see back to anything any more. It's like everything has been changed by what happened. It's as though it never happened at all.

"I've got nothing to do in here but think and I think about it every day and every night. I try to think back and say 'well it must have been this' or 'it must have been that'. But I can't say why. I just don't know." His words flowed easily for the next two hours.

Many people have postulated reasons why John Glover did what he did. Almost all the theories take a winding path through a battle with cancer and through a drawn-out war with his mother-in-law, and then back a long way — to Britain, to the council slums of the Midlands and, ultimately, to his mother.

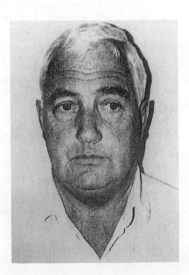

A snapshot of John Glover taken by police in the course of investigating the granny killer attacks.

CHAPTER TWO

BLACK COUNTRY CHILD

John Walter Glover was born as heavy autumn frosts and mists began to envelop England's industrial West Midlands. The infant came into the world by caesarean section at the Victoria Hospital, Lichfield, on 26 November 1932, the first-born of Walter and Freda Glover.

For the 22-year-old mother the delivery was fraught with anxiety, following as it did on two miscarriages. When the long delivery was over, she named the baby John (which meant "gift from God") and "Walter" (for his father).

The two young parents had lived locally all their lives and met over a piano in a pub in the town of Willenhall, once a quaint Staffordshire village situated between Birmingham and Wolverhampton. Like most towns in the West Midlands, Willenhall was swallowed up early in the march of the Industrial Revolution of the 19th century. Massive canal projects crisscrossed the countryside between local coal pits and factories. By the time Walter Glover met Freda Shotton, around 1929, there were 50 foundries within a few kilometres of the town, which was internationally famous for its locks.

Freda and Walter lived in a world dominated by factories belching thick black coal smoke from their chimneys, the soot settling over everything. By night, the sky glowed red from the iron furnaces. By day it was grey and the earth blackened. The area became known as "the Black Country", a name that the locals now use with pride but up until the

Clean Air Act was passed in the 1960s was somewhat less than complimentary.

Freda Shotton was born on 30 September 1910 in nearby Walsall, the daughter of a local postman. A free-spirited girl, she was kicked out of home by her parents at the age of 14. She took what work she could get and was employed variously as a servant girl, a barmaid and a cleaning maid in hotels. She developed a craving for the high life and an ambition to better her lot.

Walter Glover worked at the Chubb lock and safe foundry. He met Freda while he was playing the piano one night in the local pub.

Walter was a rarity: a quiet man of working-class stock, he could play any tune you could name. He only needed to hear it once to bring a room to life with it.

Freda saw in the handsome dark-haired Walter a chance to escape. She recognised his potential and thought that all he needed was her motivation. But Walter lacked ambition; when he was not behind the keyboard he was a docile character.

After work, Walter tickled the ivories at local pubs such as the Green Pig. From time to time Walter and a few musician mates got together and played at parties or functions. He was happy with his lot: happy to play at pub sing-alongs for anyone who would buy him a pint of beer.

The couple's courtship turned to marriage and within two years Johnny was born. When John came into their lives, the couple were living in a modest two-storey terrace opposite the Yale lock factory. The nearest open playing area for young Johnny was a centuries old cemetery rimmed by maple trees, its gravestones covered in moss.

Freda believed Walter had the potential to be a concert pianist, or at least a star of the stage, and badgered him to better himself. She tried to inspire him, tried to convince him that his talents were not mediocre. "Why can't you see we don't have to live like this?" she demanded constantly.

She devised a scheme to put Walter on the path to greatness. Whenever the family budget allowed it, she bought Walter reams of classical sheet music for him to study and practise. He took to them with a natural flair and the tiny tenement was soon filled with the gentle and inspiring music of the masters. At the first polite opportunity, however, "Camp Town Races" and his other favourites would return.

"My father was an incredibly gifted man. He taught me to sing and I believe his natural talent with music has passed on through me to my children," Glover recalled with pride.

For Walter, life was simple, uncomplicated. He could not comprehend Freda's frustrated needling when she returned home from odd jobs that she had taken to earn extra money for the family.

From the outset the marriage of Walter and Freda never had much hope — her craving for a better life would see to that. But it was her inclination towards the bedroom, not necessarily with Walter, which would finally end it.

By 1937, Freda had given birth to the couple's second child, Barry, her first and only natural birth. For a brief period they were happy, but her impatience with Walter saw the relationship deteriorate, with heated and regular arguments over her constant complaint — his lack of both ambition and money.

Some time shortly after Barry's birth, Freda met Wolverhampton businessman Clifford Naylor. He swept her off her feet, showering her with gifts, and they began an affair. He had what she desired — money and a degree of standing in their working-class community.

The affair lasted a few years until Freda walked out on Walter, taking Barry with her and leaving young Johnny, then aged eight, crying by his father's side.

In divorce proceedings, years later in 1941, she accused Walter of infidelity. Freda also cited her wasted expenditure on sheet music and Walter's unwillingness to do anything with his talent as added grounds for divorce. But Freda's accusations of infidelity against her husband were probably lies. She maintained that she came home with the children and found Walter in bed with another woman. She said she packed up the kids, put Barry in his pram and, with John by her side, walked out. John recalls no such incident.

"It was Freda who was caught in bed with another man," says Glover now. "It's a joke that Walter would have an affair. He couldn't. It wasn't in him."

At 43, Mr Naylor was 15 years Freda's senior. From a wealthy family, he was a liquor merchant who operated his business in Exchange Street, Wolverhampton. The cellars were linked into ancient vaults running under the town's old marketplace in the shadow of the medieval St Peter's Cathedral and the old Wolverhampton Police Station. Mr Naylor was the image of a typical merchant of the day — a barrel-chested man, prone to wearing tweed jackets with a gold fob watch and chain tucked into his waistcoat. His manner was full of starch and his values had been firmly set in the old ways. But for all his proprieties, he was not averse to dabbling in the black market.

Freda moved in with Naylor. John would spend time with them but Naylor did not take kindly to young Johnny. He was not of his own blood. Moreover, he was a rebellious child who did not like to see his mother with another man.

"Send him back to his father! Get him out of my sight!" Naylor regularly roared. Freda did his bidding; without a word of protest on behalf of her son, she would send John back to his father or off to stay with relatives. It was a roundabout John stayed on for the next six years.

"He didn't like us kids because we took no notice of what he said. He wasn't our father," said Glover.

Freda's lack of protection for her eldest son hurt him and caused one of the many indelible scars which flaw his memory of her today.

John grew to despise his mother's lifestyle. His descriptions of Freda are fixed in Victorian English. She was a "driven woman" and "no paragon of virtue". She had "fast and low morals". But the words most commonly used by the family to describe her were "survivor" and "opportunist".

He also grew to resent his father for not being more forceful and for his lack of manliness.

After the break-up, John and Walter continued to live in Wood Street while John attended nearby Elm Street Public School. As war broke out across Europe, father and son moved to the village of Wednesfield, eight kilometres from Wolverhampton.

Like many youngsters, Johnny snuck out from time to time to watch the night bombing raids on nearby industrial centres around the cities of Birmingham and Wolverhampton — search lights, flak from anti-aircraft artillery, fires and bomb blasts all illuminating the sky.

"You would hear the air-raid sirens, but we never worried because the Germans were going for targets away from us." One night, however, a German bomber unable to find its target and coming under attack from RAF fighters ditched its bombs over Wednesfield. Johnny was sleeping in the same bed as his father in an upstairs room when they were suddenly showered with flying glass and debris as a series of mighty explosions blasted the house. The earth erupted with successive blasts out in the small backyard gardens which separated the rows of terraces.

Through the window came a round football-sized object. John and Walter looked at it. They were covered in something red ... Blood?

"Ohh cripes!" said Walter, jumping out of bed. "A bloody German's head's been blown straight through the window."

The stick of bombs had exploded clean between the two rows of tenements, destroying the gardens. The head turned out to be a purple pickling cabbage, splattering red juice all over them as it shredded in flight through the window. Walter was a volunteer air-raid warden so he quickly donned his uniform and helmet and rushed out to survey the damage — leaving Johnny sitting in bed, terrified, with the shredded cabbage.

John Glover's first school suffered a hit shortly afterwards but Johnny had already left. He would study at five different schools by the age of 14. He was kept constantly on the move, never going far, but always moving, either with his father or to stay with relatives, or Freda. With Walter he moved to a nearby village, Wednesbury, and later to the austere new council estate called The New Invention at Walsall. It was set in rolling countryside with hedge-lined fields and within a stone's throw of half a dozen pits, both working and disused. But, as the name implied, such estates were still an experiment. This one was without shops and most basic amenities.

By late 1941, as Britain fought for survival, the separation of Freda and Walter Glover was finalised in divorce. Freda married Naylor and the following year bore him a baby daughter, Patricia.

For most families they were hard times: rationing was in force, luxuries scarce and every able-bodied person was under arms or working for the war effort. Johnny did his bit, collecting scraps of foil and milk bottle tops.

For Freda, however, the war years were one big party on the black market. Through her marriage to Mr Naylor, Freda found the life she had always craved — he had access to the sly grog, she had the personality to sell it. Her wardrobe was soon brimming with the latest in fashionable dresses and fur coats.

"Before and during the war my mother was spending 400 pounds a week having the high life, you better believe it," said Glover's half-brother Clifford.

"It was rough for everybody in those days. Freda was a survivor even in the pre-war years when she met Naylor, a total survivor. Freda lived the good life, loved living the life of Riley — they were into using people."

Not long into her new marriage, Freda's new husband lost his left leg, partly as a result of a fit of anger. As Glover recounts: "He had a nasty habit of tying his shoe laces so tightly that it restricted the blood flow to his feet."

One day in a rage he kicked a crate of Scotch and injured his toe. The lack of blood reaching the extremity quickly brought on gangrene and doctors were forced to amputate his left leg.

By 1942 Johnny had moved back in with his mother and Mr Naylor moved them all into a well-furnished five-bedroom house at 28 Lower Villiers Street, Wolverhampton. It was a red brick, two-storey terrace with big bay windows and set in a part of town that has since lost its standing but in 1942 was still modestly well regarded.

Unlike the homes of most of their neighbours who were doing it tough, 28 Lower Villiers Street offered sheer luxury for the time and place. The decor was bright and Freda saw to it that all the bedrooms were full of piped radio music. Whereas every other house in the row of tenements shared a single tap and a couple of toilets between them, number 28 had everything laid on, including an indoor toilet. It was all courtesy of black market profiteering.

"Booze was a big market during the war. You would pay five shillings for a gallon of gin," said Clifford.

"The police used to fill the vehicle up with petrol. Sidney Orphan [with whom Freda was having an affair] was a friend of my father's. He used to supply us with other things and we had a butcher called Tony from London. We never went without a damn thing.

"They lived the high life and they [Freda and friends] loved it."

Graiseley Public School was in those days a tough school where most kids learnt to fight. By his own account John was an above-average student, despite the disruptions to his education by so many moves. Frequently, he says, he topped his class, but the records no longer exist to prove it.

"I had my share of success as a student," he said, referring to his studies as well as the schoolyard pecking order.

"I never picked on other kids, but one day I had no choice but to take on the school bully and I won, not in a physical fight, but verbally.

"I beat him with words, then I was the number one kid after that," he recounts with pride.

Johnny had also learnt a few of his mother's tricks and was bringing in money from his own black market dealings. At the age of 13 he was buying nylon stockings from an Indian dealer at the Wolverhampton markets for two shillings and eight pence and selling them for three pounds. Johnny would dart around stalls and between the livestock, which was still being herded through the streets, to scavenge for empty Scotch bottles, preferably Johnny Walker. He refilled them with a cheaper brand and sold it at a tidy profit. He remains proud of his ability to earn a quid in those hard times and at a tender age. "It worked well: everyone was happy, they had their liquor and we would have a lovely side of beef for dinner. That's all that mattered to me."

That same year he suffered a major trauma when his best friend, Nigel, fell out of a tree and was killed while the pair were trying to steal apples.

Towards the end of the war, John moved back to live with his father who was lodging with Walter's sister, Harriet, at Willenhall. She was a spinster in the Victorian mould, a woman who wore dresses down to her shoes with high-necked collars, her long hair in a high bun. "She had breasts like watermelons, I suppose that must be where I developed my liking for large-breasted women," Glover said.

Aunt Harriet thought the world of young Johnny, the pretty little boy with the angelic face. He studied her as she sat for hours in a rocking chair with a plump cat on her lap, listening to Walter play the piano with a jug of beer beside him. She appeared to have a moustache, but the brown line permanently under her nose was actually a betrayal of her only vice — an addiction to tobacco snuff.

John had joined the church choir and was paid a shilling and sixpence for singing solos. His father would extract some of the money as commission until the source dried up with the breaking of John's voice.

It was early in 1947 when John was given a choice of which parent he would live with. He chose Freda.

Freda welcomed him home with open arms because, at 14, he had the "potential to earn a quid". "She was a survivor — if the means to survive included using you, that was it. But it suited me to be with my mother — a better lifestyle, more money at mum's than dad's."

So Freda pulled him out of school and put him to work, just as she had been put to work at that age. She was forever the opportunist.

"She would look after herself first, second and third, then after that her children. But in those days you had to do what you were told without question. You just had to accept what was happening. I guess it forced me to look after myself, to survive by myself. I had to do that."

At the time he was happy to be out and about earning money and he certainly never questioned the move. But as an adult, he would lament his lack of education, blaming Freda's greed for its termination.

John found work as an electrician's mate. He carried the tools, put up the ladders, made the tea and hoped that he would learn the ropes as he went along.

Freda was pregnant again, this time to a friend of her husband — a tall, handsome captain in the Royal Engineers by the name of Sidney Orphan whose hobby was racing cars. Captain Orphan was also a big player on the black market and had been a key contact for Freda and Mr Naylor.

She gave birth to a baby she called Clifford, her fourth and last child.

Freda's affair with Captain Orphan was a liaison to which, her son Clifford now says, Mr Naylor had given his blessing. "Provided that she was discreet."

Mr Naylor was by then gravely ill and in great pain, drinking Scotch heavily rather than take morphine. He agreed to take the child as his own son; but for Sidney Orphan, the price Freda extracted after the birth was Clifford's education in one of the best of the West Midlands boarding schools.

At first, no one gave a thought to Clifford being the offspring of another man. But as Clifford grew, his parentage became apparent because he looked like none of the relatives from either side.

"The whole family knew what had happened," said John Glover of the affair. "She treated him like an orphan, orphan by name and orphan by nature."

Freda's pregnancy to another man seemed to have disturbed 14-year-old Johnny and his behaviour became erratic. It coincided with his first encounter with the law. A bright lad, he might have made something of the electrician's job but the young Glover could not help himself. After only a few months he was caught lifting property from clients.

He was a "petty crim, flogged this and flogged that, saw opportunity and took it", said half-brother Clifford.

Four months after his fourteenth birthday, John Walter Glover appeared before Wolverhampton Children's Court, charged with stealing. His father had come to court in his best suit to give an undertaking to keep Johnny out of more trouble.

Young Johnny had been summoned before the court charged with stealing property valued at ten pounds from Mrs Clara Alice Chown, the wife of the Reverend J.L. Chown, of 89 Compton Road, Wolverhampton. He was also charged with stealing property from his employers worth four pounds and a date stamp valued at 15 shillings from the Wolverhampton and Midlands Eye Infirmary. John admitted the offences and asked that 13 other cases of theft also be considered at the hearing. "From the beginning of the year this boy has had a mania for stealing other people's property," said Chief Inspector T. Marsh.

"All the property, except for a ring and a brooch belonging to Mrs Chown, had been recovered," said Inspector Marsh.

The case made the afternoon edition of the *Wolverhampton Express and Star* newspaper. The newspaper report stated:

The boy, who was at the time living with his mother, who had remarried after divorce, said that he took the things, which included a vice, to start a workshop. When asked by his employers what he had stolen he returned the property.

Magistrate Grimley placed John Walter Glover on one year's probation on the first summons and adjourned the remaining charges for six months.

Six months later Johnny was placed on a bond after being ordered to pay 35 pounds compensation and his father Walter had given an undertaking that he would be of good behaviour.

It was the end of his job with the electrician. It was the last chance he would have to get a trade. His father had already offered to teach John how to be a locksmith and to play the piano, but John, seeing bigger things for himself, passed up both opportunities.

Walter would later marry the woman with whom Freda had accused him of having an affair. She was a homely woman by the name of Alice Gardner, who later bore him a daughter. The marriage was viewed with hurt and bitterness by John, who perceived it as an act of desertion. He craved a stable home. Finally, under Alice's influence, his dad had less and less to do with him.

"Eventually he didn't want to know me."

CHAPTER THREE

THE RAN TAN

've got my sailor beware on," Freda cooed seductively, hugging her
mink coat with her silk-gloved hands before stepping out for a night's
entertainment dripping in jewels.

To an impressionable 12-year-old like Brian Hesseltine, the
bleached blonde had the looks of a film star. He may have been
young, one of her son's urchin friends, but he knew Freda was high class.

"Always the best clothes and always the best guys around her. When
she was young she was attractive, see," he recalled in his thick West
Midlands accent.

The Glover/Naylor home at Lower Villiers Street was like no other
home he had been in. For a lad from a dour, working-class family, stepping
into that household was like paradise, like a small hotel, when other post-
war families were battling on meagre rations of food and fun.

Although three years John's junior and two years older than Barry,
Brian was a mate and "brother" to the Glover boys, striking up a
friendship with Barry at Graiseley Public School. "Freda treated me like a
son, and John would say to people when we went out that we was
brothers," said Mr Hesseltine. He was one of the few people to ever get
close to John but says: "I don't think anyone ever really knew him."

They were heady days of pubs, parties and fast money for boys at an
age when most were still at school. Tame perhaps by today's standards —
the word "teenager" had not yet been coined — but to them it was their
life "on the ran tan". They were having a good time. Brian used to stay at
their home most weekends and go away with them on trips to Blackpool.
It was an alluring lifestyle.

At 15 years of age, Johnny was the leader. They were "wide boys",
smart and streetwise, having been taught by Freda the various ways and
means to part fools and their money. She told them how to pick an easy
mark and they took it. But when it came to any hard work John would
always get Barry and his mates to do it. Glover: "I was the leader of the
leaderless, but smart enough to get them to do everything."

"Everything" ranged from brawling in pubs as they got older, to looking after young Patricia and Clifford when Freda went partying, or pushing old Mr Naylor — by then retired and confined to a wheelchair — up the hill to the pub.

Pushing Naylor was more difficult than the mere physical effort. The gangrene had spread to his other leg and it too had been removed. He was a bitter, legless man.

"When we would take him out he would take a swipe at you for nothing, give you a backhander for nothing," Brian Hesseltine recalled. "He was a bit ... I don't know whether it was because he had his legs off or what, but he was not very easy to get on with."

The boys would push Mr Naylor up the hill daily from their home to the Villiers Arms pub, often when Freda was entertaining her men friends at home. Although Mr Naylor was quite wealthy in his retirement, Freda had become accustomed to more luxury than his bank account could stand. She turned to what some might call selective prostitution, though others might think of less damning names.

Freda would always have a fur coat on. It was her "sailor beware", but it was not humble mariners she was after.

"She was always in with the right people if you know what I mean, fellas from the black market, always mixed with blokes with plenty of money," said Mr Hesseltine. "She was the bread and butter in the house ... John was always treated right by her ... if anything naughty ever went on in that house we would be sent out, given money to go out.

"Okay, she lived a bit of a flirty life, have you got me, but they didn't go short of anything. The food was always there, the best meat, steaks and the like, was always there. He [John] was always kept immaculate, everything was kept bright.

"You'd say nine out of ten people hadn't got what she got. That's why I used to go in there and stop in there."

Often Freda would take "her three boys" on night-time outings to pubs such as the Kings Arms in the quaint village of Claverley and the Boycott Arms on the western outskirts of Wolverhampton. Usually they would make the trip in a taxi owned by Frank Goalby. Freda's husband, whose health was fast deteriorating, was also a regular client of Frank Goalby but that did not stop Freda and the cab driver starting a long affair. Freda again had permission to have this affair provided she was discreet, according to young Clifford. He said the old man was aware of his own hopeless condition and so let things pass.

John Glover disagreed and said that all Freda's extramarital activity was strictly on the sly. Whatever conditions applied, it was a lifestyle which came naturally to Freda. "She was a good darts player and a great mixer in a pub; she was a mover," said Brian Hesseltine. "Within ten minutes of walking into a pub she would be the number one person."

The boys learnt to drink at a very early age and their big spending helped them to discover girls. "Oh yeah, the money would flow," Hesseltine said of those nights. "When we was kids, she used to get us playing cards with the rich men, you know, and they would be that drunk we would win all the while."

Freda wouldn't watch. She knew. She would just say: "Go and earn a few bob there. They're daft enough to throw it away."

"When you mix with that class of people and they have got a lot of money to throw around you take it off them because you're young kids and you don't give a damn anyway ... we was living it up."

On many a Sunday night after the pubs closed the lads would play cards with Freda's gentlemen friends back at Lower Villiers Street. The booze flowed freely and there were no restrictions on the boys' drinking.

"Everything we wanted was there and we could take girls in and it wouldn't matter. Whereas I couldn't at my house because my father was strict ... it was a bit of a party house," said Brian. "Freda was never naughty in front of us. Okay, she sent us off when she used to do the business, but it was none of my business. We never saw it, I mean we was always given money to go and have fun."

Freda regularly took the boys to Blackpool and stayed in the best hotels with a girlfriend of hers, Marjorie Craddock, with whom she haunted the nightspots. "Go down to Pleasure Beach, go and have a good time, you get out off the road and have a good time," she told the boys as she discreetly put a fiver in John's hand.

"Her and her mate would be jollying two rich blokes up, you know. We'd go off and have a few drinks and you'd end up at Pleasure Beach or around the dances. We was about 16 or 17 then. You could get away with it [drinking] if you were with the right people," said Brian.

"She was going with quite a few blokes, as many that could pay the money. She'd use them. They would be around for maybe two nights and you wouldn't see them again, you know, then there'd be somebody else. There were that many men on the scene you couldn't remember who was who. It all became a blur."

Freda's flirtatious nature inevitably created competition between men vying for her company. There were occasional brawls and more frequent near misses. "She could pull a bloke while she was with a bloke, then a little bit of trouble might start because he has noticed she has seen somebody with some more money."

Having the boys with her tended to dampen the violence but Freda's way of life almost caused serious injury one night. She and her lads were on their way to a pub in Frank Goalby's cab when they found themselves being pursued by another car. The other driver rammed the cab, trying to run it off the road. The car was driven by a local businessman — one of Freda's jilted lovers — jealous that she was with Goalby. They watched horrified as it kept coming back at them. Eventually, when the black car sped past them into the night, a shaking Freda said angrily: "I've finished with him, he's mad!"

For the boys, the news was a bit disappointing. It was the end of free lunch because the fellow in the car was the owner of a cafe. He fed them for free "because he was knocking their mother off on the side".

For all of the fast living, John was burdened by some degree of responsibility. He had a sister ten years his junior, a brother five years younger again and a mother rarely home at night. On the occasions when he did play an active part in the discipline of the kids it was in a soft way. He was cool and never lost his temper. Barry was the opposite. He would not hesitate to bring them into line with a belt and it would not take much provocation for the strap to appear. Barry was burdened by most of the work in bringing the kids up. John saw to that.

Unlike most Wulfrunians, John Glover was not a follower of soccer, nor was he interested in any other sports. His sport was girls.

Glover says his first attempts at picking up women were nothing more than drunken bravado. "Usually we would spend the night having a few pints of beer to pluck up enough courage to ask a girl for a dance," he said with a wry grin on his face. "You ended up being drunk by the time you got round to asking one and couldn't do anything more with them than just dance and hope you sobered up."

Often, other lads also fancied the one girl and they would spend the entire night jostling for her favour. "That usually meant no one got anywhere, and quite often we would all end up having a long cold walk home in the dark," said Glover.

Despite his own denials of his prowess, others had a different perspective. When Glover discovered sex he took to it with a passion. In that respect he began to emulate his mother.

"John would always have a sweetheart in one room," said Brian. There were occasions when he would have two girls in the house, one in each room, and one wouldn't know the other was there. John would use his younger brother and Brian as a foil to keep the two girls going. "Just go in there and tell them a few lies, go and have a natter with her and then I'll get rid of this one and I'll be back in there after," Glover ordered the lads.

"We would go and keep them occupied and keep them talking, then he would send one off and go back in with the other one," recalled Brian.

John never showed any inclination to older women; he would stick to girls roughly his own age. The one constant was the never-ending supply. "John had a lot of girlfriends; wherever he went he would pick one up. That was his life I suppose. He'd stand in a room by himself at a party and pick any woman, even if she had a boyfriend ... he'd have one weighed up. He was a real puller, like Freda."

CHAPTER FOUR

"TRAD MAN"

949 was a watershed in the life of John Glover. Shortly after his seventeenth birthday he left the comfort of Lower Villiers Street and took up "digs" of his own. It was his first attempt to break free from the influence of Freda.

He was "all ready to fly", with all his worldly possessions crammed into the one battered suitcase. John felt good to be out but, like most young people leaving the nest for the first time, there was trepidation: "Underneath it all, despite the way Freda was, there was still that feeling of wanting to cling to her skirt."

Glover took up room and board with a succession of landladies. While facing a packed courtroom 42 years later Glover would describe the experience only as a disaster but he found it a bit more interesting at the time.

When the leasing arrangement replaced rent with sex, the fresh-faced Johnny found the payments quite daunting. It was his first sexual encounter with an older woman. Of one such experience he said, "It was a dreadful experience, she was awful, but when you don't earn much money ... I had to pay the rent somehow."

It was a trend which continued with other landladies on the other side of the world. The biggest drawback with such leasing arrangements, however, would always be the lack of stability. So it was that John Glover came home one day, only a few months into the "agreement", to find his belongings on the doorstep.

"I suppose she didn't like the fact that I preferred her daughter to her, I guess it was the mother-daughter jealousy that did it."

Johnny returned home to Freda briefly but was not there long before he was called up to do national service. To Glover, it seemed the best thing that had ever happened. For the first time in his life he had really broken clean from his mother and all her men.

The army sent him to Wales where he completed his six weeks of basic training before being posted to the 62 Heavy Anti-Aircraft Regiment in

Lincolnshire, the home of the Royal Air Forces Bomber Command. He lived there for the rest of his two-year military service at The New Barracks, Lincoln.

It was a "settling period", he would later say. He enjoyed the army, the drill, the organisation. It was a framework in which to fit his life. He liked being told when to get out of bed, when to get into it and when to make it. He liked having three regular meals a day. The army was in effect moulding a character that previously had no direction, no shape. It was the "first real home" he ever had.

Gunner Glover turned out to be a fair soldier, specialising in radios, radar and other electronics. "I was a radar operator because I was smart, I could see pretty early on that in the artillery you've got to lift a lot of heavy shells, 50 pounds some of those things," Glover said. He says he rose to be a bombardier, the equivalent of a corporal, but certainly the records show that a few months before demobilisation he was still a gunner — a private.

He loved the camaraderie and the friendships offered by the army. It was the only time he would ever have close male friends.

Despite his professed feelings of warmth towards the town and the army, John Glover was still the wide boy from Wolverhampton. In May 1952, a spring shower was soaking the historic city of Lincoln when Gunner Glover went to leave the NAAFI (Navy/Army Air Force Institute) in Park Street with a few drinks under his belt. Looking out the door into the narrow, ancient streets of the town centre, Glover cursed the weather. It had been fine when he got there and he had no coat or umbrella.

He turned around, took a raincoat from the unattended cloak room and walked out again. With the mackintosh came a nice pair of gloves and a scarf that the owner had left in the pockets.

It was some weeks before Corporal Frederick Bateman returned to the NAAFI. He thought he would check the cloak room for his missing coat, just in case it had turned up. With some surprise he saw that it was there. The young Royal Air Force corporal rang the police and waited. By the time Glover had returned, the police were waiting with him. When Glover asked the girl behind the cloak room counter for the coat, he was arrested.

On 31 May 1952, Gunner Glover appeared before the Lincoln City Magistrates Court charged with stealing clothing worth seven pounds. In its late edition that day, the Lincolnshire Echo reported that Glover pleaded guilty and that his commanding officer had commended his military performance as "good". The magistrate fined him four pounds and ordered him to pay one pound restitution for the scarf, which he said he had disposed of. The gloves were in the pocket of the coat.

Seven months later, Glover and two of his army mates left the NAAFI just after 10 p.m. full of drunken high spirits. They were walking down the road when one of Glover's friends, John Iley, left them to go to his girlfriend's house nearby. It was very cold and Glover did not feel like walking. They talked about stealing a car, jokingly at first but then more seriously. Glover showed his bravado by opening a van and pulling out a big, warm coat. As they walked along Brayford Wharf North, Glover saw a car. He and his remaining friend, Peter Fisher, got in and started it up.

With Glover driving, they went to find their friend, John Iley, at his girl's place. Glover and Peter Fisher told the pair of them that they were coming for a joyride but the girlfriend would not have anything to do with it. Iley jumped in and the three drunken lads roared off up the steep hill which rises out of the canal and dominates Lincoln's topography. They drove up Lindum Road and left past the Gothic cathedral which sits high above Lincoln. Driving slowly past the gargoyles and flying buttresses, Glover gave in to Iley's nagging and let him have a drive ... on the condition that they swapped seats without stopping.

So just as Glover accelerated through Newport Arch — the last remnants of a Roman wall which once circled and fortified the top of Lincoln's hill — the pair swapped seats at 65 kilometres an hour. They had not gone far, however, before the siren of a police car sounded behind the old stolen car. Later, at Lincoln City Central Police Station, all three made statements admitting the offences and declared that they had been drinking. "All this was through having so much to drink," Iley said.

The next day — New Year's Eve, 1952 — Gunner Glover appeared once more before Lincoln City Magistrates Court, this time charged with stealing a car. Both the Lincolnshire Echo and the Lincolnshire Chronicle carried stories of the escapade. The Chronicle recorded the incident with the headline: Soldiers "Fell To Temptation — Costly Escapade With Car". The Echo ran the story on the back page under the headline: "Soldier Took Lincoln Car 'For Joke' — 2 Disqualified."

Glover told the three justices of the peace and the city councillor lined up in front of him, acting as magistrates in the ancient style of court proceedings: "It was more or less a joke which finished up in bad taste. Many times we have joked about taking a car." He added: "I'm towards demob, and you get that feeling towards New Year — looking forward to a good time. We had a few drinks and we started 'mucking about' the car parks."

Once again, Glover's battery commander gave a glowing character assessment to the court. Glover was fined 12 pounds and disqualified from driving for a year and was ordered to pay 10 shillings costs.

The two civil offences had marred an otherwise good military record. What action the army took on the matters is not known. Glover was demobilised several months later and left Lincoln for Wolverhampton. He had considered staying on in the town, such was his fondness for it, and says if he had not gone to Australia it is where he would have settled. He admired the beauty of the place, the complete opposite of a city like Wolverhampton. He also considered staying on in the army but felt it had already done its job in shaping him and his destiny. He had been moulded perfectly, he thought, and he was itching for a change.

Glover left the military with "no qualifications except a driver's licence" (which he later regained after disqualification). He went back to his boyhood home of Wolverhampton and picked up where he had left off. He was driving deliveries and back in with his mother, but the relationship was tense at best.

While he had been away, in 1951, Freda's second husband, Clifford Naylor, had finally been killed by complications arising out of the gangrene which had already taken both his legs. His funeral and wake produced extraordinary scenes which probably would have made the old drunk laugh. He had ordered in his will that the wine cellars be opened for the wake. Nine hundred people turned up to pay their last respects and in the process drank the huge cellar dry. All the best booze was gone.

Mr Naylor's death left Freda unfettered by any sense of moral obligation she may still have had towards him but she was shackled suddenly by declining living standards. Young Clifford, aged two, and Patricia, seven, were fostered into cottage homes. Clifford then went to the Kingswood Camp, a country school for underprivileged children, until Freda was in a position to have them both back. One of young Clifford's earliest memories was of sitting outside a nightclub with a bottle of soft drink and a packet of crisps to keep him quiet, waiting for Freda to come out. The memory is etched deep in Clifford's mind because it happened so frequently. He was, however, rarely alone. There were plenty of other kids whose parents were living it up inside as well and they formed a little coterie, free to roam the streets.

Glover gained employment with a local company selling Tiser soft drinks and other non-alcoholic beverages, including a herbal drink that "could kill a dead dog". He was soon delivering soft drinks to local stores.

He then went to another job with the council-run transport service as a ticket collector on the locally manufactured trolley buses that ran the narrow streets of the town, powered by overhanging electric cables. Johnny "the clicky", his mates called him, and he says he was the fastest on the buses.

Around this time he took to body building with another conductor, Tony Otter. His already stocky frame grew considerably bigger but he was still small in comparison to Otter. The two almost came to blows one day over a girl but after some heavy pushing and shoving, John backed down. It was the end of that friendship.

SOLDIERS "FELL TO TEMPTATION"

COSTLY ESCAPADE WITH CAR

Three young soldiers from the New Barracks, Lincoln, who had often joked about taking away a car for a ride, at Lincoln City Magistrates' Court on Wednesday, pleaded "Guilty" to a number of charges arising from their taking a car without the owner's consent and driving without a policy of insurance.

They were John Walter Glover (20), who was fin____ without a policy disqualified from ing licence for taking away stealing an ove and ordered t further charge of gloves bein sideration; Jc who was fin____ without a and disqualif from holding for driving v £1 for aiding in taking Peter Fisher £3 for aid use of a vel of insuranc and abettin the car.

Det.-Con that on plaint w owner of Graham) was _____ later, h driven a followed little la Riseholn the car had b "I don talking Police all in

All t admitt declar The p and the demobilisation was no____ caused them to fall to temptatio They expressed regret.

An officer gave the men goo military characters.

Supt. T. Pickworth, who pros cuted, said Glover had admitte other offences, the last being o May 31 at Lincoln City Magi trates' Court for stealing mackintosh and a pair of glove the others having clean records

The magistrates were Coun. E. Seely (chairman), Mrs. A. Race, Mrs. M. Hooton and Dr. A. Slater.

£4 Fine For Theft Of Clothing

NATIONAL Serviceman who stole an R.A.F. co____ coat, gloves and N.A.A.F.I. in Po coln, was fined magistrates toda ordered to pay £1 Before the cou Walter Glover (19 62 H.A.A. Regiment Barracks, Lincoln, guilty to stealing worth £5, belonging Frederick Bateman. It was stated by that the corporal left N.A.A.F.I. cloakroom. property was missing. When the corpora visited the N.A.A.F.I. he nised his coat in the cloa The police were calle Glover was seen to ask f raincoat. Glover later adr the theft. He said he had posed of the scarf. The g were in the pocket of the c Glover's officer said that military character was rate

Soldiers Took Lincoln Car "For Joke"—2 Disqualified

THREE young soldiers, of the New Barracks, Lincoln, were fined a total of £23 at the City Magistrates' Court today on charges relating to a car taken and driven away from Brayford North last night. Two were disqualified from driving for a year.

____unner John Walter Glover ____), pleaded guilty to taking ____thout consent the car belong ____; to George Barlow Graham ____ driving it without an insu____ ____ce policy and ____ ____ and disqualified from driving for a year. Glover to____ ____ ____strates ____ Joke ____ taste. ____ joked

WOLVERHAMPTON BOY'S "MANIA FOR STEALING"

FROM the beginning of the year this boy has had a mania for stealing other people's property," said Chief Inspector T. Marsh, when a 14-year-old boy appeared before a Wolverhampton juvenile court today.

He was summoned for stealing property valued at £10 from Mrs. Clara Alice Chown, wife of the Rev. J. L. Chown, of 89, Compton road, Wolverhampton; property from his employers, value £4; and a date stamp, value 15s., from the Wolverhampton and Midland Eye Infirmary.

He admitted doing all this and asked for 13 other cases to be taken into consideration.

HAD TO VISIT HOMES

Inspector Marsh said that in the course of the boy's duties he had to visit people's homes, and it was from these he stole.

All the property, excepting a ring and a brooch belonging to Mrs. Chown, had been recovered.

The boy, who was at the time living with his mother, who had remarried after divorce, said that he took the things, which included a vice, to start a workshop. When asked by his employers what he best stolen he returned the property. He had since gone to live with his father.

The boy was put on probation for one year on the first summons and the other two were adjourned for six months.

A 15-year-old boy who stole a lighter from a fellow employee and 11s. in cash was ordered to pay 15s. costs and return the

money to the person he stole from.

It was said that the boy was seen to give a girl a light with the cigarette lighter, and when questioned about the theft he admitted it.

FATHER'S £5

After taking a £5 note from his father's savings, an 11-year-old boy had it taken from him by another boy; he asked two friends to get it back, and when they did so he gave £2 to a 13-year-old and £1 to a 14-year-old boy. This was said when the youngest boy was summoned for stealing the money and the other two for receiving the money knowing it to have been stolen.

All the cases were dismissed on payment of 15s. costs.

____ ____ where they ____car. Then they drove off to wards the Cathedral, where Iley began to drive. By this time the fact that the ____car was missing had been ____orted to the police, and soon ____er the ____ car was seen on __n- ____h road. It was stopped on ____eholme road. Both Iley and Fisher made statements to the police. Iley ____d: "All this was through ____ing so much to drink." ____her said: "We had often ____ed about taking a car, but ____ever got anywhere."

Newspaper articles in the *Lincolnshire Chronicle* and the *Lincolnshire Echo* detailing John Glover's earliest convictions for theft.

MODERN-MINDED MOTHER wc

MANY a mother could take a leaf out of Mrs. A. Glover's book. For Mrs. Glover, whose home is at 28, Lower Villiers-street, Wolverhampton, is the most modern-minded mother I have met for a long time.

This time last year her eldest son, Johnny (26), set sail for a new life in Australia. She was very sad at the time, but her only comment was: "Johnny has his own life to lead and he must do as he pleases."

Now, just 12 months later, her second son, Barry, who will be 21 in May, is going out to Melbourne to join his brother. 0 DEC 1957

OWN LIVES

Yesterday Mrs. Glover told me: "Barry will go immediately after Christmas. Of course I shall miss him very much. But I would never stand in his way.

"I must let young people today live their own lives.

Barry, who is a trainee chef, hopes to get a job with his brother when he arrives in Melbourne.

"If the boys want Australia, they leave Wolverhampton.

SIXTEEN-YEAR-OLD Barry Glover, of Lower Villiers-street, Wolverhampton, turned the tables on five girls who took part with him in round three of a national cookery competition for teenagers in Wolverhampton last night by winning first prize of and a certificate of merit.

He also qualifies to go on to round four in the contest, to be held in Wolverhampton next month, when will compete with six girls from throughout the West Midlands.

Round five will take place in London, and the final prize for the teenager cook in the country will be £100, to be used for training, hobby, education or travel.

COURSE MEAL

In six miniature kitchens in the demonstration hall of the West Midlands Gas Board in Wolverhampton last night, Barry and the five girls from Dudley, Bilston, Willenhall, Sedgridge and Tividale, cooked a three-course meal consisting of baked haddock fillets with anchovy and a Bakewell tart.

The dishing of the fillets and the sauces was left to the choice of each competitor, and Barry chose fishballs, tomatoes and mushrooms as the garnish and Brussels sprouts as the vegetable.

The competitors, watched by a group of parents and friends, were given half to two hours to cook the meal.

Mrs. L. Hunt, catering adviser to the Miss ...

Conditions were good. In fact, the money's good. ... everything brothers Glover have ... are good. ... their ambition is to ... But ... and come ... to ... a doctor to give ... need a condition. their condition. us case of home-

he threw up his job and has become a chef-apprentice at a Birmingham hotel.

Second in last night's round of the contest was Miss Margaret Harris (16), of 21, Dudley-road, Tividale; and third, Miss Helen White (16), of 22, South-avenue, Stourbridge. They received £3 and £1 respectively, and certificates of merit.

Mr. F. C. Briggs, divisional general manager of the gas board, p ...

Johnny sets his star wc

DURING the next few months the local jazz set will lose three of its most popular personalities. They are television field engineer Johnny Glover (25), of 28, Lower Villiers-street; Bob Webster (24), 5, Goldthorn-avenue, Wolverhampton, and Phil Rowe, of Newhampton-road West, Wolverhampton. Johnny has set his star for Australia, Bob goes back to sea in February and at about the same time Phil emigrates to Canada.

Johnny is the first to go. He leaves 21 DEC 1956 for Melbourne on Monday.

Johnny decided to start his new life several months ago.

"My social life was so full I couldn't settle down to a career. I made up my mind to break away and start all over again," he told the "Chronicle."

He was offered a job as a television field engineer in Australia—where television is only a baby.

The Person who will miss him most (of course) is his mother and his 20-year-old brother.

Brother Barry has a job in catering and hotel management, who is taking a full training and hopes to join his brother in Australia if all goes well.

A CASE OF HOMESICKNESS

HAD a letter this week from Barry Glover, the lad from Lower Villiers-street, Wolverhampton, who emigrated to Melbourne, Australia, last year. OCT 1958 wc

He says: "Tell Wolverhampton's young people there is plenty of opportunity for them out here providing they're willing to work hard."

But he adds: "Going to a strange and big country is no holiday. You have to have guts and determination."

... aged 26, left his Villiers-street home two years ago, intending to settle in. He is now a television ... Barry ... months ago—and has a week job as a sheep at one of the bush farms. ... both of them are saving ... for the fare home. It will ... John is lucky. that ... to fly. He saved ... £200 practically his contract expires ... it's ... and his ... the end of the year. He hopes ... amount, and ... in Wolverhampton. ... towards the end of Christmas. ... hopes to be back ... is ... soon after ... as this one were origi ... But ... brother Barry started by the Glover brothers ... some months ago.

... his ambition is to make a ... the whole family in Australia.

... as a farewell party on ... He Johnny's home for a ... This followed a ... and company jazz at Castlecroft Hotel.

John Glover's new life in Australia was well documented in the Wolverhampton newspapers.

On 24 August 1953, Johnny the clicky had another encounter with the local constabulary. On a complaint from passengers he was cited by a bobby on a charge of "Driver of trolley bus by negligence, endanger the lives of passengers". Glover denies he was ever the driver of a trolley bus and says if there was such an incident it must have been when he was backing the trolley bus into the sheds. Whatever happened, Police Constable Laurence let Glover off with a caution. While the incident did not appear on John Glover's future police record it disturbed PC Laurence enough for him to note it down in the Wolverhampton Police Report book.

Glover celebrated his 21st birthday in November 1953 at the Barley Mow public house with a jazz night. He had found himself hanging out with the local jazz crowd and he fell into a spot as the drummer for a traditional jazz band. He loved his music — "strictly trad, man" — and he found the drums came as naturally to him as the piano did to his father.

He says that he was backstage once when Nat King Cole was performing at the Wolverhampton Civic Centre. John walked into the wrong room and stumbled across a room full of celebrities of the day with Nat holding court in an impromptu jam session. Everyone in the room had to sing and when it came to Glover's turn he sang "Nature Boy":

There was a boy, a very strange enchanted boy
They say he wandered very far over land and sea ...

He softened his voice for the final verse.

The greatest thing you'll ever learn
Is just to love and be loved in return ...

About a year after Glover's return from the army, Freda put young Clifford into the best school in town, the Royal School, courtesy of his real father, Sidney Orphan. For Freda, it had the dual advantages of getting the youngest out of her hair and giving him a good education at the same time. The rest of the family, and the whole town, saw the school for what it was in this case — "the orphanage".

"The rest of the family wanted to know why I went to such a school when they couldn't. That's how I received an education, thank God. The rest of the family always thought I was a bit of a toff because I spoke correct English whereas they talked with a Midlands accent ... Foony they tork, lark thess," recalled Clifford.

Most of the students at the Royal School lived locally and went home on weekends. Clifford, too, lived almost within walking distance but most weekends he had to stay in because Freda was too busy to have him home. "I was in a 90 kid dormitory on my own. I'll never forget those horrific days. John was about the only one to come and see me up there. He bought me this huge f___ing pink bear ... it looked a bit like the pink panther. I will never forget it.

"I was five and I kept that damn thing till I came to Australia. I left it at home back in the UK. But Freda sold everything, including the bear. Nothing had value to Freda unless it had a dollar sign on it."

Ten days after Freda's 44th birthday, John Glover had another one of his little "jokes" go wrong.

On 11 October 1954 he appeared in Wolverhampton Magistrates Court charged with stealing. The *Express and Star* newspaper, in the lead story on page 12, reported:

HANDBAG THEFT FROM GIRL "A JOKE", W'TON COURT IS TOLD

As a result of what they termed "a leg pull" two Wolverhampton men and a youth appeared before Wolverhampton magistrates today charged with stealing a handbag and a purse from a 16-year-old girl yesterday afternoon.

They were John Walter Glover, 21, of 8 Rupert Street, Anthony Edward Crump, 18, a private in the Worcestershire Regiment, of 16 Silver Birch Road, and Deryk Woolley, 21, of 11 Silver Birch Road. They pleaded not guilty.

The charges against Crump and Woolley were dismissed, and Glover, who it was said had been in trouble before, was put on probation for two years.

It was stated that the owner of the bag, which had a purse containing 13s 7d inside it, was Miss Betty Harrison, 16, of 95 Lowe Avenue, Rough Hay, Daraston, and that she and a girl friend went to a Wolverhampton cafe at 2.25 p.m. yesterday.

While there, the three defendants came up and spoke to them, then when they left Glover picked up the handbag and walked out with it.

The two girls followed them and got the handbag back in Dudley Street. The purse was not inside, and when Miss Harrison asked where it was Glover handed it to her.

She examined it and found that it now contained only 1s 1d inside instead of the 13s 7d. She asked where the money was and the youths then started accusing each other. They walked away and she then complained to police.

Police Constable Jobling saw the defendants in Victoria Square where Glover said: "I've got the money," and handed him 26s 11d in loose change adding: "It was only a joke." Glover told the Magistrates: "It was only a leg pull, I intended to give her the money back later."

Taxi driver Frank Goalby had, by this time, left his wife and was living with Freda. They would go on to have a fiery 16 year common-law arrangement that ended only when Freda finally agreed to marry him.

"He had a tough life with Freda. Freda was Freda ... Freda robbed him blind. He was not a bad man, Frank. One mellows over the years. He used to knock Freda around, but he never hit me," recalled Clifford.

Clifford's memories of John from this period are those of an admiring younger brother who was given special treatment. He recalls being driven out into the narrow, hedge-lined lanes of the local countryside and being taken into village pubs like The Arms at Claverley. "John would stand me up on the bar there as a kid and I'd sing carols at Christmas there. They used to pass the hat around under the guise of collecting for some bloody charity or other — the John Glover charity."

He recalls being taken to the coast to swim. John put him on his shoulders and dived deep, "like a submarine", and came bursting up to the surface with Clifford half-drowned and being dragged by the hair. He loved every minute of it. And, unlike Barry, John never hit him.

One of John's many girlfriends through this period was a pretty 16-year-old from a brand new housing estate on Plascom Road. John soon discarded her and went off hunting for other targets. But this girl soon loomed back large in his desires after Glover found out that she was seeing his mate Brian Hesseltine.

Brian was working as an apprentice bricklayer and she went to the same technical college every day, "all dressed up, quite attractive girl, and she used to always wink at me". He plucked up the courage and told her: "I'll meet you at the cinema on Sunday night. Yeah? Luvly."

"But I didn't know that Johnny Glover had been going out with her, you see." Glover got wind of the liaison and sent a message to Brian, via Barry: "Lay off the girl or you're going to get it."

The news came as quite a shock to Brian. He had practically lived with John and the family for the last eight years and suddenly he was being threatened over a girl Glover had not seen for months. "I had to get somebody to go and have a little talk in his ear hole. His words were that I would cop it. My message back was that he'd cop it worse."

Brian's message was no idle threat. He had two older brothers known in that corner of Staffordshire as "hard men". "He got the message and so the next thing you know he was talking to me again."

Freda had come to use the boys as almost her own personal bodyguard. She was still dragging them around town even though they were old enough to make their own way. "If a fella had trouble with her he'd never come in the pub because we were all young and we could take care of her," Brian explained. "Seen a couple of near misses. But they wouldn't stop in because there was always John, Barry and meself. We were sort of coming up to 17 and we could take care of ourselves."

In fact, of the Glover brothers, Barry had the worse temper. "Barry was a fly-off-the-handle type of fighter whereas John was calm and calculating: if he ever got into a fight, he always kept his cool," said Clifford.

"John and Barry were two very hard-case lads in their day. Barry was a boxer. When they went out, if John got into a fight with a couple of tear-arses, he'd kind of step back and Barry would finish it."

It was the "teddy boy" era of greased hair and knee-length drapes (jackets) with suede lapels and collars. Brian and Barry took to the new fashion like so many of their working-class peers — but not John. He preferred the look of the upper class, always wearing well-tailored grey suits, one for every day of the week. They told him he looked like something out of the Ivy League with his polo-neck jumpers. He bought his clothes in the best shops.

"You know, he was that kind of chap. He did not fit in with the era. He was sort of a step better," recalled Brian. "He used to get all of his clothes from a shop called Lou Blooms, that was the sort of shop where you looked the part and you paid for it. But he never drank or smoked much so he always had a few bob."

Glover had begun to refine his speech and, when he wanted to, would affect a softer accent, above his own class. He was happy to let people think he was university educated. The image was aimed at one thing — women — and it worked. "John was not a great mixer with blokes. He was a loner. You know, he kept his self to his self and if he went with a girl she was always a pretty one," said Brian.

"Barry and I would go to rock'n'roll places, but John used to go to sophisticated places. The women there were a bit more high class, they looked classier, and the dancing was to jazz bands."

Glover says he let Barry and Brian Hesseltine hang around with him because they were handy back-ups in case he got into trouble. In many respects, the younger lads acted as a back-up to John just as the three of them had been a back-up to Freda when she was the centre of too much attention. And, just like Freda, he would send them off whenever he brought a girl back to Lower Villiers Street. Certainly there was never any question in Brian or Barry's minds that he might have mistreated the girls, but they were rarely welcome in the same house, let alone in the same room, so they never really saw John's charms in action.

"I knew one girl he courted, she went to Australia, he was really mad over, and she left and married another guy," Brian said. "She was the first girl he thought the world of ... I am almost certain that is why he decided in the end to go to Australia, to look for her or bump into her."

All those who knew John Glover then stressed that he rarely drank much. His youngest brother only saw him drunk once. "Barry and John came home one night drunk and John threw up all over me, the son of a bitch, and then made me clean it up," said Clifford with a laugh.

Despite his disinclination to violence, there was one unusual incident on a New Year's Eve in the mid-1950s. Barry had thrown in his job as a dining-car attendant for British Railways and landed a job as an apprentice chef at the Station Hotel in Birmingham. He got the whole family invited to a New Year's Eve party in the hotel's plush ballroom under the swinging chandeliers.

John had been there only a few minutes before he had singled out the prettiest girl in the room. There was one problem: she had a boyfriend with her. Not one to let such a detail get in his way, Glover soberly and calmly walked up to the fellow and head-butted him square on the nose.

In the commotion that followed as staff raced over to sort out the mess, it was Glover who took up the running. "Look what he has done to my suit!" The staff looked at the two. Words of accusation flew about who started what, but it was the immaculately dressed and well-spoken John Glover who was believed. He was a cut above his opponent. He simply did not look the type to head-butt someone at random — and he was sober. The other fellow was thrown out and John moved in on the girl.

While John Glover was not regarded as one to pick a fight in a town and era where such might have been considered the norm, one family member would years later tell police that Glover had come home on more than one occasion with blood on his clothing. No explanations were given or sought.

Fifteen days after the incident at the Station Hotel, Barry won the local heats of a national cookery competition for teenagers. Barry beat off the competition of five girls, cooking a meal of stuffed haddock fillets with anchovy sauce, tomatoes and mushrooms and a bakewell tart to win the four pound prize.

The whole family had gone to watch the cook-off and cheered when he was declared winner. None cheered louder than Freda, who pocketed the prize money as soon as they got home.

John and Freda's fights were getting more regular and loud. Freda objected more to the type of girl he was bringing home than the fact they would disappear into the bedroom for long stays; John objected to the volume of men with whom she was coming home.

For an impressionable younger brother who only ever saw family life during school holidays, Clifford remembered Christmas as the worst time. One year, John punched Frank Goalby's son at the dinner table — flattened him during a row between their two parents. Another year, Clifford turned to his sister Pat and whispered about how well things were going and predicted that it only needed a few more drinks. Sure enough, by the end of the night, John had almost broken his big toe kicking a solid oak table in a fit of rage.

"Christmas in our house, it was always a war. Every bloody Christmas there was always a blue." The cause of the arguments was usually Freda's men. "Freda lived with various men over the years. We had more uncles than there are people in Australia," said Clifford.

The arguments got worse and more frequent. It was in the atmosphere of bitterness and recrimination that John Glover picked up the *Express and Star* one day to see an advertisement: "Conductors wanted, Melbourne, Australia". He jumped at the chance to get away. It was "a chance to be John Glover". The passage was virtually free and the pay was almost double his Wolverhampton wage.

This was at a time when migration to Australia required little effort beyond getting yourself to the nearest Australian consulate, passing a brief interview and signing on the dotted line. Thus, John Glover found himself employed as a tram conductor in Melbourne without ever talking to a tramways official. The most gumption he showed in the whole process was neglecting to correctly fill out the section of the form dealing with his criminal record.

It was also going to help if his convictions were made more difficult to trace. John Walter Glover became John Wayne Glover, ready for adventure in the New World. The name had actually been a few years in the making. It began as a joke when John took his two younger brothers horse riding. He was showing them how it was done when Barry quipped, "You should be bloody John Wayne Glover." So that is what he became, even though "he actually looked more like Paul Newman. Very piercing eyes. He can sing, he can do anything that bloke — incredible," said Clifford.

Immigration officials had everything organised. All John had to do was find his way to Southampton, on the south coast of England, to catch the boat. He made his first visit to London on the way.

The *Wolverhampton Chronicle* lamented his departure with a story on 21 December 1956, in which "Johnny" had not hesitated to spin a few yarns. Accompanied by a pop star-style photo, it reported:

JOHNNY SETS HIS STAR

During the next few months the local jazz set will lose three of its most popular personalities. They are television field engineer Johnny Glover, 25, of 28 Lower Villiers Street; Bob Webster, 24, 5 Goldthorn Avenue, Wolverhampton, and Phil Rowe of Newhampton Road West, Wolverhampton.

Johnny has set his star for Australia, Bob goes back to sea in February and at about the same time Phil emigrates to Canada.

Johnny is the first to go. He sails for Melbourne on Monday.

Johnny decided to start his new life several months ago.

"My social life was so full I couldn't settle down to a career. I made up my mind to break away and start all over again," he told the Chronicle.

He was offered a job as a television field engineer in Australia — where television is only a baby.

Person who will miss him most (next to his mother of course) is Barry, his 20-year-old brother. Barry, who is taking a full-time training course in catering and hotel management, hopes to join his brother in Australia if all goes well. Johnny's ambition is to make a home for the whole family in Australia.

There was a farewell party on Saturday at Johnny's home for a host of friends. This followed a Murray Smith and company jazz session at the Castlecroft Hotel. Such sessions as this one were originally started by the Glover brothers some months ago.

Freda was actually pleased to see him go but Barry, her favourite son, was intent on following his brother, while her nine-year-old son Clifford was saddened. He felt a void in his life because John was his most regular visitor in "the orphanage".

"I can always remember John driving off after his visits in a big black car. About 100 metres down the lane he'd stop the car and spin it around so it was facing me. He had style. Then he'd flick his arm out the window and wave ... he always did that." Even 40 years later the memory brought a quiet tear.

Brian Hesseltine, who had joined the army and just been sent to Malaya to fight the Communist insurgency, thought John would go off and make his fortune. "I always thought that if he did marry, it would be to the richest woman in Australia and he would do well with his life."

John Wayne Glover left England on board the P&O liner *Strathnaver* on Christmas Day, 1956. He thought he was leaving behind the emotional baggage of 24 years of resentment and pain. But packed discreetly in his mind was a picture. It was an image which had once been real. He had seen it years earlier and laughed it off. The actual photograph had gone, long destroyed, but the picture in his mind was not so easily lost. It would flash into his head on innumerable occasions over the coming decades; it would devour his soul; it would sabotage his life. He would be driven to try to recreate it on at least six occasions.

The picture was of Freda. It showed her face down, her dress pulled up over her head with her legs splayed and her genitals visible. It was already old when John Glover first saw it. The photographer had died afterwards. There were no suspicious circumstances.

CHAPTER FIVE

TEN POUND POM

O nly a moment; a moment of strength, of romance, of glamour —
of youth! ... a flick of sunshine upon a strange shore, the time
to remember, the time for a sigh and — goodbye! — Night —
Goodbye ... !

— JOSEPH CONRAD, 1902.

It was the beginning of February 1957. The Melbourne Olympic Games
were two months gone when the dashingly handsome John Wayne
Glover got off the boat at Princes Pier. The voyage had taken just over
four weeks. His story is that of thousands of other young migrants hoping
to make good in the Antipodes. He says he had 30 shillings in his pocket
and had refused an offer of a substantial loan from another immigrant
whom he had befriended on the way. Perhaps more smartly dressed than
the other men on the boat he was, nevertheless, just one of the thousands
of "Ten Pound Poms" who had taken up the Australian Government's
post-war offer under the subsidised Empire Migrant Resettlement scheme.

Immigration officials were at the wharf to meet Glover and the
handful of other tram conductors they had recruited with him. The city
had found it hard to find enough people prepared to brave the early
mornings and late nights on the open "toast rack" trams, battling rush
hours so cold some mornings that their numb fingers could not handle the
coins. The north of England seemed a logical place to recruit and, at
almost twice the British rate of pay, there was no shortage of applicants.

John Glover and his fellow conductors were put straight on to a bus
and taken to a large old boarding house at Hawthorn Grove, Hawthorn,

which had been arranged as their new home. It was a beautiful street of rambling old mansions on big blocks next to cottages with decorative turrets and fancy brickwork. As John Glover walked through the carefully painted wrought iron fence he must have been thrilled with what he saw. A grand old house, it suited his aspirations to a tee. The new arrivals were introduced to the owners, a couple from the Black Country town of Birmingham.

There was, however, a catch. They were shown to their living quarters — one large bedroom with ten beds lining the walls. Half of the beds had been allocated a week before when an earlier shipload of tram conductor recruits arrived. The remaining five beds were taken by the new shipload.

The atmosphere was not unlike the army. A group of young males thrown into adversity together, it was a situation in which John Glover quickly found himself the dominant male. His weight training in England had left him the most physically imposing of all the men and he used it to advantage.

One of the other freshly arrived tram conductors, who had been living in the Hawthorn boarding house for a week before Glover, was Rex Blake. Rex was struck by the way Glover looked like a Hollywood version of a Grecian hero, with his straight nose, curly hair and sculptured physique. His shoulders sloped away from his thick, short neck but were broad enough to counteract any impression of stumpiness. Glover was an aloof character with an air of superiority but his strength of character made him a natural leader.

Being strangers in a new country, the residents tended to stick together and when they went out it was usually in large groups. John dominated the politics of social decision-making. What he said went. If he came in and said, "We're going to go to a club tonight," they went.

"You had to like John. If you didn't like him, you were in his bad books. He was very domineering," recalled Rex. "There were times there where we walked into the guest room and if he was in there you weren't game enough to look at him, because if you looked at him the wrong way he would have a go at you. He would want to know why you were looking at him in that fashion. You would have to bring up some sort of conversation where you wouldn't offend him."

On one occasion one of the conductors asked John about his family. It tripped some wire in his head. He got up off his bed and went across the room to the other fellow. Eyeball to eyeball he glowered as he pointed the finger: "Don't ever bring up anything to do with my family," he warned. "Alright?"

The other conductor acquiesced readily. He had only been making conversation in the first place.

There was one significant difference between the military and the Hawthorn boarding house — the place also housed half a dozen young women who had their own rooms at the other end of the building. John Glover, in his beautifully cut double breasted suit, made an instant impression. His shoes were always polished, his tie done up tight, everything matching, everything in its place. He was not your average tram conductor.

Indeed, his colleagues held their suspicions that Glover was too well kept, his clothes too expensive. He always seemed to have money. They suspected that he was dipping his fingers in the till but they never dared ask — it was not the sort of thing you did with John Glover. John's career on the trams was, nevertheless, short-lived. He told his roommates he resigned. Thirty-five years later he would tell a court that he worked out his two year contract but the truth did not run nearly so smooth.

He passed his conductors tests a few days after his arrival. He began duty the day after the exam and within 14 days had failed to turn up for work with no explanation and was recorded as sick. Eighteen days later he had failed to log in the ticket numbers at the start of his shift — a technique which could allow him to fiddle the books. On that day and for the next three days he was reported for having "excessive shortages" in his cash receipts. On 3 April he was excessively late for work and was cautioned. On 1 May he again failed to enter his ticket numbers at the start of his shift. Two weeks later there was a review of his absences. Asked to explain why he was sick so often, he resigned.

Still working out his time, he was in trouble again for "failure to report for duty [drunk]", then the next day for failure to report for the second part of the shift, failure to pay in his change bag and "serious misconduct". He was dismissed with no pay the following day, 22 May, three and a half months into the job.

On 3 June, the Melbourne papers were full of reports of the brutal bashing murder of Mrs Elsie Boyes, 68, near a tram shed at the corner of Chapel Street and Dandenong Road. Nobody has ever been charged in relation to this crime.

For all Glover's fastidiousness with his physical presentation there was one glaring problem which he could not solve. He had the most foul feet that Rex Blake had ever smelt or smelt since.

Glover would spend hours in the shower scrubbing them and then emerge and bury them in talc, but "within seconds of him doing that you couldn't get near him. It was rotten". Living in confined quarters with nine others, such a problem was bound to cause tensions but they were kept festering well below the surface. "Every time we brought the subject up in front of him it got his back up. Oh yes, he was very, very touchy when it came to his feet. You couldn't walk in that room sometimes because the smell was that bad," Rex Blake recalled.

The other men were embarrassed to invite girls back to their room because of it, but they certainly would not have said anything to him with a girl there. That would have increased the risks of incurring his wrath. Unlike Clifford, Rex Blake thought John Glover had a strong temper.

"I've seen him do his block, I've seen him go red with temper and actually threaten the other blokes in the guesthouse there. Everyone was scared of him. You couldn't say anything out of place in front of him because he wouldn't hesitate to just punch you out. He had a very violent temper, a very bad temper.

"We kept our mouths shut."

There was another side to John, of which the other men were intensely jealous. As much as they may have cast scorn upon what they saw as his lack of morality — which, in 1957, was a more rigid social constraint — he left them all wondering about his ability to attract women.

John Glover's ability to charm, manipulate and dispose of women had been refined and improved as he got older. There was no woman whose bed he could not get into, he would boast. There were few pieces of evidence to the contrary. He began working his way through the female residents of the boarding house and other women from outside. The landlady was also a regular, according to Rex Blake.

John had no hobbies other than women. He did not play any sport and the only exercise he had indulged in was weight training for narcissistic ends. He still did not drink very much when he was mixing socially for fear it would interfere with his "style". He kept his smooth line of gentlemanly self-control while all about him others were losing theirs in drunken abandon. His confidence was such that he did not drink as a crutch to break down any inhibitions and his sobriety only served to single him out from the crowd even more.

One woman who knew him at the time recalled his attraction. "I can remember being at a couple of parties and I'd seen him sitting back and allowing it all to happen, watching it all happen. He never used to do anything to attract women. He would just sit there and women would flock to him, I've never seen anything like it. He had an enormous presence, there were no two ways about it. "He was vain, tremendously vain, but he would not boast, he didn't have to. He knew that he had this ability to attract any woman — I mean *any* woman."

Men felt threatened by him because they could see their girlfriends "go mad for him". There were often problems at parties as the increasingly drunk and aggressive male partner watched Glover work on his girlfriend.

There was a bank clerk by the name of Margaret living in Glover's boarding house. Fresh out of home, she was a plain, pleasant girl who had shown resistance to Glover's advances, only serving to challenge his ego more. He set about pursuing her with gusto, raising the level of attention payed to her above anything that had yet been seen by his roommates. Yet she held out.

One morning at around two o'clock, the room full of conductors was dead to the world when the lights were switched on. As they squinted in the sudden brightness, they could see Glover moving into the room after a night out.

"Hey, look at this," he said loudly, with the intention of waking everyone up. "I got her, she was a virgin," he proclaimed, victoriously displaying a trophy. The sleepers roused to see Glover holding a pair of bloodied women's underpants above his head.

He might have been expecting to be feted and cheered but the tram conductors were more concerned about their early morning shifts. "Can't you see we're asleep," someone said without directly challenging him. Nobody ever challenged John.

"He dropped Margaret like a lead balloon afterwards. She was pretty upset you know. He got what he wanted from her and that was it, finished," said Rex.

It was around this time that Rex Blake got a letter from his younger sister Toni, still living in England. She too was migrating to Australia.

Toni arrived in Melbourne on 3 September 1957, her brother's birthday. A small party was put together to celebrate the dual occasion.

It was a fairly quiet night. John Glover was with his latest flame, a Spanish girl with striking dark eyes and a neckline just a little lower than those of the other girls. Things had barely got started when Rex pulled his sister aside.

"See that fellow over there, John?" he said.

"Yes."

"Be very careful."

"Of what?"

"Just watch him. He's a real Casanova and he'll use you and dump you. He's got a really bad reputation with women and I don't want you getting mixed up."

"Huh, him? Why would I get mixed up?" she asked, perplexed at her brother's warning. Sure, he was a good-looking sort of fellow, she thought to herself, "but what does he think I do with myself?" She dismissed Rex's advice as that of a big brother trying to play father.

John came towards them and Rex introduced his sister. For all Rex's trepidation, the pair simply said "hello" and Toni got busy getting to know everyone else. A gregarious type, it did not take her long before she was laughing and joking with them all.

The following night, it was arranged that they would all go out to dinner and celebrate the birthday and the new arrival a bit more formally. John was there with his Spanish girlfriend and there were rumours that she was pregnant. It was not widely known at the time but the bruises that they had seen on her face some time before came from the hand of John.

They sat at a large round table, with John and his girl directly opposite Toni who was surrounded by men. All the males were telling jokes. Toni, with her naturally jovial personality, was a willing and easy audience. John had a good repertoire of gags which were all directed at the new arrival. The Spanish girl was increasingly ignored as John focused on Toni. The more she laughed, the more jokes he would tell and the more the Spanish girl became visibly upset. By the end of the night she was in tears with jealousy but nothing she would say or do seemed to make any difference to Glover.

The dinner ended and everyone came to throw their money in for the bill. They were all there as working equals and had always contributed equally. The money was counted as they stood up. The kitty was short by the amount of one full contribution. Somebody accused Glover. He denied it. The accuser was insistent. They came close to blows until everybody started throwing in extra money to defuse the tension.

The party broke up and Glover left with the Spanish girl. It was not long, however, before he asked Toni out to see a movie. She accepted without hesitation. She was already besotted.

She was, in her own words, a young 21, "totally naive" in matters of the heart and totally without experience of men. Her brother was more than a little concerned for her. But she had never met anyone like Glover before. He had a natural charm and just being with him made her feel good. He made her feel important. When she went out with John, even though he did not splash his money around, she felt like she had really been taken out.

At the back of her head she knew that what her brother was telling her just might be right but she found it hard to believe. She saw herself as strong and able to handle anything John might be able to throw at her. Able to change him even.

The truth was that she found it difficult to ward him off.

Rex tried to warn her again. "Look, you're only 21, you don't know what you're letting yourself in for."

She just asked why.

"We've seen him do this over and over. Just don't get involved with him. Don't."

As far as Toni was concerned, it was a red rag to a bull. Keen to assert her independence and even more curious to find out what a bad reputation was all about, she charged in headlong. Toni fell madly in love and for two months she could not help but think she had proved herself right despite all the knockers. Rex had not been alone in his advice.

Early in the piece, one of the other residents, a nursing sister, had also told her to stay away. "Just jealous," Toni thought, impervious to the advice. But the nurse went on. "My sister and I have both been out with him and I'm telling you not to get involved. He's been giving my sister a really hard time. Just don't allow it to happen because he's a very dangerous guy — don't allow it to get too involved because he's dangerous."

Toni thanked her for the advice but ignored it, unaware that the nurse was really trying to tell her that John had beaten her sister on several occasions, leaving her bruised and sore. It was not the sort of thing one talked about in detail.

While both the nurses had fallen victim to John's charms, the older sister had been less affected. She had a stronger personality and handled him more readily. The younger, less worldly sister had fallen in love and was easy prey.

But as far as Toni was concerned she knew him better than anyone, even though she also knew that no one really got inside John's head. In terms of basic attraction to John, she was completely taken by him. "John was really, I still say to this day, one of the best looking men, physically, I have ever met in my life," she says. "He had extremely good teeth and hair and eyes, he had very unusual eyes. He was very good-looking and not only that but he was a very charming guy.

"He was a terrific kisser, he was ... he was a very, very sexy man, I have to tell you. Very passionate, very sexy, a very good lover, he knew how to do it. It was very good the way he would work. But there was something about him I guess, the undercurrent ... this aggression. I always felt with John that he might explode at any moment."

The couple did all the things that young lovers would do: the movies, dinner, walks along the beach at St Kilda. They would talk for hours but John would say very little about himself. Toni grew to think he was escaping from something. Not anything serious, but it was as though he was trying to leave his past behind. The only time he ever mentioned his mother it was in tones of resentment.

Toni had a close relationship with her mother and would mention her often. "I would have liked to have had a mother like yours," he told her. "Mine gave me nothing but a bloody hard time." He left no doubt in Toni's mind that he hated her intensely.

The only person of whom he spoke fondly was his brother Barry. He was happy that Barry was going to follow him out soon.

All the time that John was seeing Toni, he had maintained the relationship with the Spanish girl and the younger of the two nursing sisters. He kept a grip over them all and was intensely jealous of their movements.

Toni had been out one night with the two nurses, both of whom had had liaisons with John. The three girls were all good friends and had been to a movie and a dance before returning home quite late. John was sitting up waiting for her in the lounge room. The other two girls faded away into their room, leaving Toni and John. She could feel the anger in the air, see it in his eye. She was a little scared. She turned to go upstairs.

"Now hold on, I want to talk to you," he said with anger in his voice.

"What about? It's three o'clock in the morning — I want to go to sleep."

"That's what I want to talk to you about. Where the hell have you been?"

"I don't think it has anything to do with you."

"You've been out with someone else, haven't you."

"No, and even if I had it would have nothing to do with you."

He lashed out with the side of his clenched fist, hitting her below the right ear and hurling her into the corner between the wall and a piano. She lashed back with a kick in the groin.

"Don't ever do that to me again," she said, clutching her face. "Don't you ever, ever lay a hand on me again!"

Suddenly his face went soft and his eyes opened wide. Like quicksilver, he had changed. "Oh God, I'm sorry. What have I done? I didn't mean it ... you know how much I love you. I would never do anything to hurt you or harm you. I just got upset because I didn't know where you were and I was worried about you."

Toni listened and went to bed. She was in shock that it could come to this. She hated him for it and she declared that she would never forgive him. But his words of apology had been so sincere. He had seemed so earnest. By the time morning came she found she had been drawn back to him uncontrollably and she hated herself for it. His aggression had not come as a complete surprise. She had watched it manifest itself in other ways over the three months she had known him. Now it was turning on her. She had always seen herself as an independent type but now John Glover's hold on her heart was endangering it.

When she was away from him it was not so bad. She began to talk more to the two nurses and they told her for the first time that he had beaten the younger sister worse than he had beaten Toni. She had also been in his grip and found herself at his beck and call. The Spanish girl, too, they said had a similar time of it and John had continued both relationships on the side while Toni was still his "official" girlfriend.

Common sense told her to break away from him but he had her in a grip which simply tightened every time he came into her presence. The relationship dragged on through the Christmas break and for the next three weeks, Glover's behaviour was superficially impeccable. He had sensed a certain coolness on Toni's part and that made him more aggressive in his efforts to keep her in his grip. It became emotionally wearing. His moods were swinging radically from charming to insanely possessive.

Toni could not take it any more but she was not strong enough to break it off. She was afraid of her own emotions. There was only one option left. She had to run and, once decided, she did it immediately.

Toni bought the first ticket to Sydney available. It was the next day — not soon enough, she thought. She had to keep it secret.

She did not tell her brother until just hours before leaving for the airport. He asked her why she was going.

"Oh well, no reason at all."

"Has it anything to do with John?"

"Yes, well it has a lot to do with him as a matter of fact. I think I am getting too involved and I'm worried about him. I'm concerned about the situation, that I can't control my emotions when I'm around him."

Rex nodded his agreement.

"Whatever you do don't say anything to him," Toni pleaded.

"Don't worry about that, I won't be telling the bastard anything."

She left for Essendon Airport. Her flight was not due to leave for almost three hours. Toni just wanted to get away from the house.

She sat in the open waiting area of the airport which was then little more than a shed. She had hardly had time to open her book when a message came over the public address system. "Paging Miss Toni Blake. Please report to the information desk."

She went over thinking Rex must have called. There was a phone call waiting but it was John.

"Well?" she inquired.

"What are you doing at the airport?" he asked with a tone of desperation.

"How did you know I was here?"

"Never mind that, just tell me what you're doing at the airport."

"I've decided to go to Sydney."

"Why? It's a bit of a sudden decision isn't it?"

"It's not a sudden decision," she lied. "I've never had any intention of staying in Melbourne anyway, so I've decided to go to Sydney."

"There's got to be something behind this."

"There's nothing behind it."

Glover was not to be stopped. "That's it, I'm coming out straight away, I'm getting a cab. You're not getting on that plane. I'm going to pull you off the plane and we are going to talk things out."

"There's nothing to discuss and there's no point in you coming out, the plane's just about to leave."

"I'm still going to come out there."

"Look, don't waste your time," she said as she hung up on him.

She was ragged. She couldn't wait to get on the flight, but she had lied when she said the flight was just about to go. He had a full two hours to get to the airport and Toni had no doubt that he would.

She was scared. His voice had been threatening but at the same time seemed to convey real concern. She thought that he was just worried that he was losing his grip on her. She knew how that might make him react. Sitting hidden from view, she waited for him to arrive.

But John never arrived and she got on the plane. Toni never saw John again. She would think about him often in the following years and fully expected that he would go on to be successful in whatever he did.

John for his part continued to talk about Toni for at least a few months after she left. She was the one that got away. He put her memory on a pedestal.

After making such a deep impression upon his arrival in Australia, John's aura was beginning to wear thin with his new friends. After facing the pain of rejection by Toni, John's influence within the group was also waning. Where before he had brooked no argument when it came to setting the group's social agenda, the dissenters were beginning to rally. He was finding himself going out alone as the others simply avoided him.

It was not long, however, before Barry Glover turned up in Melbourne so John, who had obtained work making stereo speakers, had his old mate to knock around with. Barry arrived in February 1958 but for some reason, relations were not as friendly as they once had been. They fought from the first day.

It was not quite meant to work out that way. Freda's ability to create situations to her own advantage demanded that the two boys work together to create a home for her to retire to.

On 20 December, around the same time that John hit his girlfriend, Toni Blake, an item appeared in a column of the *Wolverhampton Chronicle*, headlined "Modern Minded Mother".

It read:

Many a mother could take a leaf out of Mrs A. Glover's book. For Mrs Glover, whose home is at 28 Lower Villiers Street, Wolverhampton, is the most modern-minded mother I have met for a long time.

This time last year her eldest son, Johnny (26), set sail for a new life in Australia. She was very sad at the time but her only comment was: "Johnny has his own life to lead and he must do as he pleases."

Now, just 12 months later, her second son, Barry, who will be 21 in May, is going out to Melbourne to join his brother.

Yesterday Mrs Glover told me: "Barry will go immediately after Christmas. Of course I shall miss him very much. But I would never stand in his way. Young people today should be allowed to lead their own lives."

Barry, who is a qualified chef, hopes to go into business with his brother when he arrives in Melbourne.

"If the boys are successful, I shall pack my bags and take my other two children out to join them," says Mrs Glover.

Six months later, things did not seem to have panned out the way Freda intended.

Freda had got on the phone to her friend Roy Castles, who wrote the "Talk Of The Town" column in the *Chronicle*. She fed him a photograph of sun-tanned John and Barry, both wearing singlets and wide smiles, reading a copy of their home town paper in Melbourne. Castles wrote:

A CASE OF HOMESICKNESS

The money's good. Conditions are good. In fact, the brothers Glover have everything they want. But their ambition is to leave Australia and come home to Wolverhampton.

It doesn't need a doctor to give a diagnosis of their condition.

It is a serious case of homesickness.

John Glover, aged 26, left his Lower Villiers Street home two years ago, intending to settle in Australia.

He is now a television engineer. Brother Barry joined him six months ago and has a 17 pounds a week job as a sheep shearer at one of the bush farms.

Now both of them are saving hard — for the fare home. It will cost 200 pounds to fly.

John is lucky. He's practically saved that amount, and his contract expires towards the end of the year. He hopes to be back in Wolverhampton soon after Christmas. But brother Barry is still struggling. He has another six months to work on his contract.

He used to be a chef at the Castlecroft Hotel and a cook at the Royal Hospital.

In fact, John Glover says he never had any intention of returning to England. There were times when he did not like the new country but he had decided from the beginning that it was the place where his future lay. He did wonder whether he was attracted to the place or the money it afforded him, but he certainly never had any intention of leaving.

Barry had bought himself a motor scooter and joined a club, and would take his scooter on runs into the country. One Saturday night in 1959, he was riding the scooter when a car loomed out in front of him at an intersection. Barry careered into the vehicle's side and smashed headlong through the closed side window of the moving vehicle. He was carried down the street, half in and half out of the window, until the centrifugal force hurled him out as the car rounded a corner and sped off.

Barry was left for dead lying in a ditch with the most horrific injuries to his head and spine. He remained motionless by the roadside overnight until found the next day.

Freda received the news from John. She was desperate for more news and for someone to lift her injured son's spirits, so she turned to the local newspapers for help.

In July 1959, the *Express and Star* carried a story:

IF YOU ARE GOING TO MELBOURNE —

If anyone from the West Midlands is going to Melbourne, Australia, in the next few weeks, will they take a personal message for a Wolverhampton mother, whose son is lying critically ill in hospital there after a motor scooter crash? This is an appeal made today by Mrs Freda Naylor ...

Mrs Naylor told the Express and Star *that although she has sent five cables, she feels that a "personal message" carried by someone from the West Midlands would help him to rally round once he had regained consciousness.*

Barry was unconscious for five weeks. Doctors fought at his side to bring him around. He was fed through a tube and it was months before he could talk. He was eventually released from hospital into the care of John in November. By then, Freda's appeals for help for her son had prompted the Villiers Engineering Co Ltd to dispatch their Australian representative from Ballarat to Melbourne to visit him and see if there was any way he could help. The paper had been talking about offering Freda a free flight to Australia as a public relations exercise but, unfortunately for Freda, Villiers made the offer unnecessary.

Police eventually tracked down the driver who had left Barry for dead. He was brought to court on a string of serious charges. The court was soon in uproar, however, after John Glover calmly sidled across the court room and started punching the defendant. He was eventually restrained and charged with contempt of court, but was let off because of the extenuating circumstances.

Such signs of brotherly affection did not manifest themselves all the way through Barry's ordeal, however. John had been a tower of strength for his brother through the criminal action against the driver and then through Barry's battle for compensation. Barry was eventually awarded 7000 pounds in mid-1960. He intended to go back home as soon as he got the payout. John booked them both on a ship back home. Barry would, after all, need watching with that sort of money at his disposal.

Unfortunately for John, Barry found out that his brother had been a bit too comforting and supportive of his girlfriend, Dianne, during the long convalescence, according to Clifford. The two had a blazing row. Barry was at John's mercy because he was so weak but he still managed to cancel his brother's ticket. Their relationship was never the same, and they have hardly spoken since.

On Saturday 10 November 1960, Barry arrived back in England. Freda and 13-year-old Clifford were waiting at the Southampton dock when the ship berthed. They could barely recognise the frail figure coming down the gangway.

Three days earlier Freda had announced Barry's return in the *Express and Star*. "Of course we are all very excited about it," she told the paper. And the 7000 pounds? "Well, I thought we might go into the hotel business. With the closing of the Star and Garter there seems to be plenty of scope for another hotel in Wolverhampton," said Freda.

Brian Hesseltine had returned home from fighting in Malaya and had been surprised to find that Barry had gone to join John. He had continued to spend weekends at Lower Villiers Street even after the boys had gone. He had become accustomed to the free and easy lifestyle. Brian was staying at the house when Barry came home.

He was shocked by the sight of him. Barry had always been a firebrand prepared to use chairs or anything else at hand to win a fight, but the accident seemed to make him even more aggressive.

He told Brian that he and John had not got on too well in Australia and that he was worried about his brother. "John's goin' off the hooks, you know, off the ways. He's goin' to get into trouble the way he's going on. He's lookin' at young girls through binoculars like," he told Brian. "And he's got them calling at his house before they go to school of a morning."

Brian was surprised. John had always been oversexed, he knew, but had always pulled more women than anyone he knew. "Yeah ... in Australia, being a hot country, they do get a little bit excited quicker don't they, you know what I mean," he said, trying to explain away what he had been told. "Some of the young ones they look a lot older than what they should do," Barry answered, "but he's doing a binocular job all the while through the windows. The fool's gonna get his self in trouble."

Unknown to Barry, his brother had already been caught prowling with the binoculars by police. They had let him off with a caution but recorded the incident for their own intelligence records.

Just as she had done with his prize money from the cooking competition, Freda took control of Barry's compensation money. She put it into a small hotel in Blackpool, the Windsor.

While the town died a death of bleak misery every winter, in summer it bloomed. It was where Freda felt most at home. She loved the carnival atmosphere generated by the hordes determined to have a good time if it killed them. Her life on the ran tan was slowing — she was 51 years old — but she still loved the place.

Freda brought Frank Goalby up with her and she pulled young Clifford out of the Royal School to be with them. It was an attempt at stable living and it worked to a degree, but Barry still had to be watched. If he went out at night, someone would have to literally sign him out to vouch that they were going to look after him. He was inclined to suddenly switch into trancelike moods where his behaviour did not bear logical examination — put simply, he got himself into a lot of fights.

Back in Melbourne Glover had gone from making speakers to working in a warehouse as a clerk, and finally had his driver's licence endorsed to allow him to drive in Australia. Soon after he took on deliveries.

CHAPTER SIX

THE ELEVENTH COMMANDMENT

I n December 1960, John Glover got a job with the Australian Broadcasting Commission as a rigger on the outside broadcast unit. It involved driving a truck and helping set up the equipment wherever there was a television shoot to be done outside the studios.

The life of parties and girls continued as normal and he took up room and board with a couple at 16 Kintore Street, Camberwell. It was the suburb where the television serial, "The Sullivans", was set but the foliage in Kintore Street was more lush, the big old bungalows more elaborate than those in the bare street featured in the opening credits of that show.

John Glover was going with a girl called Phillipa McNicol who lived a few miles away in Prahran. He says he also took up with the landlady, a young-looking middle-aged Scottish woman called Jessie.

Things went fine for Glover in his new job for almost two years, largely (it would seem in hindsight) because he obeyed the eleventh unwritten commandment of villains: thou shalt not get caught. In May 1961 he stole two spotlights from the ABC. For the next 12 months Glover gave full reign to his kleptomania. When he saw things he didn't have he just took them — some were of practical use, others were not. In June 1961 he pinched a fan from the outside broadcast unit while on a trip to Mount Buffalo. In early December he stole a set of bongo drums from the Channel Two Ripponlea studios. The drums belonged to ABC band drummer Billy Hyde. On 21 December 1961, he went to a staff Christmas party. Some time after 1 a.m. when there were only a few people left, he saw a trombone belonging to a member of the ABC show band, David Rankin. He stole it even though he didn't know how to play it. He put it in his car then went back inside. He had a few more drinks before he saw a Byer tape recorder (worth 200 pounds) and stole that too. He then took an amplifier, a microphone, cords and a box of tapes while the rest of the party continued to finish the last of the booze.

In April 1962, he took a kerosene heater while in the bush doing scenery shots. In June 1962, he took an electric drill from the ABC workshop. His year-long spree of theft had netted him 500 pounds worth of goods from his employers and workmates.

Glover's relationship with Phillipa McNicol had been turning sour. She was pregnant to another man and the two were fighting constantly.

He was at her place on the night of 11 September 1962. They had a blazing row. He accused her of running around with every bloke in town. Just like Freda, she was stuffing up his life. He was furious. He had to get out. Jumping into his car, he sped back to Camberwell a bit after 10 p.m. He parked the car and went wandering, fuming, paying no attention to where he was going.

Mrs Myrtle Ince had just garaged her car in nearby Victoria Street after returning from the city. The 73-year-old widow had turned out of Victoria Street into Berrick Street and was walking past a nursing home when a strong arm suddenly gripped her neck.

It pulled her backwards as another hand was clasped tightly over her mouth. She was dragged to a flower bed below a large old cypress tree in the grounds of the nursing home.

The attacker flung her down on her face as she continued to struggle. Her last memory before passing into unconsciousness was of a hand disarranging her clothes.

Mrs Ince came to her senses slowly. Lying in the flower bed, she looked about trying to establish her bearings. She crawled over to the cypress tree and pulled herself up. Her watch showed that it was about an hour since she had parked the car.

Her shoes were sitting off to the side of the flower bed with her bloomers next to them. She pulled her jumbled clothes back into order and put her bloomers back on. She headed home in a daze but had not got far when her sister found her. The sister had gone out searching and when she found Mrs Ince she took her back to the cypress tree where they recovered her spectacles and hat. No money or valuables had been stolen but she could not find her car keys. Mrs Ince was bedridden for four weeks with bruised cheeks, tongue and neck. She was tender around the lower ribs and both sides of the chest and suffering deep shock.

Glover's relationship with Phillipa McNicol continued. They managed to get things back on a cordial footing and avoided more fights for a while. On 4 October, 24 days after Mrs Ince had been attacked, Glover took Phillipa to dinner in Melbourne. The couple returned to her place in Prahran at 7.30 p.m. They sat watching television and chatting with Phillipa's flatmate for almost three hours. But eventually the old argument rose to the surface. She was still pregnant. That had not gone away as Glover had somehow hoped; the rage welled up inside him again. He stormed off, jumped into his car and drove. He drove out of Prahran on Malvern Road, left on to Burke Road at Glen Iris then up into Camberwell. But before he reached his usual turn-off, he turned right on to Riversdale Road at Camberwell Junction, heading towards Canterbury. For no apparent reason he turned right again on to a back road, Christowel Street, and then the first right into Stodart Street. It was a dead end. He stopped and fumed. The forces driving his brain were unable to come to grips with the fight, with his whole predicament.

Valerie Alice Bird was not the brightest of girls. In 1962 she was called a "slow learner"; today she would be called "learning impaired". She certainly was not seriously retarded. At 25 years of age she had managed to find work in various low-skilled jobs and was still a regular at Camberwell Girl Guide meetings. She had left such a meeting at the hall on Trafalgar Road with two other guiders at 10.30 p.m. on Thursday 4 October. The three girls walked to the corner of Riversdale Road and then Val Bird left them, walking to her parents' home on Marlborough Road via Christowel Street.

A lot of local parents had banned their daughters from walking that street at night. Women had been molested there over the previous few years. It was one of those streets with a reputation. Certainly by day it looked innocent enough, with nice houses and well kept gardens, but the trees which gave it such a pleasant feel by day obscured the streetlights by night, leaving it dark and eerie.

Val Bird had either not heard or not heeded the warnings about the street. This night she knew she was in danger when she saw the dark figure of a man on the other side of the street.

He did not cross to her side straight away. She saw him go behind a tree; she had already picked up her pace as she became aware of footsteps behind her, too scared to look around but too late to do anything about it.

She had just crossed Stodart Street when the man grabbed her from behind with one hand over her mouth and the other around her chest. She felt the sticky coolness of rubber gloves on her face as she struggled and tried to scream before lapsing into unconsciousness.

When she came to, Val was in the front yard of someone's house, her twin-set cardigan and jumper pulled up around her shoulders. Totally disoriented, she started screaming. She knew she had been attacked, but she did not know how long ago and she did not know where in relation to the yard where she now sat. A woman came running out and helped her into the house. Blood stained her torn clothes and her face was throbbing. The woman tended to her bleeding mouth as Val Bird did up her bra clip and tried to reassemble her torn petticoat and singlet. Even as she examined the scratches on her neck and the bruises up her right leg, there was a commotion outside.

Other neighbours had heard the screams and men had come rushing out into the street as John Glover ran the 25 metres back to his car. Glover dived into some bushes in the yard of the last house in the dead-end street just metres from his car and waited for the commotion to die down. It did not.

Still hiding about 20 minutes later, he saw two policemen going through each of the six houses in the dead-end part of the street. Worse, he could see that they had singled his car out as not belonging in the street. He was watching as they milled about the car, waiting for the attacker to return to it.

The only way he was going to be able to get to it was to join the hunters. He went to the back of the house and knocked on the door with a plan in mind. He apologised for getting the chap out of bed but said he thought he had seen a prowler in the yard. Unaware of the night's events, the man took Glover around the back yard searching for the prowler. When they did not find anybody, the man walked Glover around to the front of the house to show him out.

The plan was working. All he had to do was make it look as though he was a friend of the neighbour and get in the car. But the police challenged both men before they had got past the gate. Glover was done.

Detectives Ed Snell and Leon Smith were on the late shift that night, the only detectives covering the large chunk of Melbourne south of the winding Yarra River.

In the early 1960s, Melbourne had its major crimes, but they tended to be well spaced and, despite the huge population in their territory, there were still nights when there was little for Snell and Smith to do. Other nights they were run off their feet.

Cruising in their late-model Holden as Thursday night turned to Friday morning, they got a call on the radio: "Possible offender for an assault on female". They were told to go to Camberwell police station. They arrived at 12.45 a.m. and found a 29-year-old English migrant, John Wayne Glover, sitting in the watch house. He was polite and obliging and fully prepared to admit having attacked the girl guide but they were not sure whether to believe him when he said he did not use a weapon. They left him in his cell and searched the scene before returning an hour later to formally interview him.

Glover told Detectives Snell and Smith about the argument; about jumping into his car and driving; and about pulling into the dead-end street. "What happened then?" Snell demanded.

"I sat in the car for a while thinking over what happened and then decided that I was doing no good there so I decided to go for a walk. When I say I was doing no good I mean I was not cooling off after the argument with my girl. I thought if I went for a walk I might cool off."

"What then?"

"I walked back to the intersection and turned up to the right. I walked up the street and then turned and was walking back towards the car when I saw a girl walking towards me on the other side of the street."

"What did you do then?"

"I walked over the road to where she was and I just attacked her."

"Can you explain it more fully to us?"

"I remember grabbing hold of the girl and I think we both fell over."

"Anything else?"

"That is the honest truth, I just don't remember."

"What is the next thing you remember doing?"

"Running away from the girl. I heard someone shouting 'stop' or something like that. I realised what I had done and I wanted to run away."

Glover explained how he was caught and was then asked about the cut to Val Bird's lip and her torn clothing.

He said he did not remember any of it.

"I don't know, I just got hold of her and we fell to the ground. I could have done anything, I don't remember, I wish I could."

"Can you give any reason for attacking the girl?"

"I was in a bad temper when I was walking along the street but that is no excuse."

"What did you intend doing to the girl?"

"I can't say, I just attacked her. It was not premeditated or anything, I just did it."

He was told he was going to be charged with indecent assault and assault occasioning actual bodily harm. Asked if he wanted to say anything more, he replied: "I want to say that I am sorry for what I have done and if there is anything I can do to repay the girl for what I have done to her I will do anything in my power to do so."

Glover spent the night in the cell and was released on bail the next day. He had only just left the court and was walking down Lonsdale Street when he was approached by two detectives. They introduced themselves as Detective Sergeant Andrew Fry and Detective Ken Evenden, then asked him to accompany them to the Criminal Investigation Branch's Camberwell office to talk about an assault on an old woman three weeks earlier.

They put him into their car and drove him from the city to Camberwell in silence. Once in the office, Detective Fry turned to Glover and explained: "Just over three weeks ago a lady was assaulted by a man in

Berrick Street. This was just around the corner from where you live. Can you tell me anything about it?"

"No ... I didn't do it."

"Mr Evenden has had a talk to your girlfriend and she says you left her last night in a terrible temper and that is when you assaulted another girl. She also says that on Tuesday night about three weeks ago you left her in a worse temper than you did last night. I put it to you, Mr Glover ... " he paused and stared at him, "that the same thing has occurred. You went off and attacked this woman in Berrick Street."

Glover looked at him, looked away. The policeman went on:

"You know whether you did this thing or not — what's it going to be? We can make things difficult for you, Mr Glover."

Glover held his gaze better this time. He sat and looked, silent. The detective tried again, moving his head a little closer and placing equal emphasis on each word: "Did you do it?"

"Yes ... Yes, I did."

"Why did you do it?"

"I don't know. I had a row with Phillipa, not about anything much, we just lashed each other with words and I went off. I was boiling up inside and went for a walk to cool off, that is when it happened."

"What happened?"

"I grabbed her from behind and threw her to the ground. I just went berserk somehow. I don't know, I found myself running. Just running anywhere. I wondered 'why am I running?' and I stopped. I found I was calm and I went home."

Asked if he removed Mrs Ince's bloomers, Glover replied: "If I did I can't remember."

Glover was asked to make a statement and he agreed. Andrew Fry recorded it on the typewriter. Glover recapped what he had just told him and then said he could not understand why he did not report the incident.

"It was the flash of time I could not account for that made me so frightened. It was just fear I suppose. I went to bed then. Since then I have been waiting for someone to knock on the door. I just did not have the guts to report it ... I am thoroughly ashamed of what I have done to this lady and will [sic] anything I can to atone [sic] for it."

The interview out of the way, Detective Sergeant Fry delegated Ken Evenden to take Glover home and search his belongings. Fry came along as well, but let Evenden do the work. They got to Glover's room and started going through his belongings.

"Who owns this drill?"

"I've got it on loan from work. They know I have it."

"Who owns the spotlight?"

"It's mine."

"Whose drums are these?"

"They're mine."

The detectives also noted a kerosene heater and an electric fan but did not mention them.

Detective Evenden got down under the bed. "Who owns the tape recorder?"

"I borrowed it from Channel Two."

"Did anyone tell you you could have a loan of it?"

"A Mr Griffen knows that I have it."

"Oh yeah. How long have you had it?"

"About three months."

"That seems a long time to have had it."

"They didn't want to use it."

Evenden went further in under the bed. "Whose microphone is this?"

"It's mine."

Detective Sergeant Fry pulled a trombone from behind a cupboard in front of the fireplace. He asked Glover if he played it.

"Yes, but I don't get much chance here though."

The policemen went back to the office and rang the ABC. Their records could not tell them if all the equipment was stolen, but it appeared that at least some of it was. It was enough for them to take possession of all the suspicious items. Glover was not going anywhere.

He applied for bail but with no close family ties and no one willing to put up substantial surety, the magistrate remanded him in custody.

When it was established a few days later that all the equipment was stolen, Glover reverted to his tried and trusted excuse that he had been using since the car theft in Lincoln almost ten years before: "I took the trombone as a joke, it must sound stupid," he told the police. "At the end of the party when most of the people had gone and there was [sic] just a few groups standing around, I saw a trombone near the piano and I decided to take it to play a joke on the owner. I intended to use it for a while and then return it. Notices were put up about the recorder missing and I got too frightened to return it — all of the property.

"I now realise what a fool I have been and am thoroughly ashamed and sorry."

On 16 October, a magistrate committed Glover for trial. The Melbourne *Sun Pictorial* newspaper ran a small item under the headline: "Two Women Allege Attacks". Bail was refused again.

On Monday, 3 December 1962, John Wayne Glover appeared before the Supreme Court charged with one count each of assaulting Valerie Bird and Myrtle Ince, and one count each of indecently assaulting both women. He was also charged for all the stolen goods found in his bedroom. He pleaded guilty to all charges and was convicted.

Luck was on his side once again. Perhaps it was his clean-cut demeanour and ability to convince others of his contrition, but he was released on a five year good behaviour bond with an order to seek medical help. The fact that he had already served two months in remand would have also contributed to the decision against incarceration.

The decision shocked Detective Sergeant Andrew Fry, who was to go on to have a distinguished police career. He had a gut feeling about Glover and was moved to warn other police of a potential danger. He wrote prophetically in the police files: "This man will commit more offences against women".

Following the court case Glover was thrown out of his Camberwell lodgings. He says it was because he found out the landlord had a special peephole to watch Glover's bedroom antics with the landlady and any women he brought home.

Glover found a bedsit in Windsor. Not long after the suburb was plunged into terror.

Irene Kiddle, a 61-year-old Australian champion bridge player, was found dead in a laneway between two blocks of St Kilda Road units on 22 March 1963. A widow, she had been attacked from behind in the most public of places while walking home from a card club. It was a motiveless attack. She had been stabbed three times, twice in the back and once in the side. Her purse was found near her body with ten pounds and eight shillings in winnings still inside. A bloody knife lay near the body. It was clean of prints.

A young man with sandy coloured hair had been seen earlier on the night of the attack, loitering in the laneway. He was never found. The murder remains unsolved.

John Glover kept his job with the ABC after his conviction and two months spent in prison awaiting trial.

On 30 May 1963, he and a workmate, John Russell, were working on the broadcast of a major surfing competition at Torquay when they started to hit the bottle heavily. Rolling drunk by the end of the day, they piled a rack of surfboards on to the back of the van before heading into the city that night.

"We could hardly see the road, it was a nightmare ... lucky to be alive," said Glover of the incident.

They were caught and fined 25 pounds. It too was only "a joke", they told a magistrate.

"We both lived bohemian lifestyles. I never thought what I was doing [the thefts] was wrong, it was the lifestyle ... if I saw something I didn't have I just took it," he said.

John Glover and the Australian Broadcasting Commission eventually parted ways, but whether it was connected to Glover's sudden interest in surfing is not known.

He was living in St Kilda, and going with a girl by the name of Catherine Pulsford who lived nearby in Middle Park. He found work as a television installer and repairman with an outfit called Hopman Television at St Kilda and, while it may have been a step down from being on the road with the ABC, it held certain advantages for John Wayne Glover — it put him back into peoples' homes.

At 14 years of age such temptations had been too much for him. Sixteen years later, his act was more refined — but more perverse. During this period he never owned a television. He would tell customers their set was going to take a week or two to fix and then use it himself until another set came along. But it was not television he was interested in watching. It was the customers — the women.

For John had not put the binoculars away. Any female client was at risk of getting a return visit from the television installer at night. Young women, middle-aged women, old women — he knew where their rooms were. In his own words, "it was a good thing for me to do at the time". He enjoyed the feeling of them not knowing he was there. He admitted to masturbating outside their windows.

On Wednesday 28 April 1965, a clean-shaven Glover appeared before South Melbourne Magistrates Court charged with being found unlawfully on a premises. He was peeping and police knew it; however, that was the most serious charge they could bring against him. But it was enough to land him a three month prison sentence because he was only three years into his five year good behaviour bond. He served 35 days.

Clifford had never forgotten the dashing older brother who had left such an impression during his visits in boarding school. By 1966, he too was desperate to make a break from Freda and to catch up with the hero figure of his childhood.

He had just turned 19 and had been out of school only a few months when his BOAC flight touched down in Sydney. While he had set up home in Sydney, he did not waste much time in booking a $42 air ticket to Melbourne for a weekend. All the illusions in Clifford's mind that John had built up over the years were not deflated by the experience of meeting him again after almost ten years.

It was a weekend Clifford would never forget, coming as he did from the somewhat dour background of the Royal School. John had organised a round of parties for them to visit and an impromptu bash at his own bedsit in Grandview Road, Prahran.

"It was a fabulous bloody weekend. Lots of parties and lots of girls. It was the first time I ever got drunk. He was screwing the landlady and he was not paying rent. He had all these ladies and he set me up that night with a chick. He had all these women, they were gorgeous."

Clifford became a semi-regular visitor to Melbourne over the next year or two, driving down in his Morris 1000. He was rarely let down by John's

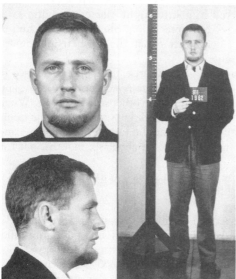

opposite: John and Gay Glover on their wedding day, 1 June 1968.

above: A newspaper photograph showing John Glover's family in 1959, after Barry Glover's motor scooter accident: (left to right) Patricia, Clifford, Freda and Barry.

left: Mug shots taken of John Glover in 1962. He was charged with indecent assault and assault occasioning actual bodily harm after the attack on Valerie Bird.

ability to organise a good time. John certainly never told his younger brother he had spent time in jail — that did not fit with the well-cultivated image.

But he was back in trouble again in September 1967. Glover's account is the only one available of the incident. He says a tram collided with his car, ripping up the panels on one side of the vehicle. The tram driver then allegedly came at him with an iron bar. Glover finished him in three punches, he says.

He appeared before the Prahran Magistrates court charged with assaulting the tram driver. The charge was dropped six months later with the court ruling that, despite his past offences, he had taken steps to keep his nose clean.

Glover was by this time working behind the counter as a sales assistant at a Melbourne wine shop. He was still not drinking very much, but he made sure his house was never short of a bottle in case friends or a young lady dropped around.

Around this time John was going out with a girl from South Yarra. She had a flatmate who had come down from Sydney to get away after a serious relationship had broken down. Before John's girlfriend knew what was happening, her boyfriend was paying more attention to her friend, Gay Rolls, than to her.

The affair grew into a full-blown relationship. Gay Rolls was not the first person to see potential in the poorly educated boy from Wolverhampton but she was the first to harness it. Gay picked up on John Glover where the army had left off 15 years earlier. Where it ordered him to make his bed, she directed him into night classes studying sales techniques, management and wine appreciation. She encouraged him to think of himself as capable of doing better than the nowhere jobs he was still doing. She was the drill sergeant.

To Glover's relatives, Gay came as a surprise. They had been used to seeing him with an endless supply of glamorous women. Gay was plain but, as Clifford noted, she had something the others did not have. When John first came to Sydney to meet Gay's parents and saw their home nestling in the harbourside hills of Mosman, he turned to his brother and said: "This'll do me fine, son. I'll be here in about six months, put the champers on."

They were standing on the balcony upstairs overlooking Quakers Hat Bay. "What do you mean?" Clifford asked.

"I'm coming up."

John told Clifford he intended to marry Gay six to seven months before it happened. Clifford asked his brother why. John said: "Only child, her parents are getting on, she is going to end up getting it [the house]."

Clifford recalled: "She was all over him like a bloody rash as usual."

Before Gay and John were married they had two engagement parties:

one in Sydney and one later in Melbourne. In Sydney, John "came up with four empty suitcases just to take the loot back," Clifford recalled.

Perhaps in a sign of things to come, the future father-in-law, Jack Rolls, was ordered to bed in his own house during the Sydney party. "We were passing him drinks, scotch and dry, through the window all night. He had a merry old time in there," said Clifford.

Gay's parents never totally approved of their daughter's relationship with John but they did not stand in her way. "The feeling was that Gay had been around for a long time — she was in her late twenties and finds this attractive charming guy — and John was extremely charming, but Essie [Gay's mother] saw straight through John right from the start, saw that he was a commoner. Essie was very snobbish," said a family friend.

On Saturday 1 June 1968, a wet, windswept autumn day in Melbourne, Glover married Jacqueline Gail Rolls, 27, the only child of Jack and Essie Rolls, a well-off but not especially wealthy Mosman couple.

The Tet offensive in Vietnam was dominating the papers of the day along with the visit by the then Prime Minister, John Gorton, to the United States for historic talks with President Lyndon B. Johnson. Towards the back of the Melbourne *Age*, in the social pages, the marriage at South Yarra was reported among a half dozen other photos of newlyweds on the social page. Although ill, Jack Rolls had journeyed to Melbourne for the ceremony with his wife.

The honeymoon bed was barely cold, just 17 days into the marriage, when Glover appeared before a Melbourne court charged with stealing from his employer — the wine merchant. Certainly his house had never been short of a good drop, but whether the ill-gotten booty was served to the guests at the nuptial celebrations is unknown.

He was 35 years old and grey streaks were starting to appear in his hair. The official charge — larceny as a servant — was the exact same one that the Wolverhampton Juvenile Court had dealt with 21 years earlier. He had been sacked from his job as a driver–salesman with no explanation and stole in retaliation, he claimed. Taking the circumstances into account, the magistrate placed Glover on a good behaviour bond of $200. He told him that if he paid $30 into the Prahran poor box and if he could make it through the year without trouble, the case would be dismissed.

At around the same time as John's marriage, Clifford rang home to Freda, whose light fingers were also bringing some trouble.

"I am a bit busy now, dear," she told him. "The police have just knocked on the door."

"What for?"

"I think it has something to do with this fur coat I'm wearing."

She rang some of her good friends in the right places and any embarrassing charges were, of course, avoided.

CHAPTER SEVEN

MOTHERS

Gay and John Glover moved into a cottage at in East St Kilda. For all that was said about John's cynical motives, he did appear to have genuine respect and admiration for his wife. He was kept busy with his wine appreciation and his sales training courses.

Meanwhile, John's younger brother in Sydney had continued to keep in touch with his new in-laws, Essie and Jack Rolls. He found them both to be "fabulous" people.

Having no family, Clifford would visit the couple regularly. For Christmas 1968 they invited him and a few of his English friends over for lunch. They were all far from home. Essie made a beautiful egg nog — thoroughly alcoholic — and everyone got quite merry. It was an open house and Clifford felt he was always welcome.

John and Gay moved up to Sydney from Victoria in early 1969 at the invitation of Jack, who thought they might be helpful in an emergency as his illness progressed. Gay was at home in Mosman. She grew up there and went to school there and John adopted the place as though he had done the same.

Dominic Lopez was a fresh-faced 30-year-old alderman on Mosman Council when he first encountered Glover within a few months of his arrival at the Rolls household. He was among a small group of aldermen supporting residents in their opposition to a series of street closures and changes in traffic direction around Quakers Hat Bay and Beauty Point. He was introduced to John by Jack and Essie Rolls, whom he knew. They were ardently opposed to the council move, which was aimed at stopping streets on the northern foreshores of the municipality from being used as a handy short cut in peak-hour traffic.

To Mr Lopez, who would eventually go on to become Mayor of Mosman, Jack and Essie Rolls were "beaut people — real Mosman people".

John and Gay's original intention was that they would stay with their in-laws until they got enough cash together for a deposit on their own

The Rolls/Glover home in Wyong Road, Mosman.

home, but they soon had another mouth to feed with the birth of their first daughter, Kellie, in 1971. Fiscal reality crept into the plan and Essie and Jack agreed it would be a good idea to help the kids out. They put another room on top of the house. Essie and Jack would move up to the new third storey while Gay, John and Kellie would have the run of the house. In an instant, the decision had catapulted John Glover into the spot where he had been intending to land all along, right from the time he had first walked into Lou Blooms, the plushest clothes shop in Wolverhampton.

He had made it.

There was, however, a price. John Glover never struck up the same rapport with his mother-in-law that his younger brother had found came so easily. Indeed, the relationship was curt at best.

It did not take much for Essie to inform John whose house he was living in and remind him that he was little more than a guest, dependent on the goodwill of her and Jack — something which could be given and taken away.

His pride chafed at being the subject of such cruel fate. He had landed, but it was not quite what he had expected.

Glover took to the Mosman lifestyle as if he were born to it. Within a few years he had joined the Norths Rugby Union Club and the Mosman Returned Services Club.

"When I first met him he appeared to be just an ordinary person. One of the local residents complaining about different situations, and then, you know, you'd forget him except I used to see him regularly at the Returned Servicemen's Club", said Dom Lopez. "Gay's parents didn't want her to marry him, but they accepted it when she did.

... He seemed to be very community minded, seemed to take an interest in things and was always obliging, wanting to help people."

John found work in Sydney as a sales representative for Golins Wines and Spirits. It was a milestone. For the first time, he was "one of the suit and tie brigade".

With Gay's guidance and encouragement Glover began to improve his lot. "I became John Glover, sales representative," he said. "Instead of driving a delivery truck I was driving a company car — it was a fillip to me. I was very successful at it. I was always a gentleman when it came to business."

In that respect, as he approached 40, it seemed like his life was, at last, going somewhere.

Shortly after John and Gay moved in, another slightly older couple, the Thierings, moved next door with their three teenage children. Glover sometimes invited Barry Thiering over to share a few beers and sometimes he accepted.

They had kids in common and they developed a friendship but Dr Thiering, a chaplain, thought he never really got to know Glover. His speciality was counselling so his whole business was about getting inside people's heads. John Glover's was impenetrable. He never talked about his background and the chaplain believed he had been a sailor. He acted like a sailor. He called the verandah the deck. He had a lifebuoy on the wall and he wore clothes with a maritime flavour. Glover also convinced a few members of the Mosman Returned Servicemen's Club that he had been in the merchant navy and had sailed around the world.

The day they met, Glover was cracking jokes mostly about mother-in-laws. Dr Thiering thought that the naval background accounted for the way he was a "wise cracker".

While they were not close, Thiering came to regard John Glover as a personality. He liked him.

Over the next few years Barry Thiering would hear just about every mother-in-law joke ever written. But John never laughed. Maybe a chuckle or a sarcastic snigger about something that made him angry but nothing from the heart, no belly laughs.

John still never got drunk as far as anyone could tell. Some small pink capillary lines had started to appear on his face, giving him the appearance of a drunk but as far as everyone was concerned, he was not. He and Gay might have the odd beer or half a bottle of wine.

Essie Rolls (*left*), John Glover's mother-in-law.

To Dr Thiering, Gay was the strong partner. "Like her mother, but more intelligent. Essie seemed like just an organised little old lady. She might have been a dowager queen, the way she ran the place in a hands-off sort of way."

Essie was a local character. "Like Dame Edna Everage on amphetamines", was how one neighbour described her. Her hair would be rinsed regularly in shades of blue and wisteria and her trips to the hairdresser were not just outings, they were events.

She knew Mosman as only someone who had lived there all her life could. She knew the gossip and would spread it around — sometimes malevolently. She was sharp and would not miss a beat. Her friends recall her as a marvellous person who loved to mix and socialise and who was always generous. She became, they say, a prisoner in her own home, which was taken over by John. She liked a drink and would have a tipple of gin upstairs in her room. It was after a few drinks that Essie really made her presence felt in the neighbourhood.

The first thing the Thierings saw when they arrived for day one in their new home was a note on the garage door: "Dirty black men run out of this house". It was disturbing. They were not a dark coloured family and it did not make any sense. But after a few years living there, they began to realise it was probably Essie. She had a fixation against blacks. There were mysterious nights when Essie's neighbours were visited late at night by police who had received reports along the lines of "Aboriginals running through garden" or "man with a knife in house". There was always a strong suspicion that Essie on the bottle was the culprit.

Neighbours with dogs also suspected Essie of being behind another strange phenomenon. They would wake to find the milk bottles that they left out the night before for collection had been ignored by the milk man because of the dog droppings inside. It was thought that Essie was getting revenge for certain dogs defecating on her lawn.

While Essie held sway in the house, it was in the garden that John Glover asserted his territorial needs. He took to the ritual of the great Australian yard with gusto. He would spend long hours on his patch. It was kept immaculate, all cement and squares, no weeds and everything trim and in its place. Except for a small plot in St Kilda, he had never had a garden before and his methods in keeping this one drew more stylistic inspiration from military handbooks than gardening guides. Anything that grew out of place was poisoned. Nothing lived there except that which John Glover ordained.

He owned large quantities of hydrochloric acid with which to clean moss off bricks.

One day when Paul Thiering and his brother were pulling up some daisies at the orders of their mother, John peered over the fence: "I've got some good poison, I'll bring it around. It'll knock out the roots and kill them properly."

After that the two boys would walk around the yard and let little comments fly over the fence like: "Let's poison this tree. No, no, let's poison that one," trying to bait their neighbour.

They saw him as a somewhat pathetic figure. "He would come home after he did his job and spend his whole weekend cleaning out the house, getting every single leaf out of his gutters and blaming our trees for all of them. He would spend hours doing this, every leaf in the yard, every Sunday morning, cleaning his big, big car, always a Falcon or a Holden or something like that — a perfectly clean car."

It was with one of these vehicles that a wayward Thiering frisbee collided back in the early 1970s. This was the worst thing in the world. Glover angrily yelled: "Do you know how to cut back and polish a car?"

"Uh? ... no."

"If that frisbee hits it one more time I'll have you doing it all afternoon."

The two teenagers laughed. They did not see him as a threatening figure. They saw him as a joke, the sort of person who made strong statements but who gave little reason for them to be believed. A coward.

On another occasion a teenager who lived further down the road and who had a reputation as a larrikin became the focus of John's suspicions. A streetlight just down the hill from the Glover house had been broken. John considered it to be his streetlight and he was going to catch whoever broke it. He got it into his mind that the larrikin from down the road had done it and he was going to make him pay.

He complained about it so much to anyone who would listen that people would joke that John was hiding in the bushes all night trying to catch him in the act. Said one of his neighbours: "He never caught him but one day John was complaining about this guy and saying how he was going to go and get him, when the guy walked by on the other side of the road and John did nothing. As far as we were concerned he was all talk. He had this big chip on his shoulder the whole time. We used to say that John treated the street like it was his street. Anyone new that came into the street, he would check them out to make sure they were suitable."

Freda was not getting any younger.

She had one operation for breast cancer and it was doubtful that it had been successful. She decided she wanted to be with her two sons in Australia and she wanted her daughter Pat to go with her. She thought the cancer was going to kill her and wanted to pull the family together.

She had married Frank Goalby in 1968 after living with him for 16 years but he was quite happy to stay in Wolverhampton. That was all right. He was expendable. The divorce went through in 1971 as the immigration paperwork began.

John filled in all the appropriate family reunion papers and told them he was getting everything ready at his end. He was playing the dutiful son. But his real reaction to the news was more like that of the little girl in the movie *Poltergeist* who greets the arrival of the evil spirits with a mixture of fear and fascination in the words: "They're here!"

He had, according to his brother Clifford, done little to prepare for the arrival of Freda, his sister Pat, her husband Brian Tocker and their two children at the tail end of 1973. Clifford and his 20-year-old bride Leonie put them up in their two bedroom house in Croydon Park, in Sydney's inner-west. It was hardly Mosman but John did make the effort to travel over a few times in the first couple of weeks. He was playing the big brother, checking up on them. But the enthusiasm died after a while and Clifford and Leonie were left with the burden.

At the couple's wedding reception John had spent most of his time playing the "toff" from Mosman. Rather than mix with Clifford's more knock-about mates, he had spent much time chatting to Leonie's boss, wealthy eastern suburbs socialite Florence Broadhurst. Leonie had worked for her since she was 16. At 72, Ms Broadhurst was a well-connected woman of independence who produced exclusive hand-printed wallpaper at her Paddington factory. Glover would later ask Florence to make blinds for his home.

Leonie's 21st birthday party was held shortly after the family's arrival. Gay and John could not make it. It was celebrated at the working-class Yagoona RSL club, some 25 kilometres south-west of Mosman, in that netherworld of suburbs where John had no desire to venture. As far as the family was concerned, John had become "a two bob snob". "He wanted to distance himself from the family because of the way he was, just the way he spoke," said Leonie. "This damn upper crust. I knew where he came from. The family were surprised when they came out here and they saw where he lived."

For all the family's perception of snobbery, there was another reason for him being reluctant to bring the two sides of the family together.

John *never* let Gay and Freda alone together. Freda knew too much. She had in fact threatened him on occasions that she would tell Gay what she knew. John had retorted with a similar threat. He would tell everyone about the pornographic photographs of her taken in the front room back at Lower Villiers Street, Wolverhampton. Impasse — but he still never ever left the two alone together.

Within three months of their arrival in Sydney, the new immigrants moved up to the Central Coast, a one hour drive north of Sydney. Clifford and his family followed them up there some years later. When Freda came down to visit John in Sydney, he put her in a motel.

The same year as Freda's unexpected arrival, Gay gave birth to the couple's second daughter, Marney.

The Thiering's yard was a more haphazard collection of native trees and rocks than the symmetrical arrangement at 18 Wyong Road. It was home to a big old blue tongue lizard. Glover saw it one day and told them: "Here, I'll take care of it for you. I'll bash it over the head."

"There's no need for that, John — we like it," his neighbour, Dr Barbara Thiering, told him.

"Well, if it comes over here I'm going to kill it."

"We like blue tongue lizards, it's fine — it's not causing any problems."

"Well if it comes over here, I'm going to bash it over the head."

Another time, a cat chased a possum into the Thiering house and with no one else in the house to help, Nerida Thiering called John over to help get it out of her bedroom. He came over with just a sack and a smile on his face — always the good neighbour. He ventured into the bedroom and re-emerged five seconds later with an even bigger smile. There had been no rummaging of furniture or any noise at all.

"What happened to the possum?" she asked, looking at the bulge in the sack.

"Oh. I killed it."

He had silently, quickly killed the thing with such precision she had no idea how he did it. She did not even see the weapon he used.

"I only wanted you to get rid of the thing," she said in amazement.

But perhaps the best early illustration of Glover's lack of respect for life came one day in the late 1970s. Dr Barry Thiering had just put the car in the garage after bringing his daughter Nerida home. It was the beginning of winter and darkness was falling as they began their way up the steep set of stairs that lead to the Thiering home. Nerida was a few metres in front but was hidden from view by the fading light and the thick bushes and trees that cover the yard.

The preacher heard a scream from his daughter. Nerida had seen a man dressed all in black appear right in front of her. Instinctively she had dropped to the ground, reared up on her back and kicked the interloper. He came stumbling down the stairs towards her father, a big man whose solid frame had been used to great advantage on the rugby field in his younger days.

"I saw this dark figure come by and I grabbed him. I'm really a mild-mannered reporter but sometimes I like to rush off to a telephone booth," he recalled.

"We've sort of rolled down the steps together, he's only about ten and a half stone so I've got a bit of an advantage. He's all in black, black woollen cap, black gloves and black running shoes. We're locked in this embrace and I hear this guttural noise, this strange noise from the primeval past and I realise it's me, fighting for my daughter and my home and all of that."

The whole neighbourhood had heard Nerida Thiering's screams and people started appearing from everywhere. They were greeted by the vision of Dr Thiering grappling with the man in black on the grassy side of Wyong Road. "I'm just looking for my dog, I'm looking for a dog," he kept trying to explain to the disbelieving group.

About five people had formed a small ring around the intruder, trying to decide what to do with him. Barry Thiering told someone to call the police. "It was a community thing of helping out. We all felt pretty good," recalls Paul Thiering. But the neighbourly good vibes were soon shattered by a scream next door, from the Glover house: "The jewellery's been stolen."

John Glover appeared on the scene armed with a mattock handle, which he kept under his bed for emergencies. "Everyone sort of naturally let John take control because John had that sort of reputation in the neighbourhood," said Paul Thiering. "He was the policeman, the upholder of moral values. All the neighbourhood thought that. Anyway, without any warning whatsoever and amid this crowd, John just walked up and went bang on the back of his head."

Barry Thiering picked up the story: "It made the most amazing noise, the sound of this mattock handle hitting the guy's head — the hollow sound of a coconut being hit by a cricket bat. He hit him at least three times. I was actually quite concerned, being a man of peace."

The intruder was rolling around on the ground in agony. "Don't hit me, don't hit me," he was begging in genuine fear. Glover hit him again, then another time. The group of respectable Mosman citizens watched John Glover in action. They were horrified.

"You bastard, you've robbed me," Glover snarled as he lined him up for another whack.

"Don't hit me."

"Stop it, stop it John! You'll kill him!" came a voice from the crowd.

Dr Barbara Thiering turned to John: "You are putting yourself in the wrong, John. Just leave it to the police! Don't you realise you are going to affect the police case if you keep hitting him?"

He started arguing with her and everyone around stepped back. The man had been disturbed in the Glover's house and had taken a few small items. He had jumped from the second floor and ran across the Thierings' yard before he was caught.

There was mass confusion. Barry Thiering remembers ordering Glover to sit on the burglar while they waited for police. Glover sat on him while the preacher lay down next to them hyperventilating from his exertions.

Paul Thiering remembers his moral outrage at being associated with the act of senseless violence; he just wanted to leave. All the while the arguments were raging. Barbara Thiering was lecturing John on ethics and morality.

In the confusion, Glover got to his feet while the crowd was telling him how to behave. The man in black miraculously rose and sprinted away. Paul Thiering started to chase him. Then he thought, "What do I do if I catch him?" He stopped, gasping for breath as the intruder rounded a corner and disappeared into the dark.

Everybody felt somewhat foolish at having let the intruder escape, but not John Glover. "I got him," he boasted without remorse. Barbara Thiering, a theologian of international repute for her theories on the Dead Sea Scrolls, was still trying to instil in him some sort of sense of the correct way to behave when the police turned up, a minute or two later. They searched for a while and then left. There was nothing more they could do than circulate a description and check with hospitals.

"I felt a fool but I had handed responsibility to John," said Barry Thiering. "We can blame everything on John now," he laughs.

On Sunday 17 October 1977, Leonie's friend and employer Florence Broadhurst was found murdered in a private annex to her Paddington wallpaper factory. Then aged 78, Ms Broadhurst had been bashed viciously around the head with a piece of timber; her killer stuffed her bleeding body in a washroom. The murder baffled police. It seemed that Ms Broadhurst admitted the killer to the apartment while working late on Saturday by herself.

It appeared that she had been attacked while preparing two cups of tea. Her fingers had been broken and rings valued at $100,000 stolen. "We [her employees and former staff] were made to feel like suspects. We were all fingerprinted," Leonie recalled.

John Glover was convicted in April 1978 of shoplifting socks and other clothing from a retail store. He was sentenced to 20 days in jail or a $100 fine.

About the same time he lost his job; he was then working for Nestlé. The company claims it has no record of his employment or the circumstances of his departure so it is not known if it was related to the shoplifting conviction. His earlier job selling wines with Golins had ended when the company folded. Glover had found work selling smallgoods with Mayfair, but this had not lasted long and he was retrenched with a number of other workers. By Glover's account, he soon obtained work as a sales representative with Nestlé, selling and maintaining confectionery vending machines.

One of his duties was to ensure that the vending machines in Sydney's Long Bay Jail Prison visitor rooms and prison staff canteens were well stocked.

Without employment, he took himself along to a modelling agency and put his name down with an eye to doing advertising work to earn extra money. They wanted to charge him $300 for his portfolio shots but he refused and told the agency that if he was wanted, they would do the shots for nothing. The bluff came off and it was not long before he had done his first magazine shoots. An offer for television followed.

The agencies saw something in Glover. His silver-grey hair gave him a look of maturity and respectability while his face was still quite young and handsome. His eyes said "trust".

His first television commercial was for American Express. John Glover's job was to pat his breast pocket and pretend he had lost his wallet. His words were not going to be used but the director told him to mouth something.

The result? He says deaf people might have a sly giggle at his performance, his clearly visible words being: "F___! Someone's stolen my wallet!"

(American Express have been unwilling to confirm whether the tape exists. Their advertising agency, Ogilvy and Mather, deny that Glover ever appeared in any ads for American Express, claiming to have employed a look-alike actor. If so, both Glover's family and friends were fooled by the likeness.)

"He thought he was a movie star, he loved it," was how one friend recalled the period when the commercial was showing. "It was the entertainer coming out in him."

By 1980 Glover was back on his feet. He had been taken on as a sales representative by Melbourne-based company Petersville Pastries, who sold Four'N Twenty Pies. It was a modest, straight wage with no commission for extra sales, but had one major perk — a company car with 24 hour use.

John Glover had, by 1980, found another passion in life — poker machines. His visits to the Mosman Returned Servicemen's Club and Norths Rugby Club became more regular.

In 1982 Glover's membership at Norths Rugby Union Club was terminated. A number of complaints had been received about his wanderings through the unattended gymnasium and squash centre dressing rooms. Money had gone missing from bags and suspicions ran deep that he was the culprit. However, there was not enough evidence to call the police.

Freda moved into a Gosford retirement village in the early 1980s. It was one of the better places in a town overflowing with retirees. It had a waiting list five years long ... Freda talked her way in within three weeks.

Once inside she was unstoppable. She got to work harnessing the untapped energy of hundreds of underemployed knitting needles. A mad knitter herself, she had her group of little old ladies making handbags and other items and was paying them $6 a bag. She had them "working their little tails off" and would collect the bags every Friday, making sure each of her girls was up to quota. Then she went down to the Gosford Bowling Club to sell them for $28 a throw.

As bowls was the main recreational activity in town, Freda had become a keen bowler. Just as she had been a proficient darts player at home, she quickly took to the lawn game.

It was on the greens of Gosford bowling club she met Samuel Roger Underwood (Roger to his mates), a suntanned Aussie who was hard of hearing as a result of an accident in the surf 50 years earlier. Roger and Freda became a mixed doubles pairing of some repute and took their share of prizes. Roger's wife was dying and had been sick for a long time. Freda became a regular visitor to her in hospital and was her friend in her final months.

Roger's wife had been on at him to remarry as soon as possible after she passed away and often picked out appropriate mates for her husband. Freda was the final choice. Roger admired her. She was a "very jovial woman, very active ... a good mixer, a good organiser. She started a mahjong club within the Gosford sailing club. She had a will of her own."

Seven months after the death of his wife, the wiry, retired dental technician proposed to Freda while they were on holidays in New Zealand. Freda and Roger went by train to Sydney shortly before the ceremony to meet the in-laws and to get the official nod from John. Roger was struck by the appearance of her children. "None of them were alike. They all had different fathers," he said.

When the couple were married by a celebrant in July 1983, John Glover stood by his mother's side and gave her away. The newlyweds were both 73 years old.

Florence Broadhurst pictured in 1977, two weeks before her death.

John seemed very happy for the two of them and wished them well. Gay was there with the girls.

After the marriage they moved to a unit on the side of a hill overlooking East Gosford. But Freda's days of dancing were numbered. The couple already knew the cancer was back and it would eventually take her life. Freda had never expected to make it as far as she had. She was riddled with the disease and had no chance of beating it.

By 1984, Glover's job with Four'N Twenty pies took him out of Sydney. The company had decided to try to drum up new business on the Central Coast. It was an enormous run which had no boundaries. So long as he brought in business he could go where he pleased; he did not have a daily accountable schedule mapped out for him by his boss. Occasionally, he would drop in and say hello to his sick mother and Roger.

Glover's "pie run" on the Central Coast came to an end in 1986, confining his operations to Sydney.

In the same year Freda and Roger made a will. Freda asked Clifford to read it over for her to see if it was all right. "You'll finally get your inheritance," she told him, straight-faced.

He read it, then read it again. There was something horribly wrong ... his name was missing. Everyone in the family got something except him. "I have just read the thing, Freda, and I'm not even bloody mentioned."

She was unfazed. "Well, Pat will get something out of it."

"I think from that day on I closed Freda out, I closed her off," said Clifford.

When it seemed that Freda was going to go in 1986, Barry Glover came back to Australia for the first time since 1960. By then Roger was driving Freda up to Newcastle twice a week for chemotherapy as she slowly wasted away, but clung relentlessly to life. It was a terrible time for them both.

For the most part, over almost 20 years, things were pretty good at the Glover's end of Wyong Road. John was a typical father, ferrying the girls to netball and to music practice. There was always music coming from the house. Marney and Kellie had both inherited their father's latent musical abilities — a direct line of descent from Walter. Glover spent thousands of dollars on a top-of-the-range oboe for one of the girls, according to Roger Underwood. But they did not need instruments: their singing voices were what passersby would most often hear.

The whole family loved music and attended orchestral concerts together, finishing up at cheap restaurants, preferably Italian. Gay and John had been doing it since their courtship and the girls just became involved with them.

There were those idyllic summer days when the whole family would troop two doors down to the house of a couple, the Caspers, who had a swimming pool that they allowed the Glovers to use at will. There were no fences bordering the back yards of those few houses and the Caspers' pool became a focus for a small group of friends. In the early years, John taught the girls to swim there. They were peaceful days, a million miles from the Black Country.

There were those there who still thought him an object of ridicule, however. "He would always make these comments which were just slightly anti-social, out of touch, with a sense of coldness. He was different from other men in that he didn't know how to play any games, didn't play any sport. He was in a household of women — two families, his wife and Essie upstairs," recalled a neighbour.

There were days on the weekends when John would be in a jovial mood. He would walk up and down the street chatting about nothing in particular with whoever was outside. This was how he was remembered by many people.

Yet inside John Glover was an angry, brooding man. All the while there was the focus of his hatred — Essie — looking down from her commanding position on the third storey. It was her house and, even as his tenure there stretched over a decade, she never let him forget it. "You can go," she would yell at him. "This is my house. This is Gay's house. You can go," neighbours recalled.

"She treated John like a lackey and she made sure she let him know he was not of her class — she was a well-to-do wife of a successful Mosman businessman — and that she always disapproved of Gay for marrying John," said a person close to the family.

It was castrating for his ego. "Beneath it all, he looked tremendously angry. He was always bitter and angry ... an isolated person. He had no real male friends as far as I am aware. We never saw any of his friends come over, it was only Gay's friends. John was downstairs in the garden but always being hen-pecked, you could just see it. She would be talking at the top of her voice so everyone could hear it ... Essie lording it over everyone."

A lot of people said she started to go senile but she largely remained lucid to the end, just becoming more cantankerous. She had been a modestly large woman but she grew thinner as her last days approached. By the mid-1980s she was going downhill.

It came as some sort of relief for both John and Gay when they moved her into a nursing home — first at Neutral Bay and then at the Mosman Nursing Home, just up the road from Wyong Road. Reports from some staff members suggest she was a well-known, domineering figure who ran the nurses ragged. Others recall her as a very pleasant woman.

Every weekend, John and Gay would visit her. "John playing the dutiful son-in-law. He was the upstanding citizen regardless of how much he might have despised her," said a family friend.

CHAPTER EIGHT

DARK SIDE

Apart from his garden, John Glover established one other niche for himself. It was just inside the doorway of the Mosman Returned Servicemen's Club. There, he plied the same 20 cent poker machine and drank his customary Gordon's gin and tonic. He was recognised by all the regulars and known to many of them. Some called him "The Captain" because of his dapper dress and reserved demeanour.

John Glover rarely sought conversation with other members, preferring to sit with his drink and religiously put his coins through the pokies. But he was, according to one of his drinking buddies, Alderman Dom Lopez, "Mr Pillar of Society". Lopez had seen him do all the good work, putting in the hours. And he charmed those old ladies who attended the bingo regularly. He was the "lover boy" who would always offer a lift home and always provide the charming line in chatter when it was required. When their backs were turned, however, he was likely to turn to one of his male acquaintances and utter some crudity.

Glover had many acquaintances and few friends. The friends tended to be more like allies anyway. They did not have to be confidants or pals, just carry the same opinions.

The 1980s were a terrible time for John Glover. He bemoaned the downfall of his suburb as the new money started to flood in when the stock markets went crazy after 1985. He talked to his neighbours about how yuppies were ruining the neighbourhood. They were pushing prices through the roof and average young families could not afford to buy a house there any more. He hated their outward display of affluence that he could not match. He fretted when the Porsches and BMWs started multiplying and the big new houses replaced the more homely bungalows.

Added to that were the old women — the widows who occupied the large houses that should have housed a family. The suburb was being overrun by them. It was being ruined by the twin assaults of yuppies and Mosman matrons — or so John Glover said.

He complained about the construction of a new retirement village at Spit Junction called The Garrison. A large complex of 82 units, it was a disaster in John Glover's eyes. "There's already too many old people in Mosman," he said. "Gee there are a lot of nursing homes here. I go to a lot for work. Essie is in one. They're everywhere. The whole suburb's going to the dogs with them and the yuppies."

One neighbour recalled his last conversation with Glover. It was about "all these trendy advertising executives" laying waste to his beloved surroundings with their fast money and cars.

Across the road from the Glover house was one such source of John Glover's ire. One of his allies, a Mr Britten, had lived in the street for years in a little old brick house painted white. After Mr Britten, "a nice old fellow", gassed himself in his car, the new owner built a large orange house. John called it a monstrosity and would complain at length about the "black Porsche driving" owner.

The new owner later built a large orange wall around the place with a security intercom system. It was not John Glover's idea of how Mosman should be. One morning the street awoke to find the word "friendly?" daubed across the orange wall in black paint. Glover may not have been the only one in the street to dislike the wall but he certainly became the prime suspect for that piece of vandalism.

The only times anyone can remember John opening up and displaying any feelings was when he talked about his daughters, Kellie and Marney. He would express his real delight in their progress at school and in their music — getting the opportunities he thought he was denied.

Kellie was such a gifted musician, with a beautiful soprano voice, that Glover was more than happy to pay for her music lessons with a prominent local music teacher, Irene Kurtesz. Mrs Kurtesz, like John, saw great potential in her student, and pushed her hard to get her up to the standard of the Conservatorium of Music. During winter, John often came over to walk Kellie home from music lessons. He would sit listening and occasionally ask questions about music style. His own interest was being sparked.

In 1987 Glover was diagnosed with breast cancer. At first he had been horrified to learn that he had contracted what he considered to be a "woman's disease". It offered little solace to him that five per cent of all breast cancer cases were males. With Freda deteriorating before his eyes from the very same affliction it scared the life out of him.

He contacted relatives in Australia and overseas to try to find out if there was a history of the disease on either side of his family. He needed to allay his worst fears. The Glovers, he learnt, lived to ripe old ages.

But he was still scared. He was only 54 years old. He thought he was going to die well ahead of his time, and he didn't want to go the way Freda was headed. She was dragging him into the grave with her, he thought.

Everybody noticed a change come over John Glover when he was diagnosed with the cancer. He began to open up and express some of his feelings for the first time. "Oh yeah, I've had this problem, I've been diagnosed with breast cancer. Is that possible? I didn't know men had breasts," he told one acquaintance, who remembered it because it was one of the few times he had seen him express any real emotion. He looked worried and depressed.

"Most of the time he had a charming look on his face — a smile that said everything was fine — but you could see the worry coming out in his face ... Most of the time with John it was bland, grey interaction."

But Glover was not being as open as he might have been. The breast cancer was only a small part of his worries. The operation to remove the cancer was successful and doctors were confident there would be no recurrence.

Playing more on his thoughts was the fact that he had become impotent with all the emotional turmoil. It was linked to the onset of a prostate condition and repeated urinary tract infections.

On the surface he continued acting normally and Gay was totally understanding; she accepted they were progressing in years and told him there was more to a relationship than sex, Glover recalled.

Her assurances, however, had only a limited effect on her husband, whose whole personality had once been based around his sexual libido. Now, it was based more on his feeling of importance from the fact he lived in Mosman. He attributed this to his wife, so his inability to satisfy her sexually — to maintain his side of the bargain — was a great stress.

Glover was failing to keep up his end of the bargain in other ways, too. He later boasted about how attractive he was to women at the club, some of whom he thought of as "predators". The predators were the numerous middle-aged women who were either widows or unhappily married and whom he perceived as being available for the taking.

He had a long-standing affair with one woman in her eighties. A bright, outgoing woman, she looked 65 and was one of the local characters. She was alerted to Glover's impending arrival by a short message down the phone: "Put the kettle on!"

One afternoon, around September 1988, Glover dropped into the club for his habitual after-work drink and a spin on his favourite poker machine. This day he made the chance acquaintance of Joan Sinclair, a well-off divorcée who had been attending a function at the club.

To those who knew her, Joan Sinclair was a friendly, gentle, warm-hearted person — exactly like you'd want your grandmother to be. In 1952 she married Alan Sinclair, a builder who made his business into a great success. They had three sons: Roger, Rod and Ross. The couple divorced in 1972 but remained lifelong friends. Her children grew up and she lived alone in Beauty Point.

The neighbourhood children loved Mrs Sinclair. Her home was a refuge and playground for them. She rarely used her tennis court, preferring to watch the game on television, but would let the children play on it and swim in her pool on hot summer days.

Joan Sinclair adored her two grandsons and often looked after them. She became involved with their school, Beauty Point Public, helping at school plays and functions.

The relationship between John Glover and Joan Sinclair was to change from one which involved a few fumbled attempts at sex play — hampered by Glover's impotence — into one of pure friendship. The pair would see each other at the RSL or for lunch from time to time — always on weekdays.

Shortly after their meeting Joan Sinclair introduced Glover to her youngest son, Ross, aged 27, when Ross made a surprise visit to her home. They chatted briefly and Joan later explained that John visited her on an irregular basis. Eventually Glover came to meet all her sons. They did not approve but at the same time it was their mother's business so they did not interfere. Glover's own family was completely in the dark about Mrs Sinclair's existence.

Glover's mother Freda had been transferred to the Neringah private hospital at Wahroonga on Sydney's northern outskirts when John met Mrs Sinclair. To those who saw Freda it was clear she did not have very long to live.

The twice weekly chemotherapy had lasted a year but it was no longer enough. It was getting too much for Roger to take her up to Newcastle all the time. John had driven her a few times but he hated seeing the pain and suffering. He "couldn't bear to see a three legged dog".

On 30 September 1988, Freda's 78th birthday, Clifford received a phone call from his mother at the hospital, saying she was broke and asking if he could pay for her funeral. Clifford agreed.

Then she matter-of-factly broke the news to him, news that he had always suspected but had wanted to hear from her lips.

"Clifford, I've not got long for this world," she said. "You've always wanted to know."

"Yep!" he said, half expecting what she was about to say.

"Your real father is Sidney Orphan. Remember, you met him once or twice at Blackpool." Hardly pausing for breath, she continued: "I've spent your inheritance. There is nothing. I have got nothing of your father's or your real father's."

Eleven days later Freda was dead. Both John and his sister Pat were at the hospital at different times on the day. In the atmosphere of grief, something peculiar happened. When she died Freda had $20 in her purse. Freda never went anywhere without $20, according to Clifford. On this, her last day, her daughter Pat lent the money to her.

Pat, Roger and John were all in her room. Pat went out of the room to get her bag. When she returned Freda was dead and the money was missing from her purse ...

Pat thought that Roger had been alone with Freda when she died but she later told police she learned John had been the last person to see Freda alive.

John broke the news to Clifford by phone. "You don't sound upset," he said to Clifford.

"I don't?"

"It was not very pretty."

"I imagine not."

"Are you coming back for the funeral?"

"I don't need to. Freda and me, our relationship is now complete."

"She was your mother!"

"She was the mother of all mothers," Clifford replied.

John did not sound upset. Clifford sensed he was looking for some kind of reaction from him. Clifford did not go to the funeral.

"We said our goodbyes over the phone."

Two days later Freda's body was cremated at the Palmdale Crematorium near Gosford. Glover wept uncontrollably. Her ashes were scattered across Frederick Park where she had married her fourth husband, Roger.

Three and a half years later, Glover would say he was saddened, but felt no great remorse at his mother's death. To him she was like an empty soft drink can.

"I felt nothing."

Glover had bought an electric keyboard the year before and taught himself to play. He had picked it up quickly and all the tunes which had filled the home of his father came flooding back, unprompted, through his own fingers. He, too, loved playing for anyone who would listen.

Around the time of Freda's death, John went next door for a small celebration to mark Paul Thiering's son's first birthday. "John just mooched around in his usual sort of way," Paul Thiering recalled. He looked depressed but he played some music for the group.

"You could see he loved it. It was one solace he had. When John played the organ he didn't play it for himself, he used to leave the window open. He wanted everyone to hear. He loved it, you could see that."

John was openly saying by this time that he wished his mother-in-law would hurry up and die. She was suffering dementia and it was sad to see her deteriorate. "Even my wife said that," Glover later told police.

He had begun to experience strange sensations and he blamed Essie for exacerbating them. At the work Christmas party he had undone his fly and made rude suggestions to female staff. "One side of me was all right,"

Glover would later recount to police. "The other is dark, evil. I can't control it."

This side of John never surfaced in front of his family or neighbours.

Two months had passed since Freda's death. John and Gay continued to visit Essie at the Mosman Nursing Home each weekend, but the roulette wheel in John Glover's head was already spinning.

There had been an incident there in the previous weeks. Nobody could prove anything but it was suspected that John Glover had interfered with one of the patients in an indecent way. Glover was found wandering through the building and had said he was lost. It was a very small nursing home built on a square pattern, so it was difficult to lose one's way. There was no proof and so it was decided to move Mrs Rolls to the front of the building so there could be no more reasons for her son-in-law to lose his bearings.

But the staff did not have too long to keep the other patients out of harm's way. Essie was going downhill fast. She still had them running in circles, but she was becoming weaker, her demands less frequent.

On Wednesday 11 January 1989, John paid his last visit to his mother-in-law. He couldn't stand to see the dying woman and ended up leaving Gay and her mother alone. He left the nursing home, jumped in his car and drove off. Where he intended going is unknown but after a series of turns he found himself 200 metres away in Hale Road, driving past an elderly woman.

She was the embodiment of his fantasy waiting to happen. He drove past her and parked in Ourimbah Road. He jumped out of the car and began walking back towards where he had seen her in Hale Road.

Mrs Margaret Todhunter, aged 84, had just been to lunch with old friends when she saw the portly grey-haired man walking towards her.

She had lived in Mosman most of her life, but in her retirement had moved to Queensland. She was back in Sydney on holidays visiting relatives and catching up with friends.

She left her friend's place between 4.30 p.m. and 5 p.m. and started walking to her sister-in-law's house in Macpherson Street. She walked across Spit Road and along Ourimbah Road, then became confused with her directions, turning left into Lang Street, right into Military Road and right into Hale Road.

Walking back towards Ourimbah Road Mrs Todhunter noticed a man six metres away walking towards her. While she gave him no thought, his appearance left a vivid impression on her. In the seconds that followed, she noted that he was the same height as her, 170 centimetres tall, and had fair tanned skin which gave him a European appearance. He had greying hair which seemed to be dark and she noted that the front of his hair was sticking up as though it had hairspray on it. He was clean shaven and appeared to be in his late 40s or early 50s. She noticed his large upper body with big shoulders, chest and waist. She also remembered that he was very well dressed.

The pair walked past each other, Mrs Todhunter with her white vinyl clutch handbag tucked snugly under her left upper arm. They were just over a metre apart when the man turned on her. "I felt a brush on my left shoulder. I turned my head to see what it was when I felt a dull thump on the top of my head."

The blow knocked her to the ground, causing her to land on her hands and knees and momentarily stunning her. In that instant he snatched her handbag from her grasp and ran. She yelled: "You rotten bugger!" Her handbag contained $200, her Commonwealth Bank passbook, a return coach ticket in her name to Brisbane, a small red address book and her pension cards.

By the time she rose to her feet with blood running down her back, the man was nowhere to be seen. She then staggered into a private hospital, four doors away. Staff contacted police and stemmed the flow of blood before she was taken to a nearby doctor's surgery for 14 stitches to the wound.

Police who interviewed Mrs Todhunter after the attack found her description of the punch to be a bit odd because the serious wound required so many stitches. It seemed more likely to them that something was in the hand of the attacker to open up such a cut.

She was shown a book of mug shots the following day but did not recognise anybody even remotely like the respectable-looking chap who hit her. The matter was filed and there was little else the police could do unless the perpetrator was caught doing something similar.

John Glover drove straight home. He had $200 in his pocket and he left the handbag in the boot of his car overnight.

The next day, as Mrs Todhunter tried to identify her attacker to police, Glover disposed of her handbag while on his work rounds. Eight days later, Essie passed away.

CHAPTER NINE

A MUGGING GONE WRONG

Gwendoline Mitchelhill had led a quiet and comfortable life. She was the sort of outgoing person who found it easy to mix and could have had her pick of the eligible young men on the lower North Shore. But her attentions were centred on Colin Mitchelhill, a rakishly thin young man from a well to do family. For Christmas 1928, he gave the 21-year-old Gwen a palladium ring with the somewhat cold engraving "Gwen from Colin 25/12/28". It featured two small diamonds flanking a larger diamond.

They married in the mid-1930s and, despite the ravages of the Depression, Colin kept them living well.

By the time Colin had turned 30 he became the owner of the hardware business in which he worked. The business, which included a foundry, thrived. Orders for brass castings and all metal workings were in plentiful supply.

For most of her life, Gwen Mitchelhill was in the enviable situation of having hired help. She became known as an entertainer and the host of many a bridge party. She was an independent woman who went her own way more than most in those days, but she could afford to.

Curiously, in 1950, Essie and John Rolls, with their 10-year-old daughter Gay, moved in to a house in Bullecourt Avenue, just four doors away from the Mitchelhills. Whether the two families ever met is unknown but it would seem likely, given the outgoing nature of the two women and the propensity of Gwen Mitchelhill to entertain.

Gwen Mitchelhill raised two children, Toni and Phillip, who were

Gwendoline Mitchelhill, the granny killer's first victim.

born during the Second World War. Later the family sold the house and moved to the other side of the peninsula, to Clifton Gardens, swapping a view of peaceful Quakers Hat Bay for that of Sydney Harbour.

For holidays, Colin would pack the family up in the car, along with a few relatives, and head west to the Blue Mountains, as did most fashionable folk of the day.

The years rolled by; Colin died, leaving Gwen Mitchelhill a comfortable widow. Her interest in card games continued and she became a regular at a game in Manly. She was also a member of the Mosman Returned Servicemen's Club and attended bingo games from time to time. Mrs Mitchelhill moved to a fifth floor unit with panoramic views in the Camellia Gardens apartment block, 70 metres from the club.

"How is everyone today?" a cheery Mrs Mitchelhill said as she entered the Silhouette Beauty Salon in Military Road, Spit Junction.

The very sight of this matriarch of the North Shore made the young beautician, Cheryl, freeze in dread. Mrs Mitchelhill wasn't the best of customers. She was extremely demanding, wanting more and more for the money she was prepared to pay. Although better off than others her age, she displayed the frugality of a pensioner, accounting for every cent.

It would make Cheryl boil up inside. Cheryl would try to rush her through to get her out. Her facials took one hour and ten minutes but she would expect more and then would want to negotiate the price.

"My dear, I do think your fee is exorbitant," Mrs Mitchelhill would quibble. "Well, if you want to spend $39.50, then this is what you're going to get, you can't have all the trimmings for $39.50," Cheryl would reply. But Mrs Mitchelhill never paid more than that. She always got Cheryl to take the money out of her purse, and the young beautician could see for herself that Mrs Mitchelhill always had plenty of cash on her. It made her wonder why she seemed so mean.

But on this day, Wednesday 1 March 1989, Mrs Mitchelhill was cheerful, greeting Cheryl like an old friend. Her mood took the young woman aback — perhaps it was her pleasant morning outing at the Marian Theatre with a friend that put her in the good mood. Punctual as usual, she had arrived precisely at 2.30 p.m. for her regular facial.

Gone were her usual complaints — complaints about the price of a loaf of bread, money, people, queues and bus stops. This day she was very happy. For the first time in over a year she felt well, she explained.

Mrs Mitchelhill chatted away about her dead husband, her former home in Clifton Gardens and her children. For the first time she did not ask Cheryl to take the money from her purse — nor did she quibble about the price.

At 3.40 p.m. she left the salon for the ten minute stroll along Military Road to her home, first stopping briefly at Raimond Hairdressing Salon to make an appointment for the next day.

John Glover finished work early that Wednesday afternoon. As was his custom, he drove to the Returned Servicemen's Club to relax over a drink before going home. After finishing a drink and putting a few dollars through the poker machine, he left at 3.50 p.m.

He had barely turned left out of the front entrance of the club when he saw Gwendoline Mitchelhill, 82, walking towards him along busy Military Road, a walking stick supporting her. In that brief moment something strange happened inside his head. Whatever it was, it compelled him to act.

Glover dashed to his Ford station wagon, which was parked nearby. Under the driver's seat was a claw hammer. He kept it there to fit a dolly wheel to a company caravan that he took to trade shows to display his array of Four'N Twenty goods. He stuck the hammer under his shirt and fitted it into his belt before walking quickly back to where he last saw Mrs Mitchelhill. He could still see her. He closed in.

Mrs Mitchelhill was walking along the driveway towards the foyer of her block of flats when Glover caught up to her. She rounded a corner where the front security door was hidden from view of the main street, oblivious to the fury about to explode behind her.

As she stepped away from the view of passersby Glover struck, punching her once with all his might. Her frail, 48 kg body fell to the ground, six ribs shattered from the blow. He pulled out the hammer. Mrs Mitchelhill was still conscious. She stared up in horror then turned her head away as he raised the hammer into the air. It came smashing down on the back of her skull. Then he hit her again with his full force. She was semi-conscious. As if in a dream, Glover set to work, oblivious to the noise of construction work in the adjoining lot. He picked up her cane and placed it to one side, parallel to her legs. Then he removed her shoes, placing them neatly next to the walking stick. Her handbag was next. He examined her purse and placed the handbag next to the other items. Her stockings were torn off and he moved to strangle her with them when the sound of a bell distracted him.

Looking through the glass security doors into the foyer, he saw the light above the elevator door, indicating that the lift was about to open. He straightened and fled the scene in a casual sort of way, striding quickly and confidently along the busy shopping street and back to his car.

He drove to Wyong Road, but instead of going home, he turned down the steep hill to Joel's Boatshed — two blocks from home on Quakers Hat Bay — where he stopped to examine his booty. There was no one around. He examined the contents of the purse and took $100 before flinging it into nearby bushland. Glover got back in the car and drove home, then changed and threw his shirt, socks and underpants into the washing bag before sitting down to dinner.

Two young brothers, aged 11 and nine, had popped in to visit their great-aunt at her Camellia Gardens unit after school. At 3.55 p.m. the pair headed off home, hopping into the elevator as their aunt said goodbye.

When the lift came to rest on the ground floor and the doors opened, they saw a sight which would torment their minds for the rest of their lives. Outside the glass security doors four metres away was an old woman struggling to support her weight with her hands and knees. Blood was gushing from her head, horrifying quantities of scarlet liquid covering her face, staining her clothes and splashing on to the tiles.

They stood in stunned silence only briefly before bolting back into the lift to fetch help from their great-aunt. By the time she came down with another woman, the old lady had crawled towards the doors and was sitting up against the glass in a pool of blood. She was still clutching her keys and she mumbled something about them to the women.

An ambulance was called and arrived in minutes, the officers working quickly to stem the flow of blood. As they moved her on a stretcher to the waiting ambulance, both officers noted that her personal effects had been placed away from the body but gave it no further thought. They assumed they had been placed there by one of the neighbours. Just before they left for Royal North Shore Hospital the senior ambulance officer asked the residents who had gathered at the scene to clean up the mess about the woman's handbag and stick. It was only on the way to the hospital that he began to think that the circumstances did not gel.

Mrs Mitchelhill was rushed straight into an operating theatre. Blood was building up on her brain and they had to relieve the pressure.

By early evening, the senior ambulanceman felt uneasy. He called local police and told them that he was suspicious — he could remember seeing Mrs Mitchelhill's handbag sitting open near her body.

Doctors who worked to try and save her life were equally concerned. They too notified Mosman police. "You know, this is a bit suss. I don't think that she's fallen over and done this to herself," one of the doctors told police.

Two uniformed officers went to the hospital and began to gather information on who the woman was and where her injuries had occurred. Slowly their routine inquiry began to look more like a murder investigation. At 8.30 p.m., with Mrs Mitchelhill close to death, Constable Phil Compton notified Mosman detectives of the suspicions and they in turn contacted the Physical Evidence squad.

At 8.45 p.m. Mrs Mitchelhill died.

Late that night Detective First Class Constable Ted Littler from the Crime Scene unit of the Physical Evidence branch went to Camellia Gardens and met up with Detectives Goymour and Campbell. An earlier doorknock of residents who went to Mrs Mitchelhill's aid had revealed that no one had touched or opened her handbag.

More puzzling was that nobody could find a purse. No old woman would go out without a purse, it was thought. Relatives arrived and told them she always carried a red purse containing significant amounts of cash and credit cards.

An extensive search of the crime scene that night had failed to turn up any clues, the area where the attack took place having been hosed down, scrubbed with detergent and sopped up with newspaper. There was nothing to be found. The scene was photographed and measured. There was a distinct lack of drama and hype from the neighbours. "Nobody seemed that interested," recalled Littler.

When Detective Senior Constable Paul Mayger came into work the next day at the North Region Homicide office in Chatswood, he was pretty pleased with the way things had been running. He had been temporarily in charge of Homicide and for the months he was there, nothing had gone unsolved.

When he walked in on the morning of 2 March 1989, there was a message waiting for him on the Netmail, the computerised police bulletin board. A woman had died from head injuries and her purse was missing. It seemed interesting.

The hospital confirmed that the injuries suffered by Mrs Mitchelhill were not entirely consistent with a fall. Among other things she had two serious black eyes. It looked as though the woman had been hit on the head with something but they could not be sure. They would have to wait until the postmortem later that afternoon. Mayger rang his wife, Chris, to tell her that he would be late. She was not impressed. The couple's second child had been born only a few months earlier and she also had a six-year-old to look after.

The press had already got hold of the story and when the first edition of the *Daily Mirror* hit the streets it ran a story saying bag snatchers had killed an unidentified 82-year-old woman. Almost as an afterthought, it mentioned that a fall might also have killed her. By midday, Mrs Mitchelhill had been named in the late edition of the *Mirror* and the story updated to include a quote from a relative: "I just hope they catch the killer before someone else gets it."

As dictated by police procedure, Mayger went to the postmortem. It was something to which most detectives have long closed the emotional side of their minds. The bodies become objects. On Mayger's very first day as a rookie cop, he was sent to the morgue to watch a postmortem. It didn't worry him too much. He had worked in an abattoir as a kid on school holidays so had seen "a fair bit of blood, guts and gore. We had blokes in there, six foot six, just falling over."

At 26 years of age, Mayger had been older than most new recruits to the force. He had not been in the job long when he realised the only challenge for him would be as a detective — and what could be more satisfying than tracking down a killer? However, the opportunity to join the Homicide Squad did not present itself until 1986, after seven years as a local patrol detective.

It was the old days in NSW policing when Homicide was still under the umbrella of the CIB — the Criminal Investigation Bureau — which included other major crime squads such as the Armed Hold-up and Vice Squads. A detective would apply for a spot and Homicide would do a bit of investigating into his background to see if he (and they were almost all "he") was any good. It was virtually a club. Sometimes young up-and-coming detectives, if they were good operators, would be invited to join.

Mayger was accepted in 1986, a time when the CIB was under intense pressure after years of corruption allegations. The Police Commissioner,

John Avery, had set in motion his plans to dismantle the bureau and other branches of the force which had been the subject of similar allegations for more than ten years.

Dissatisfaction was rife among senior officers over changes in promotion structures and resignation rates went through the roof. It was a time when a clean young officer could do very well filling in the vacuum.

Paul Mayger had been encouraged to join the force in 1976 by a friend who had warned him: "You're going to see some pretty nasty things ... you've just got to look at them as objects." As he stood there 13 years later watching Mrs Mitchelhill being dissected, the advice had long since passed into his subconscious but it was nevertheless followed to the letter. She was inanimate, and that was that.

Standing beside Mayger in the autopsy room was plain-clothes Constable Megan Wilson. Originally from the rural city of Wagga Wagga, the 26-year-old officer was in her final year of a two year training program as a candidate for detective school. She had joined the police three years earlier and her first posting had been to Mosman, a backwater of a police station regarded by officers elsewhere as a sleepy hollow. After 12 months the constable had transferred to North Sydney detectives and then been posted back to the five man Mosman detectives branch. As a uniformed officer she had seen bodies before, victims of road accidents, but this was her first murder investigation.

Because it was a suspected murder, the postmortem became a clinical flow of information between doctor and policeman. "From the angle of those blows do you think he is right- or left-handed?" Mayger inquired. "How many times did he hit? Was that bruise before or after death?"

In the case of Mrs Mitchelhill, the suspicions were based very much on the nature of the blows to the head and chest. As soon as Dr DuFlou removed the top of Mrs Mitchelhill's scalp, it was obvious she had not fallen. When the top of the head was removed with a small circular saw, it showed that she had suffered three distinct blows to the crown. There was a crescent-shaped fracture and two straight lines that ran perpendicular to each other.

The postmortem showed massive injury to the chest — six ribs were broken — and deep bruising on her face. Dr DuFlou noted that her bones were made more brittle from osteoporosis, but that she would have had to have fallen down, then stood up and fallen again and again, to suffer the injuries she had. Dr DuFlou found that she died from head and chest injuries.

There was no longer any doubt they had a murder investigation on their hands but the crime was already more than a day old. Mayger went back out to Mrs Mitchelhill's unit with Ted Littler and Detective Barry Keeling to go over everything more thoroughly, on the off-chance that something had been overlooked. The missing purse made it seem plain that the murder was the result of an overly violent mugging and the second search of the scene and further discussions with neighbours presented no other suggestion.

Local Mosman detectives, including Constable Wilson, had already been hard at work establishing Mrs Mitchelhill's movements on her last day and talking to people she encountered. The canvass of family, neighbours and businesses established her movements up until she made the hairdressing appointment with Karen Davis at the Raimond salon. Ms Davis told police Mrs Mitchelhill was in fine spirits, happy to be back on her feet again. It was the last known conversation Mrs Mitchelhill had.

Constable Wilson canvassed the workers on the building site overlooking the spot where the attack occurred; they had seen nothing.

She could not believe how the murderer got away with it. It would have taken just one builder to have turned around and he would have had full view of it. But none did.

While it looked like a mugging gone wrong, it didn't fit because there had been so much violence. And surely her shoes had not just fallen off.

When Mayger came to look over Mrs Mitchelhill's last steps, there was only one oddity in what had happened to her all that day. As she paid the bill for her facial, a man came in wanting to tell fortunes by handwriting analysis for $5 a time. The man, in his mid-30s with short cropped dark hair, a deep tan and tight jeans, was making his way through all local businesses asking shopkeepers and customers alike. Mrs Mitchelhill brushed past him on the way out. The fortune teller left shortly afterwards.

Mayger was very interested. He had what appeared to be a drifter in contact with the victim at the right time. More importantly, it was somebody who was obviously after a quick buck. The "fortune-telling man" became the focus of the investigation. His description was released on the Friday, two days after the murder. But Mayger's hope that the fortune teller was the murderer sprang more from the fact there was no one else who seemed likely to have done it than from any firm evidence. Nobody had seen the old woman walking the last 200 metres to her home.

Mosman is an aging suburb. It boomed in the 1930s after the Harbour Bridge was finished in 1931. Beautiful old homes were already being built and connected to the city by more than 20 ferry services, but it was the ready vehicular access which sent the young middle class to the stunning peninsula. Sixty years later the survivors were old, frail and plentiful. No one was likely to notice an old woman struggling back from the shops.

The police were also hampered in their early attempts to track down people who may have seen Mrs Mitchelhill by the lack of a photograph. The family refused to give them one because one of her last wishes had been to die in dignity, free from any fuss. This was construed by the family to mean privately.

Paul Mayger's run as acting head of Homicide was short lived. Four days after the murder of Mrs Mitchelhill, Detective Sergeant Dennis O'Toole was transferred to Chatswood to take over from Mayger as head investigator for the North Region Homicide Squad. It was a fairly routine sort of move. O'Toole, "Miles" to his mates, was told there was a vacancy there if he wanted it and he accepted. He was not one of those cops with a burning ambition to be in Homicide, but thought that five years in the Drug Squad was enough for anybody. He wanted a change.

He had been officer in charge of the North Region Drug Squad in his home town of Gosford on the Central Coast where he was living with his wife and four daughters. The O'Toole family was comfortably settled in a place by the water just outside town. With their own private jetty and the peaceful surrounds, the O'Tooles could not tear themselves away to head back to the suburbs. The Sydney to Newcastle F4 Freeway allowed O'Toole to drive between home and his new base at Chatswood in a little over an hour each way.

When O'Toole walked into the Chatswood office for his first day, there was nothing special happening. The Mitchelhill investigation was in full swing but every other unsolved murder on the North Region's books had been taken as far as it could go. They all had rewards posted and as far as a detective was concerned rewards were only applied for when investigations had hit a brick wall.

O'Toole got to work familiarising himself with each case on the books and, in particular, the murder of Mrs Mitchelhill which up until then he had only read about in the newspapers.

The fortune teller still seemed like the best bet. It took them a week to find him. A lot of people had seen the fortune teller around over a period of weeks. Police reasoned he must have been living locally and started looking at all the cheaper accommodation in the area.

"It's not until you work on a case like this that you realise Mosman is not the place you think it is," said Mayger. Behind all the big houses and the obvious wealth is an under class. Big houses have been turned into boarding houses, doss houses and hostels. Police checked them all and eventually turned the mystery man up in a boarding house at Cremorne Point. O'Toole and Mayger went straight down to interview him.

"Where were you on the afternoon of Wednesday the first of March?" asked Mayger.

The fortune teller could not recall.

"We've been told you were telling fortunes down Military Road."

"Oh yeah, that's right."

"That was the day an old woman was murdered; can you tell us anything about that?" O'Toole asked, his sharp eyes contradicting his approachable manner.

"Yeah? I didn't know anything about that."

Detective Sergeant Dennis O'Toole leaving court on
29 November 1991, the day of John Glover's conviction.

"You were one of the last people to see her alive."

"Bullshit?" The man seemed genuinely surprised.

The interview went all morning and the man was unable to offer any
alibis or any recollection of Mrs Mitchelhill. The detectives nevertheless
walked out satisfied he had not been involved. His character did not seem
right. He was not eliminated completely because he could not give an
alibi, but Mayger and O'Toole could both sense their efforts would be best
expended elsewhere. It was a gut feeling.

A week after the murder, the family were sifting through Mrs
Mitchelhill's belongings when they realised that two rings were missing.
One was the palladium diamond ring Colin had given her for Christmas
61 years earlier. The other was an anniversary ring he'd given her in even
more prosperous times. The ring itself was 18 carat white gold and
platinum encrusted with sapphires. It was decked with eight large
diamonds and three smaller diamonds. The engraving on the first ring
would make it easy to trace. It was hoped that the murderer would be
stupid enough to try to pawn it. The investigators found themselves doing
the familiar round of pawn shops but nothing was turned up.

The Mitchelhill case dropped out of the news quickly. Within a
month, media attention would be focused on the murder of a policeman

and the wounding of another in a busy Sydney street during a shootout. In the ensuing hunt for the killer, John Porter, police shot dead an innocent Aboriginal man, David Gundy, an event which would dominate the police news for months.

On Wednesday 26 April, the night before the Gundy shooting, a 64-year-old retiree, Ray Roper, was attacked in Mosman. Mr Roper had been walking along a dimly lit street at 11.30 p.m. when he was hit hard on the head from behind. He was rugged up against the cold, wearing an overcoat and a large straw hat on his head. His attacker, a young man, had fled when Mr Roper reacted to the blows by shouting obscenities. Was it the killer who had mistaken Ray Roper for a woman? The head of Mosman detectives, Detective Sergeant Bob Goymour, thought so. When he saw the incident report he sent it straight to the Homicide Squad.

It was the second night of rehearsals for the Mosman Musical Society's 1989 production "No No Nanette" when John Glover wandered into the Mosman Community Services Centre.

Society president Ian McCann was overjoyed at the stranger's request to help behind the scenes. Volunteers who did not want to be stars were rare. Glover was instantly made "rehearsals secretary", which involved collecting fees and registering attendances and absences. The show was booked to play Mosman Town Hall in June. McCann had set a tight schedule, with cast meetings every Monday evening.

Glover performed his new role diligently.

CHAPTER TEN

REPEAT OFFENDER

The marriage of the widowed Mrs Winfreda Hoggard to Sir William Ashton changed her life dramatically.

She was a slightly built talkative woman of 56 who moved on the fringes of artistic circles. He was one of Australia's foremost artists who had been knighted the year before — for services to arts administration as much as for his ability as a painter. He was 81 years old.

Will Ashton's first wife May died in 1958. He was knighted in 1960 and, the following year, married Mrs Hoggard, a widow and retired nurse. In her youth she taught youngsters to swim and had a keen interest in yachting, polo and rugby.

The couple's marriage in St Johns Anglican Church at North Sydney was reported as a large and colourful affair with a guest list full of prominent names in the Australian art world, including Norman Lindsay, who turned up sporting pink-dyed hair.

The couple took up residence in a beautiful two-storey white Tudor-style home in tranquil Tivoli Street, Mosman. Looking out to Chinaman's Beach and across Middle Harbour, the house was surrounded by tall blue gums and a large oak tree.

Whatever happiness the marriage afforded Lady Winfreda it did not last long. Sir William had become seriously ill in the year following the ceremony. He died two years later in September 1963. Winfreda kept her title and moved out of the big house into a small block of flats up on the ridge of Mosman, close to the shops and amenities.

To neighbours she was known as "a loner who circulated around a very

close-knit group of elderly friends". "She was a v⸍
and friendly little woman," one neighbour said. C
was known to donate handsome sums to charitie⸍
a friend of Lady Ashton for 13 years, said that ⸍
friend was always willing to help others. To h⸗.
absolute angel who walked on earth".

Her new home was a plain three-storey yellow brick apartᵤᵤ.
housing 17 other tenants. Unlike much of Mosman, nothing about ⸗.
apartment block screamed wealth. However, Lady Ashton's second floor
unit, where she had lived for 15 years, reflected a woman at home with
beautiful objects.

The walls were lined with paintings given to her by her late husband.
The furniture, cutlery and crockery were expensive antiques of the
Victorian and Edwardian periods. She was happy, surrounded by her
cherished possessions.

On Tuesday 9 May 1989, Lady Winfreda rose early. She had an
appointment with a specialist at the Sydney Eye Hospital in the city.

She made her way into the city across the Harbour Bridge by bus and
was back in Mosman before lunch to see her hairdresser, Joseph
Schorlian, an Armenian known in the area simply as Joseph the

Lady Winfreda Ashton, murdered in her Mosman
apartment block on 9 May 1989.

...sser. A short, rotund man with balding grey hair and olive ...lexion, Joseph the hairdresser has permed and rinsed the hair of ...usands of Mosman's matrons since migrating from Cairo in 1964. Lady ...shton had been a regular.

"She was a magic woman. She's all right. Very happy, very nice, very kind woman, very active, she walked by herself, with a stick sometimes, she got some arthritis or something like that," he said in his thick Mediterranean accent. Lady Ashton came in every week or fortnight: "every three months a perm, every fortnight a hairdo, every five, six weeks a haircut."

It was part of her regime. "The doctor said to me if I want to live longer I must go at least once a week to the hairdresser," she told Joseph.

Lady Ashton regularly came in bedecked in jewels on her way to the opera or ballet. Her finery set her apart from even the other Mosman matrons. One day when she came in, Joseph offered his services. "Don't you like a chaperone? Me, I'll take you to opera and make jealous other old ladies because you are going with young man." It made her happy.

"I'll do that one day," she told him.

On most occasions Lady Ashton would enter and leave the salon by the back door because it was more convenient. Her unit was only 100 metres away, separated from the back access alleys of the Military Road shops by a large bitumen carpark.

"Sometime I used to take her back, not because she thought someone would try take her things, it was polite and she was old. She was never frightened of anything," said Joseph.

This Tuesday Joseph made his usual offer. "You want I give you a hand and take you home?"

"Thank you for your kind offer Joseph, but not today, I'm going shopping," Lady Ashton said, stepping out of the front door of the salon as Joseph bid her goodbye.

It was a cool, late autumn day with intermittent showers signalling winter's approach. Lady Ashton was well dressed as usual. Over her blue and white striped dress she wore a bright red raincoat, and a red and brown knitted cap protected her head. She wore a diamond ring, a necklace and a much-loved gem-studded gold watch. To support her frail frame she had her mahogany walking stick.

The murder of Mrs Mitchelhill a month earlier had not fazed her as it had some of Joseph's other customers. One elderly woman who lived in Camellia Gardens was so terrified that Joseph had taken to escorting her to her door. By the end of the year Joseph would be seeing many more frightened customers home.

It was around midday when Lady Ashton stepped out onto the footpath of Military Road and commenced the 150 metre journey to the Mosman

Returned Servicemen's Club. Her destination was her twice weekly bingo game at the club.

She sat by herself and despite her regular attendance at the games, none of the other players knew her. "She was always friendly and smiling, but so frail — one gentle push and she would fall over," said club employee Sharon Hancock.

Lady Winfreda left the club around 2.30 p.m. and went to pay her gas bill at the Commonwealth Bank on the opposite side of the road. As always she was in good spirits.

She left the bank and crossed Military Road at the Raglan Street traffic lights. A friend spotted her and called out to say hello but Lady Winfreda did not hear. She would be seen alive by just one more person — John Glover.

Glover had finished work early that afternoon and set his car on a course for the club. He had been depressed for some weeks. For some unexplained reason, this day he did not take the quick back route along The Avenue to the club but found himself on a slightly more circuitous path, cruising along Raglan Street. As he looked for a place to park an old woman wearing a red raincoat caught his attention.

She was walking at a slow pace with a walking stick, away from the late afternoon pedestrian traffic of school children in uniforms, well-dressed women and men on busy Military Road. She became his total focus of attention. There was something inside him — attack, *attack*, ATTACK!!

Within seconds he had found a parking spot. No time to waste. He retrieved a pair of gloves from the glove box and stepped from the vehicle, walking briskly towards where he had last seen his quarry. She was less than 50 metres from her apartment block when he spotted her again.

Lady Ashton picked up her mail on the way into the property as was her custom. As she passed through the entrance foyer, Glover pulled on the gloves. He was on her heels but she was unaware of it. Instead of turning right to climb the flight of stairs to her apartment she paused, opened a door on her left and entered a small alcove. To her immediate right was another door, which she opened and stepped through into a rubbish room.

The tiny woman put her mail and keys on a bench next to an external door which opened on to the concrete yard abutting the shopping centre carpark. She moved over to put some rubbish wrapped in newspaper into her bin, which was sitting on a bench almost at her eye level. As she reached up a hand was thrust over her mouth to stifle any scream. Another hand clamped the back of her head. She was pulled backwards like a rag doll on to the concrete floor.

Lady Ashton was a small woman suffering lymph cancer. By Glover's account of the attack she fought desperately for her life — she "almost had me". They fell to the floor together with Glover falling on top of her. The fall may have broken her ribs but it was more likely Glover gave her a full-blooded punch or dropped one of his knees into her body. Seven of her ribs were broken, with not just a few minor fractures — they were shattered. It was a furious explosion of human force. Not satisfied, Glover put his hand on her face and pulled her head upwards before he crashed it down on to the concrete floor. He did it again. Then again. If she screamed no one heard it.

She was unconscious, her nose broken, when he got to his feet. Glover set to work in a methodical if not military fashion. It was as if he had rehearsed the sequence over and over in his head. He picked up her low-heeled black shoes and placed them neatly together near the rear wall about half a metre from her feet. As he worked he heard footsteps on the stairway, and muffled voices nearby. He disregarded them and continued with the plan, oblivious to risk.

He worked quickly, removing the walking stick from underneath her body and placing it alongside the shoes, like a soldier setting out his kit for inspection. He pulled off her nylon pantyhose and wrapped them around her neck, pulling the ligature tight with all his force before tying it off. He removed her gold wristwatch, wallet and two purses, then left. Back in the safety of his car he drove south along Bradleys Head Road, past Mosman police station. By the time he stopped at a spot with sweeping views of Sydney Harbour, he was two kilometres away from Lady Ashton's body. He arrived, as if playing a macabre joke, at Ashton Park.

Glover examined his booty, pocketed the cash and threw the wallet and purse willy-nilly around the park. His original intention came back on the agenda. He went to the club for a drink and put his ill-gotten cash through the pokies.

When he got home, he burnt the gloves in his backyard incinerator. What went through his mind as he watched the smoke rise into the sky? Was he consciously destroying evidence of his evil? Was he reliving the moment, or was he struck with fearful grief for what he had just done?

It was about eight o'clock when John Ferke decided to leave his Raglan Street unit to take in some fresh night air. A minute or two earlier he had heard a noise downstairs outside his window, like bins rattling, and he thought the woman upstairs must be putting out her garbage. So he decided to go and have a chat. That's when he found Lady Ashton dead in the bin room, her body having passed unnoticed for at least four hours.

He stood there in shock staring at the form before him, trying to figure out what had happened to his friendly neighbour. She was lying on her stomach facing the external doorway, the left cheek of her face against the concrete, her right eye still open and glazed, a look of stunned terror frozen on her face. Under her head a small pool of blood had formed. Her bright red raincoat was dishevelled. It appeared she was naked from the waist down. Her left arm was stretched across the floor.

He thought she had suffered a heart attack; then he noticed something odd — her shoes were not on her feet. Her black short-heeled shoes were together one metre from her feet, one of the shoes lying on its side. Thirty centimetres from the shoes lay her finely polished walking stick, almost parallel to her body.

Mr Ferke called out to a neighbour for help. After examining the body they called police.

When 25-year-old plain-clothes Constable Al Steel arrived at the premises, five uniformed police and the Station Sergeant from Mosman were already there. Two weeks earlier Steel had joined the station's detective squad and his work to date had comprised investigating break and enters and cheque frauds. Although inexperienced with murder investigations, Steel was struck with the glaring question: "How does she fall out of her shoes?"

All present were linking the death to Mrs Mitchelhill's and all were hoping they were wrong. "There was a gut feeling, but everyone wanted to ignore it, because once you count up two ... you start thinking, we've got nothing to go on. What the heck are we going to do?"

First Class Constable Ted Littler from Physical Evidence had been called away from his dinner soon after the discovery of the body. Local police had been warned to be on the lookout for attacks on old women and so when this one was found, they telephoned him straight away.

When he got there, he took one look at the scene. "Oh shit, this is going to be a long night." The similarities were all too plain: the location, the age, the shoes, the walking stick.

"This is what the Mitchelhill scene would have looked like if somebody had of realised that she had been murdered and not fallen," he said to a constable standing nearby. Littler got the names of the four people who had been in the bin room since the murder and called his partner. There was a lot of work to be done.

Detective Senior Constable Phil Flogel, one of the brightest young members of the Crime Scene unit, arrived at Raglan Road at 11 p.m. He had been having a few days off in lieu of overtime but he did not mind coming in for this. The whole reason he got into the Physical Evidence side of policing ten years earlier was because it gave a chance to work on big cases. From the moment he got to this one, it felt like it was going to be one of those.

A big bloke, he had a softer look to his face than your average detective. As far as Flogel was concerned, the brutality was an unfortunate side of a fascinating job. What was more important to both Littler and Flogel was that this scene had been well preserved by both the neighbours and by police.

Flogel noticed that Lady Ashton's raincoat was nylon. That was going to make it difficult to get any fibres or hairs which might have rubbed off the killer. The nylon would not have caught on to the fibre unless the killer wore a thick woolly jumper or something similar.

Detective Senior Constable Paul Mayger arrived at the scene at 10.30 p.m. and, with Flogel and Littler, headed up to Lady Ashton's second floor unit. It was a beautifully preserved reminder of the niceties that come with wealth and time. Beautiful antiques crammed tables which were themselves finely crafted pieces from a distant era. Valuable paintings adorned the walls.

As the detectives looked around, it was plain that there was no sign of disturbance. Clearly, Lady Ashton had been hit while coming home. A planned attack would have seen the thieves make off with a small fortune in valuable loot.

They headed back downstairs to the bin room to start their minute examination of the scene. Before Flogel and Littler entered the room they followed the first rule in the Physical Evidence handbook and photographed everything. Then they divided the room into grids and worked over each section, one at a time, picking a path through the room which was least likely to disturb anything left on the floor by the killer.

The pair moved around the perimeter of the room, watching their feet. Two ambulance officers and the two neighbours had already been over the scene. It was slightly tainted but it still should have revealed something.

The detectives moved over to the body at the back of the bin room. Staring up at them was one wide-open eye. They could see fine red lines below the surface of the pupil and also in the face. "Looks like a petchail haemorrhage," Flogel said clinically. "Yeah, look at that," Littler said, pointing at something brown protruding from under Lady Ashton's left ear. Flogel followed the line of his partner's finger. A piece of stocking material appeared to be sticking out of the neck. They looked closer and saw a fine line in the folds of skin on her throat.

It was the stocking, pulled so tight it had been embedded into the skin and would have gone unnoticed but for the knot under the ear. They knew the petchail haemorrhage (when blood capillaries burst from pressure in the eyes and face) was the result of strangulation, so they were on the lookout for telltale signs such as bruising around the neck.

After they examined the head, it was standard procedure to work down the body, inspecting the clothes, which could not be removed until the postmortem, and then the hands. The hands and fingers can be the most important part of a victim's body. If a victim has defended herself, there is a good chance the hands would be injured and so give an indication of the nature of the struggle. More importantly, the hands collect fragments from the attacker. Clothing, skin, blood and hair all have a good chance of landing on the hands and staying there.

They were in luck. Two or three grey hairs stood out against Lady Ashton's brown gloves. They were between four to six centimetres long and had been caught between her fingers. Looking at them in the poor light, neither man could distinguish whether the hairs were Lady Ashton's or not.

Unfortunately, hair is not the conclusive piece of forensics that many believe it to be. Hair can only be grouped into broad categories and one or two hairs alone are almost useless in proving a case against a suspect unless there are dyes present or the roots have come out.

Grey hair was the worst type of all from a forensic point of view. Lady Ashton had short grey hair so it might be hers. It seemed quite plausible that she had grasped it from her own head while trying to stop the killer pulling the pantyhose tight, but it could be anybody's. Flogel hoped there was some of the root left on one of the hairs: that might give more information and the chance for DNA testing.

There was no sign of any weapon. The walking stick had no marks on it so it was ruled out. They searched all the multi-coloured plastic bins around the edge of the walls but found no heavy objects. A clean broom was produced and the bin room was swept and the refuse poured into a small bag.

The fingerprint section turned up and got to work. In fact, the whole surrounding area was concrete so the chance of finding any sort of print was small.

The Government Medical Officers arrived and took the body to the morgue in the small hours of the morning.

All citizens and all police were logged on as they came on to the premises. Before leaving they recorded what they had done and what they had touched. It was a well controlled crime scene — almost "pristine", in the words of Ted Littler.

Detective Sergeant Dennis O'Toole was sound asleep when the phone rang at his Gosford home. He fumbled for the phone, glancing at the clock. 2 a.m. It had to be the office.

Paul Mayger was on the line. "Remember the Mitchelhill case?" Mayger asked.

"Yeah, what's happened?"

"You'd better get your arse down here — it looks like we've got another one."

O'Toole arrived at Raglan Street a little before 4 a.m. The body had already been removed. The midnight to dawn media crews were waiting outside.

CHAPTER ELEVEN

THE SOCIETY KILLER

D etective Sergeant O'Toole was busy organising the investigation as the first orange rays of dawn began to cut across the skyline. The first hours would be crucial while memories were still fresh. The postmortem would have to be early because the body was looking like it was going to be the only clue, again.

The mood of police was still confident. They would get the bastard this time, he must have slipped up somewhere. Someone must have seen something.

As the sun rose, all 17 residents at 186 Raglan Street woke to the sound of police knocking on their doors.

"Did you know Lady Ashton?"

"Did you see or hear anything unusual yesterday afternoon?"

"What time did you arrive home? What were your movements ...?"

Everyone was interviewed. Statements were taken. By mid-morning, almost everyone in the building had been contacted. Nobody had seen or heard anything.

The media had also been door knocking, talking to residents and police at the scene. John Ferke, who had found the body, expressed his abhorrence of the crime to reporters who gathered outside the unit: "Who could do such a thing? She was such a dear old lady."

At 9 a.m. O'Toole left the scene to go to the City Morgue at Glebe with Crime Scene detectives Flogel and Littler. It had been a long night and they would spend the rest of the morning watching Lady Ashton's body be dissected and examined in every way thinkable.

Detective Inspector Mike Hagan on 25 November 1989,
after the murder of Muriel Falconer.

Lady Ashton's clothes were carefully peeled off, layer by layer. Her assailant had missed something. A cigarette box containing $20 was found inside a pocket but there was no glaring clue on any of her garments.

O'Toole was particularly concerned about the similarities with Mrs Mitchelhill. Closer examination of the skulls in the postmortem showed that the massive head wounds on the two women were caused by different blunt objects — but the pathologist, Dr Joe DuFlou, could not say what objects.

There were seven broken ribs, fractured in such a way that indicated she might have been hit with one punch. She might, however, have fallen on something. The postmortem also revealed a contusion across her chest, indicating the possibility she had been hit by a stick. Dr DuFlou pointed out that a break in the bruise matched perfectly a rippled knot in the surface of the victim's walking stick. There were also bruises to her arms, indicating she had tried to shield herself from blows.

By midday the *Daily Mirror* had dubbed the murderer the "High Society killer". The paper, like the *Sydney Morning Herald* the following day, had taken the plunge and linked the attack to the Mitchelhill murder. But police were cautious, not wanting to cause total hysteria.

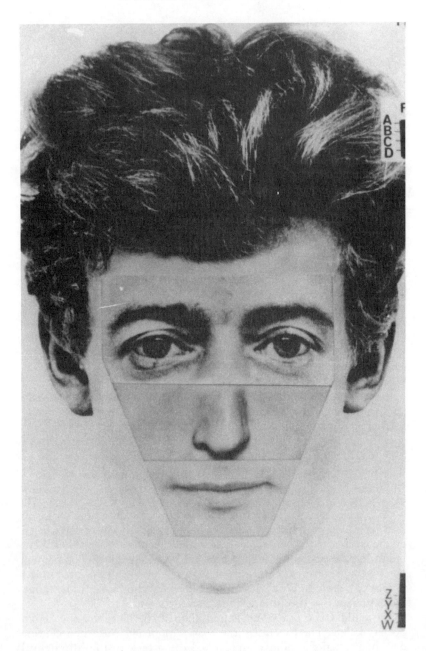

The police identikit picture of Ray Roper's attacker.

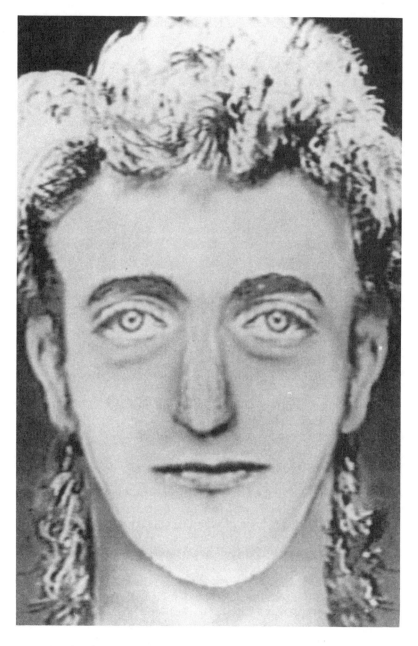

An identikit picture of a man seen loitering near Lady Ashton's unit.

O'Toole told *Sydney Morning Herald* journalist Sonya Zadel: "While we can't say for certain if the same person is responsible for both murders, the similarities between them are just too striking to ignore." He gave away his true feelings when he warned elderly women in the area to travel in groups whenever possible and to be on their guard. "I don't wish to alarm the community but they must be aware that we do have a madman out there."

Before returning to Mosman, O'Toole had consulted with his boss, Northern Region Homicide Squad Commander, Detective Inspector Mike Hagan, on the night's events and where the investigation stood. Inspector Hagan, a straight shooter by character with tinted glasses and spear-shaped sideburns running across his cheeks to the tips of his moustache, was deeply concerned and backed the serial attack theory, but urged caution.

His team had to keep an open mind in the event that they were dealing with a copycat: it was not impossible to have two similar murders in the same patrol area committed by different people. He warned against the investigators developing tunnel vision.

The canvass was extended to the rest of the street and into the shopping centre. They were looking for common threads. The same milkman, the same grocery delivery boy, a visit by a plumber, a visit to the same bread shop — all were analysed but no connections were made. Patrons and staff at the Mosman Returned Servicemen's Club were also quizzed.

O'Toole decided to play the only real card investigators had by revealing, in an appeal for public help, that police wished to speak to a young man. The man, aged 22 to 25 years old, had a mop of blond hair with a yellowish tinge; he was 180 cm tall and had a slim build. O'Toole said he was wanted in relation to other matters, but might be able to assist police with their current inquiry.

O'Toole was talking about the person who had attacked Ray Roper 13 days earlier at the other end of the same street Lady Ashton lived on.

They released a sketch of Mr Roper's attacker. A week later, a neighbour of Lady Ashton's who had gone on holidays on the day of her murder returned home to learn of what had happened. She told police she saw a "fair-headed surfie-type with long hair" at the back of the block of units at around 10 a.m. on the day Lady Ashton was killed.

Police were interested. It was not much but it was all they had. Maybe he could help them. Maybe, just maybe, he was the killer.

Another identikit was made up and circulated to all stations and to the media. It bore some resemblance to Ray Roper's sketch.

The new angle caused an instant media reaction. "Police Fear Thrill Killer Loose", "Face of a Killer" and "This is the Killer" were the headlines that accompanied the picture.

It was a disaster for the police. The combined effect of the two pictures was to have every old person in Mosman on the lookout for the pimply blond surfie. The phones rang hot. More than 500 phone calls were received in all.

Police still wanted to find him, but this was getting them nowhere. To be a young blond male anywhere near Mosman meant that you were treated with suspicion and even fear. Old people were crossing the street to avoid you.

Dennis O'Toole rang a number of newspapers and told them they'd got it wrong. "You're way off the mark. This is not the face of the killer," he would patiently explain.

"We want to see if we can identify this fellow. If he can come forward he may be able to help with our inquiries. We're not suggesting he is the murderer but we want to know who that fellow is."

The treatment of the story damaged the investigation. Each one of the sightings had to be investigated. Thousands of hours were wasted following them. The blond surfie and Mr Roper's young blond attacker were never found.

Amid the reported sightings, Mosman police were receiving a flood of calls from frightened residents and relatives concerned about the welfare of their mothers living alone. "I think someone is in my back yard, Constable. I'm here by myself, can you send someone quickly?"

There were also callers who demanded to know what police were doing to ensure safety. It was becoming too much. To alleviate the pressure, police organised a public meeting. The response stunned them.

More than 500 elderly people crammed inside the Mosman Council chambers to hear local Patrol Commander Inspector Graeme Ferguson. Another 200 were turned away, causing police to organise another meeting the following week.

Also addressing the meeting was Detective Sergeant Murray Byrnes from the Homicide Squad, who tried to allay their fears. Police were following a number of leads, he said.

Advice was given on how they could protect themselves: travel in groups, go to banks at different times and don't carry large sums of cash, keep homes locked, maintain daily contact with friends. The meeting ended with a half-minute silence in respect of the memories of the two victims.

Local business showed a marked drop in trade, particularly between the hours of 3 p.m. and 5 p.m. "The old ladies they start to be scared," bemoaned Joseph the hairdresser, thinking of the impact on Ivan's Salon, which relied heavily on the elderly.

Joseph was not the only one who had taken to escorting women home. Just after Lady Ashton's murder, John Glover was very persistent one evening about taking Alderman Dom Lopez's mother home. She was 80 and knew Glover because he could manage some of her native tongue, Italian. She told him she had made arrangements to get a lift with someone else. John persisted, saying it was no problem to him, but Mrs Lopez politely declined.

Police had announced a $50,000 reward for information leading to the arrest of Mrs Mitchelhill's murderer. Detective Senior Sergeant Ron Smith had been going over the case reports of both murders at the Chatswood Regional Crime office. Almost three weeks had passed since Lady Ashton's murder, yet the motive for the killings was as obscure as ever, blurred between the definitions of thrill kills and violent muggings. Smith dialled a forensic psychiatrist, Dr Rod Milton, and asked him to put together a psychiatric profile on the murderer.

With his tweed jackets and round glasses, Dr Milton had the look of a true boffin. He had been steeping himself in the dark side of the criminal mind over ten years of working with the police.

He insisted on having access to all photographs of the crime scenes and the bodies. Milton was a firm believer that such murderers tell more about themselves in the way they murder and leave a body than they ever would admit in subsequent confessions and interviews. In his view, the body was like a signature, giving an insight into the person who has left it, in much the same way as the state of a bedroom might tell you about its occupant.

He paid particular attention to the way Lady Ashton was lying on her stomach; the way the clothes were pulled up over her chest with the red raincoat pulled slightly back down; and the black and blue patches on her body. He studied the walking stick: the way it was placed neatly near the body and parallel to it, just as the Mitchelhill stick was reported to have been left. There was the neat placement of the shoes, the open handbags in both cases left tidily by the side.

"What was it that caused this contrast from the explosion of rage to the orderliness of the aftermath?" he pondered. There seemed to be no answer.

Milton sat there with the photos and lingered. He flicked through them in no particular order with no particular object. He was looking at the murderer's most intimate fantasy. This was not something the killer would ever admit to anyone. After he murdered, this was the memory he took home with him, fantasised about, relived in the privacy of his mind and probably masturbated over. But why?

Well, he thought, first of all we have got to have a male, can't have a woman doing this. She wouldn't be strong enough. No, women aren't that aggressive. This is enormous aggression within seconds ... that chest is just pushed in.

He looked at the tremendous risks involved. There had to be a thrill there. Like kids who get bikes and ride at high speed at great risk, this was classic adolescent risk taking. These are typically the acts of a young person, he mused.

What about the theft? he questioned himself. It's like kids pinching money from their mother's purse, it's more like a trophy ... but what about the layout? The killings were an act in themselves, he thought. They were an art form.

This, Dr Milton believed, was someone with terrible, terrible feelings towards women that were gratified by these acts.

His words began to flow on paper:

It was clear that the murders had been carried out with extraordinary violence ... More detailed examination of the killings suggested that there was a curious mixture of order and chaos. Both old ladies seemed to have been carefully targeted, perhaps followed, and then attacked in an explosion of devastating violence and rage. I use this term because the suddenness and violence of the killings were consistent with what was literally an explosion of rage — the circumstances of the killings indicated that they must have been carried out in seconds.

The degree of organisation and the apparent purpose of the attacks, to humiliate and defile women though in a relatively straightforward way, suggested to him that the offender was not grossly mentally disturbed or suffering from a psychosis.

He noted the times of the attacks in the report, both mid-afternoon, and the great risks taken by the offender and the apparent impulsiveness, despite some evidence of planning. These factors suggested to him that the person police were seeking was relatively young.

He paused and reflected on the police evidence spread out like a collage across his consulting room desk. He continued to write. "Despite the theft of money from the victims it appeared that this was not the primary aim of the killings ... it suggests the offender came from a background where money was not a major issue, ie the family was comfortably off."

Dr Milton said he thought it also unlikely that the killings were carried out in order to obtain money for drugs, the violence was far greater than would have been warranted. He was disturbed by the sexual defilement of Lady Ashton's body: it suggested a deeper motive. The removal of both victims' pantyhose and the force used to tie them so tightly around Lady Ashton's throat pointed away from the "robbery gone wrong" theory.

Dr Milton summarised his perception of the character of the killer. To the doctor, the person police were seeking was not an obvious bully, but could be regarded as a bit odd by other males. He would have acquaintances rather than friends. He would not seek help of his own accord, for his inner thoughts were so secretive and violent that he would be afraid to reveal them. He would appear superficially cool and collected, but might show physical signs of anxiety in the form of sweating when being interviewed, the report concluded.

Milton finished writing half a day after he started, confident that he had described the man the police were seeking. The report landed on Ron Smith's desk the next day. He was glad to have it. He wanted all the information he could get because he had nothing else, but he — and all the other investigators — were cynical about these psychiatric reports. "They're all very well and good but they don't give you the killer's name and address," Dennis O'Toole would say.

He was nevertheless interested. At least the theory on the killer's age confirmed what they had thought. It made it imperative to look at Mosman High School.

In an area of affluence and prestigious well-to-do private schools, Mosman High is the only state-run secondary school on the peninsula. It was also smack bang in the middle of the killing zone and close to Mosman Returned Servicemen's Club. Both killings had happened around the time school finished. It seemed to add up. There were plenty of blond youths and plenty of other kids who would have been having problems at home and at school.

Local police intelligence also told the Homicide Squad that a group of Mosman High students had been getting up to no good and had a reputation for violence. They were children of wealthy families and had come to police attention as much for their drunken parties and fights among themselves as for bag snatching and petty offences. With this in mind O'Toole went along to the school and addressed the students at an assembly. He asked them if they had seen anybody lurking around and put it to them subtly that one of their schoolmates might be the murderer.

Police were also assigned to address other schools. Detective Paul Mayger went to Balgowlah High on the other side of Middle Harbour. It was an experience somewhat removed from his training and made that little bit more uncomfortable by the fact that his stepson was in the audience.

Students came forward and named their peers, perhaps where a previously outgoing boy had become withdrawn, stopped mixing with his old crowd, or started going straight home after school where previously they had hung around. All those nominated were talked to.

O'Toole and the other detectives interviewed dozens of students. Some were visited at school, others at home and some were pulled out of bed by the knock of police at the door.

Some parents threatened legal action. Investigators could only try to tell them that two women had been brutally murdered and that nobody was accusing their son of it.

The week of Lady Ashton's funeral a report from the Crime Scene unit landed on O'Toole's desk. The grey hair found on Lady Ashton's hand had been analysed by a forensic biologist. The hair could not be classified. It might have been hers — picked up while trying to stop strangulation — or it might have been the killer's. Since all indications were that they were looking for a young man, it seemed safe to assume it was the former.

The search of Mosman's young people put one young person — described as a local character — straight to the top of the list of prime candidates. A heavily built youth, he walked the streets carrying a baton and a police radio scanner. He had been in and out of a psychiatric hospital for some time, not with any psychotic illness, but with enormous rage.

Investigations showed that he hated his mother. He would ring her and make threats to her or break wind down the phone to her. He was also a member of the Returned Servicemen's Club.

The police devoted hours to gathering information on him and tailing him, but he had an alibi for one of the killings. Police were wary: the alibi was good, but it was not inconceivable that he was being protected. He was seeing a counsellor who said he was having a session with him at the time of one of the killings.

Rod Milton was called in to try and eliminate the youth. He looked at a huge dossier police had compiled on the fellow and could only conclude that he was more than capable of such crimes. "The aggression towards his mother is horrific. You can't rule him out at all but, if anything, he is a little too disturbed," Milton told them.

In early June, a few weeks after he had given police his profile of the killer, Dr Rod Milton was thinking hard about the case. He had watched the investigation getting nowhere and would often ring up detectives to find out what was happening, hoping to catch up with new information that might help the profile.

He had been pondering the peculiar mixture of violence and orderliness found at the scenes. It was such a great contrast, there had to be meaning in it.

Milton remembered the military presence in the area. The army and the navy both had large bodies of men stationed at Mosman. The army was the sort of place to attract people prone to violence yet it also had the discipline. It made sense, the combination was there.

More importantly, soldiers had families. If it was not a young soldier it could just as easily be the son of a career man brought up on a diet of strict discipline enforced by violence.

He rang the task force and spoke to Detective Senior Sergeant Ron Smith. They had already thought about the armed services, but Milton's theory certainly lent weight to the idea.

Approaches were made to commanders to screen all servicemen and they agreed. It was a small nightmare which involved sifting through rosters, troop movements and prison records.

"The army was terrific," said O'Toole. "They co-operated with us. You come to some of those commandos ... terrific people, great blokes, but they're mad. They love killing. They're trained to kill. They are looking for a war.

"Sit down with 'em and look at their eyes. I'm not having a go at them, but we had to look at all avenues."

But as the weeks turned to months and lead after lead yielded nothing, doubts began to enter the investigator's minds about whether or not they really were looking for a young male. You could hear it in the evening sessions over a beer when they would sit around and informally exchange information, keeping each other abreast of what was going on. But the doubts that were raised were more the result of the months of thankless slog than of any firm reasoning.

The investigation was stalled.

Glover continued to turn up at the Mosman Musical Society's weekly rehearsals. By late May the company was meeting every Monday and Wednesday night.

Ian McCann had begun to hear polite complaints from female members in the cast about Glover's behaviour. Always out of Glover's earshot. "He was not obnoxiously rude, just made a few of the women feel a bit uncomfortable. Some complained that his conversation was a bit smutty. Some of them had mentioned that he had made suggestive remarks," recalled Mr McCann.

To the male members of the company he seemed a "charming likable sort of bloke in a knock-about fashion". Mr McCann thought so. "He used to tell smutty jokes in female company, and once made a dirty remark about one woman's backside." Yet despite what was said, none of the cast demanded he be thrown out.

By late May Glover had proved himself invaluable, helping to make props and scenery. But a week before the first night curtain Glover disappeared without explanation.

"I tried to reach him for ten days. All we knew was that he lived in Mosman and worked for Four'N Twenty Pies as a salesman," said Mr McCann. "Every time I rang his work I was told he was away or sick."

On the second night of the show Glover turned up with his daughters. He gave no reason for his absence but told Mr McCann he thoroughly enjoyed the show. His services were rewarded by a credit in the program.

He never came back.

CHAPTER TWELVE

BUSINESS AS USUAL

O n Wednesday 28 June — as police continued to work through the backlog of young ruffians, surfies and dobbed-in students — John Glover set off to work in his company car. As usual his clothes were immaculate, the creases ironed to military perfection.

That day he planned to drum up new business in the leafy suburbs of the upper north shore. It was a clear winter morning, brisk by Sydney standards.

That day the State Police Minister Ted Pickering had announced a doubling of the reward for the north shore serial murderer to $100,000 — $50,000 for each victim. "These women were subjected to incredibly vicious attacks. By offering such a high reward we're bound to attract somebody with knowledge about the incident," Mr Pickering confidently predicted.

Glover drove to the Wesley Gardens retirement village on busy Forest Way at Belrose, bounded on either side by a golf course and bushland. His arrival attracted the attention of staff because he entered the building through a rear entrance. Asked if he was lost, Glover introduced himself as a salesman. He was directed by a sister to the catering manager, Rod Murrell, who told him they did not need any pies or pastries. They made their own.

Glover handed over a price list just in case Murrell ever wanted any catering help. On the way out, Glover realised he had lost his good pen so he went to the reception desk. A message was put over the public address system asking if anyone had found it.

As the speakers echoed the request for the lost pen through the complex, Glover slipped into the nursing home proper and started up a conversation with one of the residents, Marjorie Moseley. Without warning he began fondling one of her breasts on the outside of her clothing.

He then turned and left the building. Mrs Moseley was distressed and reported the incident. Staff were confident that it was this grey-haired man who had lost his pen.

Police from Frenchs Forest were called but the investigation did not go anywhere. The Homicide Squad at Chatswood and O'Toole, who was based at Mosman, were unaware of the incident.

They were waiting for something to give. It came on Saturday 15 July.

Since Lady Ashton's death, a neighbour had taken to regularly clearing out the build-up of mail from her letter box. On 15 July she came across a red leather wallet containing Lady Ashton's pension card. It had not been there a few days earlier when the letter box was last checked.

Detectives viewed the discovery with hope. It looked like the breakthrough that they had been waiting for.

Rob Murrell (left), catering manager at the
Wesley Gardens retirement village at Belrose.

There was no doubt that the wallet was taken by the murderer. The question was: how did it get in the letter box?

Detective Barry Keeling told the media it was most likely that someone had found the wallet and returned it to Lady Ashton's address. "We want to know where it was found," he appealed to the finder.

The wallet was dispatched immediately to scientific for fingerprint testing and analysis. For three days detectives waited anxiously for the results. No one came forward to admit to finding the wallet. O'Toole thought that maybe the killer was taunting them.

When the results came back from the lab, there was not a trace of a print, not a hair nor a piece of clothing. Their boy was still out there, as elusive as ever.

Despite mixed bouts of depression over the preceding months, John Glover continued to go about his work as usual, checking on clients to see if they were happy with their orders and whether they wanted more.

He was his own boss, could go anywhere he pleased and did not have to keep a logbook of his daily movements. His brief: bring in as much business as you can talk up.

On 24 July, he found himself cruising on the lower north shore. At 2 p.m. he went to a nursing home in Lane Cove. He was seen in the hallway near the main entrance by the home's diversionary therapist, Stephanie. She noticed him as a well-dressed man, well presented and good looking with his grey hair ... "Not that I go for older men," she would explain.

Stephanie paid little more attention to him. As far as she was concerned, he was just one of the many people moving around the home at any time.

A few minutes later, she went upstairs and saw him in one of the rooms. "What are you doing here?" she asked as a normal matter of inquiry.

"I'm sorry, I'm lost. I'm looking for the kitchen."

"Well, it's down here," she told him, leading him down the wide staircase to the kitchen.

As she walked with him she remembered that when she had last seen him, in the hallway, he was standing virtually outside the kitchen and he must have walked straight past it. But if a notion of his sinister intent ever crossed her mind it was quickly dismissed.

Wearing his brown slacks, brown leather jacket and brown brogues, Glover turned on his charming best. Stephanie introduced him to the chef, who was similarly taken by his appearance.

Glover introduced himself and handed over a price list. His banter had worked well enough to prompt the cook to call for the matron's opinion, even though she knew what the answer would be.

"I have a gentleman in the kitchen who wants to sell us pies."

"Tell him we need pies like a hole in the head," the matron told her.

So that was that, and Glover left as the two women joked that maybe they should have bought some pies if it meant bringing the good-looking bloke back more regularly.

But the diversionary therapist, Stephanie, had doubts about what had just happened. "He was pleasant but later I thought: 'That was a silly thing to do, not challenging him upstairs'." She was worried enough to report it to the matron after he had left the building. Stephanie then went into room 28 where she found 85-year-old Lillian Tracey, who seemed to be distressed. Mrs Tracey was very jittery and her clothes seemed to be in upheaval but Stephanie could not make out what she was saying.

Then another woman, Mrs Jean McGilchrist, came in. "A man has just come in, lifted my dress and patted my bottom," she told Stephanie.

"What man?"

"A man in a brown leather jacket."

The therapist went back to the first woman, who was senile. She was laughing but scared at the same time. This time the diversionary therapist understood what she was saying. "A man put his hand down my nightie," she said, scared that he would return.

The matron called the local Lane Cove police. Mrs McGilchrist was able to give a fairly accurate description of Glover. The cook and Stephanie also gave descriptions and told the two male uniformed officers that he said he was a pie salesman.

Perhaps not believing he was a pie salesman at all, they said there was little they could do. They told staff to be on the lookout for strangers.

Nobody had thought that the man they were talking about might be capable of more serious crimes, and certainly not that he was the person responsible for the Mosman murders. After all, that was meant to be a blond surfie.

About the same time that the police were interviewing staff at the nursing home, the Chatswood Regional Crime Squad office was abuzz with news of an extraordinary case. A former police superintendent, Harry Blackburn, had just been charged with 12 serious sexual assaults dating back over 20 years. Those investigators who were not on the road watched the television news in disbelief. Most of the senior officers had known Harry Blackburn from his days as head of the Scientific Branch, which was now called Physical Evidence.

Despite the jostling encroachment of homes, high-rise apartments and office blocks, large patches of bushland remain unscathed on Sydney Harbour's shores. Some stretches of Middle Head are much the same as the first settlers saw them in 1788.

On Tuesday 8 August, a Carlingford businessman was jogging along one of the bush trails at Ashton Park where the track broke across a grass verge. As he ran out on to the clearing an object caught his eye.

It was a Commonwealth Bank savings passbook. It had the appearance of having endured several storms. He opened it and saw the name Winfreda I. Ashton. He continued on his run thinking nothing more of his find.

Not long after the jogger made his discovery, John Glover travelled to Lindfield, in the heart of the northern suburbs. He was working, but his mind was elsewhere.

He parked his car at the Northhaven retirement village and upon entering realised the retirement village was made up of self-contained units and so there was no central kitchen for him to make a sale to.

There were no staff around either, so he left. But before he got back to his car parked in the street, he saw Euphemia "Effie" Carnie struggling back to her unit with a bag of groceries.

As she passed him he pushed her to the ground then punched her in the chest, leaving her gasping for air in pain. He stole her groceries and her handbag, then strolled back to the car and drove off.

Pulling over to the side of a nearby road, he took $90 from the handbag and pocketed it before throwing the handbag and groceries into some roadside bushes. He then continued on with the remainder of his appointments for the day.

Three months had passed since his trip to Ashton Park. His excursions of assault and molestation at nursing homes had become more frequent.

He had been half expecting a knock on the door the whole time, but none came. He was growing more confident as the days passed, as his evil went unpunished.

The following day Lady Ashton's bank book landed on Dennis O'Toole's desk. The jogger had handed it in. At first glance, its appearance told detectives the odds of getting a print were extremely slim, but it was dispatched to the lab in the faint hope that some clue could be salvaged.

Foremost in O'Toole's mind was the need to get back to where it was found. It might prove to be some sort of dumping ground.

The search began early the next day. More than 20 police were assembled at Ashton Park. The jogger showed them where he found the passbook.

The searchers fanned out and then commenced an emu-bob, walking slowly in a line, eyes fixed to the ground, pausing occasionally to bend and study any unusual items. Each spot with a scrap on it was marked.

By 11 a.m. their prayers had been answered. After more than two hours, they had found two purses 20 metres apart, one brown and one yellow, along with two travel concession passes, both bearing Lady

Ashton's name. Police had not been aware one of the purses even existed. Lady Ashton carried three purses and a wallet.

Although pleased, O'Toole was concerned. It looked too easy. The items had been discarded with little attempt at concealment. "He must be taunting us," O'Toole thought.

After days of testing, none of the items turned out to reveal anything new about the killer. It was back to square one.

Apart from the Mosman youth, there was just one suspect that could not be discounted; the evidence against him seemed stronger as the other leads faltered. He was a Canadian who had returned home shortly after Lady Ashton's murder.

His game had been to rip off old people through various ruses. A confidence trickster dressed in a business suit, he had left a trail of hard luck stories throughout the Mosman peninsula, taking money from nuns, pensioners and the disabled. Then suddenly he had disappeared. Those who had known him while he was living in the area had been unable to account for his whereabouts on the days of the murders.

Canadian police were contacted and they began to trail the man. They soon arrested him when he pulled one of his scams on an elderly woman, unaware that police were watching.

It was early October and the investigators were reaching their wits' end. They would have to go to Canada to interview him while he was in custody. O'Toole began to sound out his superiors on allowing the trip.

The Wybenia nursing home at Neutral Bay, one kilometre from Mosman, was unusually quiet on Friday 6 October 1989. The diversionary therapist had taken about half of the home's 42 residents out on a bus trip.

Around midday, most of the nursing staff were in the staff room having lunch, relaxing before the bus came back. A nurse facing the door happened to glance up and noticed a man walk by holding a piece of paper as though he were reading it. He appeared to have dark hair, framed as he was against a bright light streaming through the door.

Moments later a bell sounded, signalling that one of the residents wanted assistance. "Help, help, help," sounded through the corridors.

Sister Ann Chan was checking the drug intakes of patients and could not leave straight away. She heard one of the nurses saying in an alarmed voice: "I think someone's been in and assaulted Mrs McNeil."

Phylis McNeil was blind, quite lucid but very frail. The radio had been her main source of entertainment and she had followed the stories of the murder of elderly women with interest.

Sister Chan raced in to see for herself. Mrs McNeil said something about a man pulling at her clothing, saying he was a doctor. Sister Chan could see she was extremely distressed.

Moments earlier, the bus had arrived back from the day trip. The diversionary therapist came in wondering what all the fuss was about and was told. "I think I might have seen the fellow," she said.

When the bus had pulled in, she had noticed a grey-haired man leaving the building and had looked at him carefully because she at first thought she recognised him as a friend. He was wearing a white shirt and grey trousers, she told Constable Gavin Mayo, who came out from North Sydney police. He had been called immediately and had gone alone because they were short-staffed that day.

Nursing home staff asked him not to interview Mrs McNeil because of the state she was in. Constable Mayo agreed. She was blind, after all, and would only have been able to describe the crime.

The diversionary therapist described the portly grey-haired man she had seen getting into the car and the nurse who noticed the dark-haired man framed against the light told the constable what she saw. Constable Mayo later took them to the station to view a book of mug shots but as the women looked at the pictures they agreed that all the characters looked too sleazy. None of them seemed anything like the well-dressed businessman the nurses had seen.

They were told there was little more that could be done.

Constable Mayo thought the case unusual, but did not link it to the murders which had occurred up on the Mosman ridge.

Mayo thinks he passed the report of the incident upstairs to the detectives office because that was standard procedure. The case certainly went no further than that.

Five days later, on Wednesday 11 October, Harry Blackburn was cleared of all charges. It was revealed that he had been wrongfully arrested. It was the blackest of days for New South Wales investigative police; the reputation of the entire service was tainted.

"Well, I was out of the car and I saw her before I got back to the car and I just took the opportunity. I didn't have time to get back into the car and get the hammer. Hit her face at least once into the wall ..."

On Wednesday 18 October Glover parked his car at Spit Junction, the point where Military Road veers right towards Taronga Zoo and Spit Road goes left towards Manly. A three lane highway, it is thick with traffic all day, easing only late at night. At 4 p.m., Glover needed to make a phone call at the Mosman post office on Spit Road.

It was there he saw her: an old woman walking on the other side of the road towards the Garrison retirement village facing the post office. Her name was Doris Cox, an 86-year-old widowed resident of the four-storey townhouse-style complex.

The Garrison also had a fifth level of apartments running below street
level. They could be reached via two external stairways, which led into a
winding garden maze. This lower level was obscured from its two street
frontages by thickets of shrubs and trees erected as an aesthetic buffer
against the thunderous traffic just metres away.

Glover waited for the "walk" signal before hurrying across Spit Road.
He caught up to Mrs Cox and struck up a conversation with her as they
walked together into the grounds of the Garrison. Once there, he ushered
her down the stairs onto the secluded walkway two metres below the
pedestrian footpath, running parallel and just metres away.

Down there, in relative seclusion, he grabbed her head from behind
with both hands and, with as much force as he could muster, pounded her
face into a brick wall.

Mrs Cox collapsed on to the stairs. Glover rifled her handbag and
found nothing he wanted. Blood was streaming from the crumpled body.
He put the bag down and went home, leaving Mrs Cox for dead.

At 4.10 p.m. two women walking past heard her cries for help. When
they found Mrs Cox she was sitting down, her clothes scarlet. Blood was
pouring down her face, her handbag lying open on the ground nearby.

An ambulance was called and she was taken to Royal North Shore
Hospital, undergoing immediate emergency surgery.

O'Toole had gone to work at the Mosman police station the following
morning thinking that the trip to Canada was looking more and more
necessary. He had driven from Mosman to Chatswood to brief Detective
Inspector Mike Hagan on how the investigation was progressing, and to
pick up his mail and any messages. It had become his daily routine.

The phone rang. It was a doctor from Royal North Shore Hospital.
"We've got a patient down here who came in yesterday, an old woman,
and look, we think she may have been assaulted. It's quite serious."

Dennis O'Toole raced down the Pacific Highway to Royal North
Shore at St Leonards, two kilometres south of the Chatswood Crime
Squad office. "If this is the work of our boy, then thank God one's
survived," he thought. This was the break they had been looking for.

He got there and was impressed by the liveliness of the old woman
despite her horrific head injuries. Mrs Cox proved willing and co-
operative, if a bit vague, but that was understandable in the
circumstances. She rattled off what she had done that day.

She told him that she had been to her sister's place. She gave O'Toole
the sister's name, address and telephone number. She told him how she
caught the bus back to Mosman and how she was walking along the path
and then she went home.

"But what happened on the path?" the detective asked.

"Oh nothing," she replied. "I went home."

"Can you remember anything about the path?"

"I went home."

"No, Doris, just before you got there. What happened?"

"Nothing happened."

O'Toole had drawn a blank. He got back to the office and began checking. He rang Mrs Cox's sister's number. A woman with an Asian accent answered the phone and told him he must have had the wrong number, there was nobody there by that name. He asked what number he had reached.

The woman told him. It was the number Mrs Cox gave him.

O'Toole gave the address. Yes, that number did belong to that address, she said. Then she remembered. A woman by that name had lived there, the Asian woman said, but she had died ten years earlier.

Dennis O'Toole checked with the Garrison. Mrs Cox suffered from Alzheimer's disease, a condition that causes severe memory loss.

Doctors would, however, credit the ailment for preventing her from going into shock, thus saving her life. Dr Joe DuFlou was called in to examine Mrs Cox's wound and concluded that it was similar to injuries sustained in the other attacks.

Mrs Cox was transferred to Mosman District Hospital and a guard put on her room. There would be no information from her.

O'Toole went to the Garrison with Phil Flogel. The scene had been washed down, though there were still bloodstains visible on the concrete. But it was not blood that they were after. The investigators needed something left by the killer: a piece of hair, a shoeprint, a fingerprint, even a button.

The Crime Scene unit did what they could, but there was not much to be done. The hoses and soapy water had ensured nothing was left.

The police were reluctant to say it openly, but they had no doubts that the murderer was responsible for this attack too. Doris Cox's injuries and the open handbag told them that. This would rule out their Canadian suspect.

O'Toole inquired as to why police were not informed of the attack until the following day. Ambulance officers told him that they asked the Garrison to ring police, but Garrison staff said the ambos said they were going to do it. He threw his arms up in despair.

The routine investigation began. Flats at the Garrison and surrounding businesses and homes were doorknocked. Nothing came up.

It was suggested that all three victims had visited the Mosman Returned Servicemen's Club either on the day they were attacked or shortly before. Mrs Cox had been taken there to see a lunchtime show on a visit organised through the nursing home.

The police canvass turned to the club. Most regular patrons were quizzed about their movements and whether they had noticed any suspicious characters. It was more thankless slog for the investigators.

But two days after the attack, the canvass and public appeal produced what every cop had been praying for. It was *the* big clue.

A teenage boy was seen at around 4 p.m. emerging from the shrubbery behind which Mrs Cox was attacked. He jumped straight onto his skateboard and sped across an adjacent set of traffic lights on Spit Road which had just flashed up the "walk" signal. He almost cleaned up two pedestrians as he went. He was flying and motorists noticed him too. He was aged 14 to 16, was of medium build with dark hair cropped closely at the back and sides and was wearing a loose-fitting dark shirt and shorts.

As a suspect, he looked pretty good to O'Toole because "he was all we had". O'Toole was also swayed by the fact police did not know what the murder weapon was. Could it have been a skateboard? "It appeared to be a heavy blunt object and those skateboards are pretty bloody heavy," he said during the conference next morning.

In the following days, 18 skateboarders were pulled in and interviewed. While O'Toole talked to them, members of the Physical Evidence unit were sitting or standing quietly at the other end of the room, holding newspapers or jumpers on their arms. They were secretly taking photographs for surveillance purposes. If any of the boys began to firm up as suspects, photographs would be needed so the witnesses at the crime scenes would be able to say whether that was the boy.

The skateboarder theory looked good, but the links by all three victims to the Mosman Returned Servicemen's Club could not be discounted; neither could the military.

It was late October when Glover returned to the Lane Cove nursing home in which he had molested Mrs Tracey and Mrs McGilchrist in July. Again he did not head for the kitchen but was recognised wandering in the hallway. A nurse called Sue had remembered the descriptions that had been given to staff.

"Can I help you?" she asked suspiciously.

"Yes, I'm looking for a phone," he told her.

"There's one around the corner."

"Thanks."

She discreetly followed him and watched him go into a phone booth. She thought he was pretending to make a call before he left. Matron found him wandering around outside and he said he was looking for the adjacent retirement village. She had not recognised the description and offered to walk him over. She often walked people over there because it was a pleasant stroll beneath the eucalypts, a good chance to get out of the office. Glover started up a conversation, pleasant and charming. They walked up a secluded path and she bade him farewell as he headed into the retirement village. On this occasion, Glover left the retirement village without attacking or molesting a resident.

CHAPTER THIRTEEN

A SERIAL KILLER AMONG US

O n 2 November 1989, Glover found himself working in the Lane Cove area, seven kilometres from Mosman. It was a peculiar day. A light breeze was bringing patches of sunshine and patches of rain. According to Glover's account, he saw an old woman he would later know to be Margaret Pahud, 85, walking down Longueville Road, at a point where the busy strip of suburban shops gave way to a school and then houses. She was dressed in a two-piece black summer suit and was carrying two bags of groceries.

It was about 3 p.m. when he pulled the car over. The woman turned off Longueville Road into a narrow private walkway which she used as a short cut to her home in the Ridgeway apartments in Austin Street.

Glover reached for the hammer under his seat and put it under his shirt as he stepped from the car.

He saw that a retirement village overlooked the laneway where the woman was walking. No fewer than 20 units had a clear view of what he wanted to do. A house on the other side was just metres from where Mrs Pahud was walking slowly. Cars were flashing by the end of the lane and there was a good chance a pedestrian could walk by at any moment.

But whatever was working inside Glover's head that day, it was overriding any other concerns ... tunnel vision, he had to kill again. Glover came up quickly behind the 85-year-old woman, lifting the hammer above his head only at the last possible moment. He rained down a furious volley of three blows and she probably never knew what hit her.

Knowing the risk he was in, Glover neglected his ritual strangulation.

above: Margaret Pahud, John Glover's fourth victim, was killed in Lane Cove. Her handbag (*right*) was later found where Glover dumped it, two kilometres away.

He calmly took Mrs Pahud's handbag, placed the bloodied hammer back under his shirt and walked back to his car. The whole process lasted seconds. Another dying woman lay on the ground.

Minutes later, a nine-year-old girl returning from school saw what she thought was a bundle of old clothes. She examined it out of curiosity before letting out a bloodcurdling scream.

Even as the shrill tones of her cry were ringing out, Glover was back in his car and driving down Longueville Road. He turned left into River

Road then pulled over and parked near the entrance to the Lane Cove Country Club, two kilometres from where Mrs Pahud lay dying.

Mrs Pahud's handbag was rifled and $400 extracted. It was dumped in a stormwater drain at the back of the ninth tee, just metres from River Road, which was thick with the early peak-hour traffic.

John Glover drove to the Mosman Returned Servicemen's Club where he proceeded to have a few drinks and put most of Mrs Pahud's cash through the poker machines. He sat mesmerised, watching the reels spin and spin. He was reliving the crime. Part of his victim was going into the machine with each spin.

He was playing the $1 machine at five coins a go. The money did not last long and he returned home shortly afterwards, got changed, had a shower, dined and watched television.

Detective Sergeant Dennis O'Toole was in the "murder room" of the Mosman police station that afternoon. The phone rang. It was Detective Senior Sergeant Ron Smith at Chatswood. "A woman has been found at Lane Cove, it looks like it could be one."

O'Toole got in the car with Barry Keeling and headed out.

They did not talk much. They were both hoping there were no similarities. They were both going over in their minds the implications for them if it was the same killer. It would add a whole new dimension to the investigation. It would mean the killer was mobile. The skateboarder, the best lead, would be gone.

They pulled the squad car into a spot on Longueville Road and walked a short distance to a laneway where some uniformed police were milling around.

The body had been moved. O'Toole started asking questions.

The woman had been alive when she was found. Two doctors had raced down from a surgery two doors away. She died in the arms of one of them before the ambulance arrived.

Nevertheless, the ambulance took the body to Royal North Shore Hospital and the crime scene was destroyed. Doctors at the hospital had in turn contacted police upon seeing the body.

O'Toole looked around. The Uniting Church retirement unit block, Kamilaroi, looked straight down on the scene. The killer was getting more brazen. He could not believe the guy's audacity, to do this

in such an open spot. Somebody up in the units must have seen something. There was an old fibro house on one side — somebody in there might have seen something, too.

Twenty metres away, Longueville Road dissected the laneway. Lane Cove shopping centre was 100 metres up the road and two schools were just down the road. Surely this time someone had seen their man.

The Physical Evidence unit had decided that three people would have to attend every killing of an elderly woman after the Cox bashing. The amount of work to process was increasing all the time.

But this scene looked as bad as the others. Again, it had been cleaned, this time scrubbed down with ammonia. A stream of blood had flowed ten metres down the pathway into a little drain then been washed away.

But over the fence, in a schoolyard, Physical Evidence found a length of copper pipe. It appeared to have blood on it. It looked like a weapon.

They pinned their hopes on it at first but there was no other sign the thing had been used in an attack — no hair, no skin or dents suggesting it had killed Mrs Pahud. It was hard to say for sure, but it was later decided the blood on the pipe was splashed there when the path had been hosed.

The canvass began immediately in the retirement units and the house next door. Nothing of great interest was turned up except that a neighbour and friend of Mrs Pahud's, Mrs Enid Benckie, said that at around three o'clock a gentlemanly grey-haired man had helped carry her groceries up to her unit.

She assured police he could not have been a murderer: "He was far too nice, officer."

Shopkeepers had been questioned to try to piece together the woman's movements. She had last been seen at the Commonwealth Bank in Longueville where she had been a regular. Staff knew her well. Her last transaction was to pick up a new chequebook and withdraw $400 in cash. Lady Ashton too had been to a Commonwealth Bank just before she died.

Patterns were emerging but they did little to alleviate police frustrations.

Detective Senior Constable Paul Mayger broke off from the other police late in the evening. He wandered over to the end of the lane where the media were waiting, keen to get something new. He found himself talking from the heart. "For God's sake, how many more people must die," he said in pleading for anybody who knew the killer to come forward. "How many more attacks do we have to have before we get this guy?"

Up until then police had been reluctant to say the murders had definitely been done by the same person. They still were not absolutely sure themselves and they did not want to show their hand. Officially, they said the possibility of a copycat killer or even a coincidental mugging gone wrong was still real, but in their guts they knew it was the same man and that scared them.

The death of "Madge" Pahud meant that the killer might strike anywhere and he was likely to go on until he was stopped. "If it is the same person, he's mad," Dennis O'Toole told reporters at the scene.

Police really did not have to say publicly that it was the same offender. Radio bulletins were already saying as much and by the time Mayger wandered over to say his piece, all the morning newspaper police reporters had already filed their stories saying the same.

Mrs Pahud's postmortem had been carried out early that evening. The urgency to find the exact nature of her wounds and any clues that might have been thrown up became paramount.

The wounds to her head were staggering. "The biggest hole in the head you've ever seen. It was blitzkrieg," recalled one officer present. Two of the blows had shattered her skull. Homicide police came back from the postmortem with a feeling of rage, driving them on to catch the madman.

More than 40 police, detectives and uniformed officers set out canvassing the area and that same night O'Toole relocated the investigation from Mosman to the tiny Lane Cove police station.

Craig Regan from the Police Media Liaison unit was called out to help ease pressure from reporters swarming outside the station looking for new angles. In the media office at Police Headquarters in the city, the phones were running hot. There was little to be said other than to describe how Mrs Pahud was found and the nature of her injuries. Nor would there be any release of the victim's name until relatives had been contacted, at least not until the morning.

Officially, police were still playing down the links with the previous attacks. Their stance angered one reporter who turned up late at Lane Cove police station only to be told by a young policewoman to wait outside while a statement was being compiled. Regan was inside the station attending a briefing with detectives when the discussion was interrupted by angry shouting.

"Watch your grandmother! Just watch your grandmother!"

As Regan looked out the door he caught a glimpse of the constable closing it in the shouting reporter's face.

O'Toole stayed at the scene into the early morning, picking around for clues and talking to neighbours. At 2 a.m. he got into his car and drove home to Gosford, exhausted. As the car glided up the empty freeway, his mind kept going back to his worst fear. If it was the same person, he was shaping up as someone the likes of whom none of the detectives had seen before; worse still, he had shown he could strike anywhere.

The house was in darkness when he arrived home. He climbed into bed, had 40 minutes sleep and got up again. He showered, put on a fresh set of clothes and headed back to Chatswood.

O'Toole and his team were back at the laneway at 8 a.m. to begin afresh, spreading the net wider. The whole area was canvassed. Did anyone notice anyone suspicious? Nothing.

Did anyone see a kid on a skateboard? Nothing. It was too far to skateboard from Mosman anyway. Bus timetables were checked. Bus drivers were asked if they'd seen the kid on board. Police rode on the buses around the time of day the killing occurred, hoping to find passengers that might have seen him while the recollection was still fresh in their minds. Still nothing.

Earlier attempts to establish a chronological pattern had fallen apart. The ten week gap between the first two murders had been followed by a five month gap until the Cox attack and then two weeks until the third murder. It certainly was not phases of the moon.

By midday, dozens of phone calls had been received from people who had been in the area at the time. Most of them were to report young males seen acting suspiciously. One of the reports was from a woman who noticed a dark-haired young man walk by with a mad look in his eye. She duly reported what she saw. She was passed on to the Physical Evidence unit and another identikit was drawn up.

Another youth was brought to the attention of investigators through his school. He was good on a skateboard, went everywhere on the thing. He was having problems at home, and he had the means to have got to all three murders.

A solicitor, Prue Gregory, rang to say she had seen a grey-haired man walking in Longueville Road around the time of the murder. She said she was picking up her six-year-old daughter from Lane Cove Public School near the retirement village when a man walking in the opposite direction had brushed past her. She noticed he was middle-aged, had grey hair, and was thick set and well dressed. She had to skirt around him in the street and had paid attention only because she thought it odd that a man coming from the direction of the Catholic school down the road did not have children in tow.

Her information was taken down but meant nothing. Well-dressed middle-aged men were as common in Lane Cove as the eucalypts which lined the streets. Her report was filed away with the growing mass of other sightings in the area.

"I can't believe nobody saw anything. Whoever we are looking for is going unnoticed. People aren't looking for the person we're after," O'Toole told the next morning's conference.

It was mid-Friday afternoon when Glover drove into the Wesley Gardens retirement village on the upper north shore where five months earlier he had fondled the breasts of Marjorie Moseley. He stuck his head through the servery window and asked to see the catering manager, Rob Murrell.

Murrell was rostered off that day and staff were busy and did not have time to talk to him. Glover left, but on the way out came across an old woman sitting on a garden seat outside the home. Her name was Olive Cleveland, an 81-year-old spinster. She was a quiet person who rarely took part in organised social activities at the centre.

Born in the NSW mid-west town of Parkes, Miss Cleveland had lived at the village for eight years. During that time she had survived three heart attacks, the last of which was only a few months earlier.

Despite poor health, she rarely missed her daily afternoon walk through the courtyards and surrounding fields. As on most days, she had spent Friday morning reading the papers which declared that the Mosman killer or "Society Killer" had moved on. She had dozed off in the big armchair in her room, then woke to join other residents for lunch in the dining room where staff last saw her at 12.30 p.m. After another nap she had set off on her stroll at 3 p.m., a trip that normally took her an hour.

By Glover's account, he saw Miss Cleveland, walked over to her and started a casual conversation. Whatever he said or did, Miss Cleveland was not interested. She got up and started walking back towards the front door of the building.

Glover followed close behind for a few feet, glancing quickly around him. There was no one about. He grabbed Miss Cleveland, pushed her past the doorway and around to the right of the building down a sloping laneway. He grabbed her head from behind and slammed her to the bitumen. Still holding her head, he pounded the left side into the pavement until she appeared unconscious.

He pulled up her dress, removed her thick stockings, tied them around her neck and strangled her. The dense weave of the garment caused the loose ends to fluff up, giving the appearance of a bow around her neck.

The whole process was completed in little over a minute. It was done in a completely public (albeit little used) lane overlooked by the units of residents and a back tee on the adjoining golf course.

John Glover walked back to his car and drove to the Mosman Returned Servicemen's Club. He was $60 richer.

Dennis O'Toole stayed at Lane Cove until 4.30 p.m. then drove back to Chatswood to brief Mike Hagan on the Pahud investigation, but Hagan was not there. O'Toole had been in the office for ten minutes when someone pulled a can of beer out of the fridge. Tired and tense, he accepted it gladly. He had hardly stopped since the day before.

O'Toole, Detective Senior Sergeant Geoff Wright and the other Dennis O'Toole — a Detective Sergeant in charge of robbery investigations nicknamed "Doodles" — were standing around a table in the corner of the office. "Miles" O'Toole pulled the top off his can. He was going to enjoy this beer. A phone rang.

Olive Cleveland, murdered at Wesley Gardens retirement village.

"Miles, we've got Frenchs Forest on the phone," someone called out. "They reckon they've got an elderly woman found dead at Belrose. Looks like he's hit again."

O'Toole looked around the office. He expected to see someone on one of the other phones playing a joke.

The office was empty.

They looked at each other, heads shaking slowly; dismay, disbelief and exhaustion were written on their faces. The Pahud murder was only 24 hours old and already they had another one on their hands.

"We'll get out there as quickly as possible," O'Toole said.

He in fact did not go. He could not. There was an investigation still to be set up at Lane Cove. So much work still had to be done — and he was exhausted. Mike Hagan was in his car when O'Toole called him on the radio. He headed straight out to set up the new investigation. But with whom? The officers and the resources were thin on the ground.

Geoff Wright and "Doodles" O'Toole jumped into their cars and raced up to Belrose. "Miles" O'Toole rang the Lane Cove station where most of the detectives had gathered after the day's work there. Everybody at Lane Cove thought he was joking too. Paul Mayger drove from Lane Cove to the scene to join Inspector Hagan and the others at the new scene.

Media crews began to gather almost immediately. Their scanners had picked up the call for Scientific and Homicide to attend another nursing home. The crime scene had not been sealed off with tape. Camera crews were standing on a grass verge shooting down into the laneway. A uniformed constable was all that stood between them.

Phil Flogel from Physical Evidence had been having a few days off and was busy building a deck on the back of his home. He got a call from Tony Keeling telling him there had been another killing.

"Mate, everyone's running around trying to finish up at Lane Cove, you're going to have to help us out. I'll come and pick you up straight away," Flogel was told.

They got to the scene and were faced with the all too familiar disappointment. Under the illumination of floodlights set up by the Police Rescue Squad they could see that everything had been cleaned up. The body had been found by a staff member at 4.30 p.m. It had been moved almost immediately to the retirement village's own morgue.

The scene was hosed down. Staff had at first drawn no connection to the murders happening on the lower north shore. Best not to cause a fuss with the other residents. In the absence of clues, however, the well-meaning staff came to feel they were under suspicion.

"I don't know how they thought it was an accident with her stockings tied around her neck in a big bow," Flogel complained to his partner.

The pair masked their disappointment and began to examine the area.

There might still be a footprint somewhere in a flower bed. There just might have been a print in blood.

The search proved fruitless except for a faint mark on the ramp where the body had been found. Miss Cleveland's shoes were later examined. On the side of one of them there was a scrape mark, and it was concluded that Miss Cleveland had been dragged along the ramp.

A reporter from the *Telegraph* crossed the Forest Way opposite the nursing home in search of a public phone to file his copy. With no phones at hand he knocked at the door of the first house he came to and asked to borrow the phone. Inside was a woman in her sixties whose husband was away on business.

The reporter began dictating to a copy-taker over the phone: "Sydney's north shore serial killer claimed his fifth elderly victim yesterday ... dash ... just 24 hours after the last murder, break. New par. An 81-year-old resident of the Wesley Gardens retirement ..." When he turned to thank the woman after filing his story, she was trembling. An hour later, he returned to ask if he could file more copy and found the woman had armed herself with a carving knife and bolted the windows.

As rain began to fall late that night, police held their first news conference at the scene. Craig Regan from Police Media had been called out and, like the Homicide Squad boys, was feeling tired.

Earlier, police decided not to make any public statements until it was too late to make the late evening news, not wanting to alarm the elderly residents inside the village who still had to be interviewed. Staff were also concerned about how some of the more frail residents would take it.

Detective Inspector Hagan handled the conference, confirming the murder of an 81-year-old woman, but refusing to elaborate on speculation that a stocking had been tied in a bow around the victim's neck. Hagan used the conference to appeal for public help in locating a man dressed in dark clothes and aged in his late twenties. He had been seen walking near the nursing home that afternoon carrying a metre long piece of wood.

He was the prime suspect.

That same night John Glover sat in his lounge chair watching television. Attempts to keep the story from going live to air had failed. Images of police searching the grounds of the Wesley Gardens and the previous day's footage of the Pahud murder scene flashed across the screen.

"This is terrible," he said to his wife. "They should do something about it — I hope they catch this person soon."

The following day police mounted the largest search of any investigation in NSW but the body of Miss Cleveland remained the only physical testament to the crime apart from the shoe mark on the footpath. The body had been whisked off to the morgue at Glebe but the postmortem, again, revealed nothing.

CHAPTER FOURTEEN

ARREST THAT MAN

When news of the senseless murder of Mrs Mitchelhill first rippled through the Mosman peninsula, it was greeted with a reserved mixture of disgust and concern. Who could have been so cowardly as to beat a defenceless old woman for her handbag and then leave her for dead? Murder had never happened in the conservative sanctuary of the peninsula — at least not that anyone could recall.

The ripples grew to waves, the village becoming increasingly alarmed as the attacks escalated. Public concern in areas outside Mosman began to swell with news of each new horrifying onslaught — Lady Ashton, then Doris Cox, and then Margaret Pahud.

Like the previous attacks, the murder of Olive Cleveland was violent and ugly — out of proportion with the little monetary gain it brought — but news of it broke across Sydney like a savage gale whipping in from the Pacific Ocean.

The madman was out of control.

For the Northern Region Homicide Squad this was perhaps the most difficult period since the breaking up of the old CIB. The Squad was quite clearly stretched to the limit with the Pahud murder and now it had the murder of another elderly woman on its hands.

Until then, investigations had proceeded with the five members of the Homicide Squad, local detectives and any other available detective in the Major Crime Squad office. On a good day, if there had been no bank robberies, rapes or other serious crimes, there might be 20 officers working on the case. The next day, they might be back to just the five Homicide Squad members. It was not a good way to run an investigation but it was the best that could be done with the resources available and all the competing demands in a big, violent city.

But with the deaths of Mrs Pahud and Miss Cleveland, this case had very quickly become special. "It was the hardest time I ever had after Pahud because the media really got on to it," O'Toole recalled. "We knew it was the same person responsible and we had to show our hand without alarming the people."

It was impossible to deny any longer that a serial killer was at work. The public did not need to be told, it already knew. Fear and hysteria — fed upon and maintained by every media organisation — were beyond anyone's control.

At Lane Cove, the council called a public meeting with police, aimed at providing local elderly with security information.

While O'Toole and his team worked through Saturday at both the Cleveland and Pahud murder scenes, Detective Inspector Mike Hagan had been deep in conference with his superiors. He outlined the problems the squad faced and the need for more staff. At Police Headquarters and at Chatswood the phones didn't stop ringing — a political blowtorch had turned their way, for local politicians were in turn feeling the heat from electors.

Later that day Police Commissioner John Avery announced in grave tones the creation of a 35 man task force. It was to be headed by Chief Superintendent Norm Moroney of the State Intelligence Group and was officially called Operation Command, but to those assigned to it, it would be the Granny Killer Task Force.

In announcing its formation, Commissioner Avery made a public appeal to both the killer and his family: "There is a strong possibility that someone out there is aware of a family member who may be disturbed. He or she may be fairly well aware of the potential danger that this family member poses, but may not yet have come to grips with the reality; this is now tragically apparent."

It was the first time police officially conceded that they were dealing with a serial killer. The Commissioner announced that the task force would have access to the United States Federal Bureau of Investigation's most advanced psychological profiles on serial killers and rapists.

To allay the hysteria, Mr Avery set in motion plans for foot patrols in all northern Sydney neighbourhoods with a high ratio of elderly people. He appealed for people to be on the alert and report anyone acting suspiciously in the vicinity of elderly people. A 24 hour telephone hotline was set up to gather information from the public.

A full-time media officer was seconded — the first time that a media officer had been assigned for the duration of an investigation — to deal with the flood of media calls, both interstate and international.

The task force took shape on paper that weekend. As overall head, Chief Superintendent Moroney's job involved setting up the patrols that would keep the killer at bay. Finding the officers to carry out such a job was itself a rostering nightmare.

Detective Inspector Hagan would remain the head of the investigative arm. It was decided he would be the sole spokesman for the task force unless he nominated another officer to speak. There would be no more leaks either. The public knew too much about the killer's methods. They did not want to have to deal with a copycat.

Steps were taken to introduce mobile phones. No more radio transmissions. The media and maybe the killer might be listening.

Hagan's joint deputy commanders would be Detective Senior Sergeants Geoff Wright and Ron Smith. They set up in an office three metres square at the end of the room, with responsibility for reading every scrap of information as it came in. Each morning Smith and Wright would give every field investigator a folder listing their daily assignments and then read the reports upon their return in the evening.

Detectives from the Southern and North Region Homicide Squads were seconded to the unit as were four computer experts from the Tactical Intelligence Section.

For the first time a major investigation would have access to the MIIRS (Major Investigation Information Retrieval System). It meant that officers no longer had to spend hours going back through old cross references, flicking through cards by hand. They just had to press a few buttons on a keyboard and the information appeared almost instantly on a screen before them.

The computer room team's job was to input and analyse the mass of intelligence that would flow in. Their room would be called the Incident Room and they would be led by Detective Senior Sergeant Bob Myers while Detective Senior Constable Gordon Green set up and maintained the software.

O'Toole would remain the senior field investigator. The Homicide officers would be divided into teams and paired off with O'Toole, Paul Mayger, Detective Paul Jacob and Detective Sergeant Murray Byrnes to investigate suspects.

A surveillance team, known in police jargon as the "dogs", was also assigned. Shrouded in secrecy, the "dogs" looked like anything but cops.

Not since the disbandment of the CIB two years earlier had such a group been assembled. Some privately expressed the belief that they would have already got the killer had the CIB not been broken up.

What they could not foresee was the eventual growth of the task force. By Christmas it would number 70 detectives.

With Inspector Hagan dealing with the external pressures, the team set to work. Uniformed police at Lane Cove and Belrose jumped on buses throughout the weekend, asking passengers and drivers alike if they noted anyone acting suspiciously on the days of both murders. Especially any skateboarders.

The belief that they were dealing with a skateboard rider was looking thinner and thinner, however. With no train station nearby, getting to Belrose from Mosman involved a roundabout series of bus hops — in all, a journey of some 20 kilometres. It began to look like they were dealing with a young man who had a car.

The possibility was raised that it was someone older, but still the profiles and all previous leads said they were looking for a young person.

Detectives despaired at the negative results from the crime scenes. If the victims had been young, it was more than likely the bodies would not have been disturbed. But because they were so old, people just assumed that they had fallen over.

There was still the strong possibility that the killer left the scenes with blood on his clothing. He may have used a dry cleaner to clean his clothes. So all dry cleaning services on the lower north shore were asked to hand in any items of clothing that had stains that looked like blood.

The setting up of the special hotline had brought a number of leads the first day. One was a hermit living in bushland near the Cleveland nursing home. Heavily armed officers with tracker dogs raided the man's camp and he was pulled in for questioning, only to be released later that same day.

By Sunday, the dark-haired man seen walking near the Wesley Gardens retirement village had come forward and been cleared by police as a suspect.

Two days after the death of Miss Cleveland, the familiar dead ends were being hit at both Lane Cove and Belrose. The skateboarder was out, the Mosman youth who had been under heavy surveillance was out — he told his mates he was upset when he found out he was no longer of interest — but about 600 lesser suspects were all still possibilities.

By Monday, the task force was in place, the rosters running 8 a.m. to midnight. The feeling among its members was one of apprehension and intensity.

For Detective Inspector Hagan it was a test — a test of investigation skills and community-based policing. Not only did they have to solve the murders quickly, but in the process they had to try to deter the killer from striking again.

"As we got each murder the intensity of everything we did just became higher and higher. The pressures were unbelievable," Hagan recalled.

Hagan's gut feeling told him that their suspect was more than likely still living in Mosman or was linked to the suburb by a relative or work. His chief investigators agreed. The murders were all localised within ten kilometres of Mosman, and three of the attacks were within a kilometre of each other.

He had to be in there.

Detective Senior Sergeant Geoff Wright stepped out of his office and called Detective Senior Constable Paul Mayger over. He had spent much of the Monday wading through leads phoned in by the public. "We've just had an anonymous call from a woman who reckons two young blokes staying at her place have told her they just killed a lady at Lane Cove."

She had not left any personal details but she had let her first name slip and that she was living in a Housing Commission estate at Dundas Valley.

Mayger set about locating the woman. It was like looking for a needle in a haystack.

Mosman plain-clothes Constable Megan Wilson was among those seconded to the task force. She had been at the Mitchelhill postmortem and had helped in the canvass following the first two murders.

Wilson spent the weekend talking to frightened residents at the Wesley Gardens retirement village, whose main problem was that they felt they could not go out any more. She found herself having to talk to relatives of some of the victims and was struck by the fact that many were not close to them. "They were disgusted at the way they died, but a lot of families didn't really have close relationships with the victims; perhaps it was because of their ages," she said.

Mrs Pahud's daughter, Elaine Avis, was the only one whom Constable Wilson saw exhibit heartfelt grief. "She loved her mother a great deal, she was obviously very close to her mother," she said.

Out in the field, the public seemed to really want to help. "You would knock on a door and say there had been another murder and people would just want to talk to you about it," said Constable Wilson. "They were telling you anything that they could think of which was pretty different to the normal circumstances."

On 7 November under mounting public pressure for a quick result, the New South Wales Government doubled the reward to $200,000.

That same day members of the task force went on Radio 2UE's John Laws Show, Sydney's most influential talkback radio programme. They hoped that by reconstructing the murders on air they might prompt the killer or someone close to him to come forward. Five years earlier John Laws had read out on air the grizzly details of a leaked police report on the rape and brutal murder of a Sydney nurse by the name of Anita Cobby. It had prompted the conscience of a listener to give police the lead they needed to crack the case.

The calls continued to flood in at Chatswood throughout the day.

Among them was a 65-year-old woman who claimed that on the day of the Pahud murder she had been stalked by a young man at the Ryde Plaza shopping centre — a ten minute drive from Lane Cove. The woman's description of a slim dark-haired man aged in his late twenties and driving a grey 1950s Holden led to the release of a third identikit sketch.

In newspapers and on television screens that Wednesday night the public were now being shown the faces of three different suspects: a young blond surfie, a dark-haired teenage skateboarder and a dark-haired man driving an old car.

The task force had begun to have doubts that the killer was also responsible for the 24 April assault on pensioner Ray Roper in Mosman. It did not fit his killing time pattern. Journalists were discouraged from including the picture of Roper's attacker in any stories on the murders. It only caused more confusion in the public mind as to who they should be looking for.

The next day, police released a fourth description. It followed the chance discovery of Mrs Pahud's waterlogged handbag in a drainage ditch on the edge of the Lane Cove Country Club by a jogger earlier that morning.

During a canvass of nearby homes a resident said he had seen a young man walking near the area on the afternoon of the Pahud murder. He was in his mid-twenties with light-brown, layered, shoulder-length hair and was wearing navy blue clothing.

Was it possible they were still dealing with two killers?

More than 20 police spent the day combing the golf course but failed to find any more clues. Crime Scene officers who looked at the bag knew there was little hope of finding a lead. Submersion had seen to that.

Two kilometres up the road, St Andrews Church in Lane Cove was packed for the funeral of Mrs Pahud. She was cremated later that day.

Leading criminologist Dr Paul Wilson predicted that the killer would return to Mosman.

Detective Senior Constable Paul Mayger was not happy.

"Piss off and leave us alone," he told the two quivering young druggies sitting on the lounge in front of him. It was Friday 10 November and he had spent four days tracking them down following Monday's anonymous phone call from the woman at Dundas Valley.

The search of Housing Commission units in the area had borne fruit earlier in the week when Mayger found the woman. She told him that the two young men who had bragged of killing an old woman had gone.

"Did they leave anything behind, was there anything they would have touched?" She said they had both used the phone. Mayger removed the woman's two phones from the walls and took them away for fingerprinting while surveillance officers watched the home over the next few days.

Mayger found acquaintances of the woman, executed search warrants in the neighbourhood and raided the place next door. There he found the two young men, both minor druggies, but completely innocent.

It turned out the woman had a string of convictions for public mischief and false claims. She was a single mother whose daughter had been taken from her and who had fallen back on a campaign of revenge against authority.

She was charged with public mischief. Mayger had lost four vital days of investigation time.

"I see you winning much money," Joseph Schorlian commented to the well-presented grey-haired man sitting on a stool beside him playing the "Dollar Mania" poker machine — the largest paying and most expensive machine at the Mosman Returned Servicemen's Club.

Joseph the hairdresser had seen the man many times over the years when he dropped into the club after work, but this was the first time he had ever spoken to John. The pair never exchanged full names, but found themselves chatting on and off for over an hour.

Joseph — who had mourned the loss of his client and friend, Lady Ashton — had been putting a few coins through a 20 cent machine next to Glover when they met. Glover was betting $5 a spin. His credit meter showed he had already won over $1500.

The Pahud–Cleveland murders had just happened but the pair's conversation was limited to gambling. Glover bought Joseph a scotch with the winnings, and Joseph then bought his round, a gin and tonic: "and then we start be friendly talking".

"This fellow, he was a nice man. He was a very calm man here, he was very polite, he was always by himself. Many people knew him but nobody talked to him much. He was very serious, never, never joke."

But Joseph thought that this night he should have been happy with his lot. "Why don't you pick up the money, cash the money and go home?" the hairdresser implored his new friend.

"No, I'd rather stay here. What am I going to do at home?"

Glover always drank Gordon's gin and tonic or white wine and by 1989 was putting $200 in the poker machines every night. Win or lose, he still left the club at 6 p.m.

Alderman Dom Lopez had also noticed Glover's big plunges on the pokies. "I thought because he lived in Wyong Road he must be wealthy."

Contrary to the opinion of others, Joseph observed that Glover had been drinking heavily. "You see he be drunk. He drink too much. He drink doubles all the time. He drink much and you would see his face get red, red, red. He don't talk too much. If you talk to him you don't get too much answer, he's just be himself. I never asked him personal things, but I found out from here that he was to sell the sausage and the meat pie."

Glover rarely talked about the one topic of conversation on everyone's lips in Mosman. "We talk about the poker machine, the horses, because I gamble and he gamble, we use to talk about the races."

For staff at the club, Glover was just a quiet regular who never got drunk. He would sit on his gin and tonic for about half an hour and only ever buy three or four. He brought them presents from his larder at work.

One afternoon Glover lost his cool when a blond youth walked into the club. Bar staff had never seen him act in such a way as he rushed over to the bar.

"Quick, call the police, call the police!" Glover ordered. "He looks like that guy in the paper, the one they're looking for over the murders."

When staff laughed and expressed their reluctance to ring police, Glover became aggressive and indignant. "I demand that you ring police ... ring the police! They've got to arrest that man!" The police were not called and Glover went back to playing his machine.

Two weeks into the life of the task force, the release of the three identikit sketches had led to an influx of more information than could be handled. The telephone hotline had worked well, too well, and the mountain of information would take a long time to sift through. It ranged from the plausible to the weird.

Together with Craig Regan, Nicky Gavel had been seconded from the Police Media unit to the task force for two weeks to help prepare press releases for twice daily media briefings. Journalists from as far afield as Japan, America, Switzerland and Sweden wanted details on the murder. Even *Time* magazine — it was international news.

Soon, task force members had run out of things to say and the information flow became a trickle. Detective Inspector Hagan abandoned the scheduled news conferences and began releasing information only when there was something the public needed to know.

The stories that never saw the light of day included the myriad of reports, usually phoned in, beginning: "My next door neighbour is a bit of a weirdo ..." One anonymous caller had told police that the clue to the murders could be found on a particular page of Salman Rushdie's controversial book *The Satanic Verses*. Although the task force scoffed at the idea, an officer with a high boredom threshold was duly sent to buy and read the book.

Even the premonitions of clairvoyants had to be acted upon. They came from as far afield as Western Australia, dozens and dozens of them, some believing that they had seen the killer in visions. "Well, I see him as a young man, yes a young man, who likes to wear bright things. Yes, he likes to wear yellow shirts ..."

O'Toole would just shake his head in disbelief at such leads. "I don't think even we knew how many raving lunatics there were out there in the community." Yet he could not discount any of them and hundreds of hours were wasted.

The task force also had several psychological profiles on the killer. O'Toole viewed them as "a load of garbage". From a psychiatric point of view he could see that the profiles might be interesting, but as a detective trying to identify an offender, it still did not tell him "who the bloody murderer was".

All the shrinks agreed it would be a young person. "Eighteen to 35 [years of age] gives you a fair bit of scope. They didn't give us a name, address or an occupation."

Among the calls to the special hotline was one from Sister Ann Chan from the Wybenia nursing home. She had rung the task force to tell of an indecent assault upon a blind patient, Phylis McNeil, thinking there might be a connection. She gave the details and was thanked for her information. She heard nothing more about it.

Across the Harbour at the Sydney Police Centre a section of the crime scene office had begun to resemble a laundry.

They had been overwhelmed with clothing from dry cleaners anxious to help police catch the killer by sending in anything with a stain resembling blood — beetroot, spaghetti, raspberry. Sloppy eaters across the northside experienced inexplicable delays in getting their washing back. The police had promised to get the items back as quickly as possible so as not to anger the dry cleaners or alert the suspicions of customers but it was not so easy providing a same day forensics service.

By the end of the task force's first two weeks the workload was such that on long nights, some officers took to sleeping in the office. There were no beds or changes of clothes. Across the floor, in chairs or on desks they lay with a coat for a blanket and a telephone book for a pillow.

There had been no time for sitting around playing cards at lunch. No time for lunch. They were constantly on the road, catching a bite to eat whenever they could. Their only relaxation was a beer at the end of the night in the task force office or at a nearby pub — some place where they could de-stress — because they knew they would be hard at it again the next day. At the end of each day some of them wondered if the killer would show his hand again; wondered if he was hidden somewhere in the mass of information they were now picking through; wondered if they had spoken to him.

Mike Hagan watched his team through the glass partition of his office during those weeks. He could see the pressure on their faces. He respected their dedication and perseverance, but knew they were expending more than they were physically able to give. He wondered how long they could go on.

CHAPTER FIFTEEN

HOME GROUND

Muriel Falconer had lived at number 3 Muston Street, Mosman, since 1954. It was a single-storey red brick Federation-style home. She had gone there with her husband William and son John but had, by 1989, been alone for many years.

She was a spritely woman whose youthful energy was belied by a walking stick. Although her body was showing signs of fragility — she had suffered a minor stroke — she was still climbing a ladder to clean out the guttering on her roof at the age of ninety-three. She nursed stray cats and you could not meet anybody nicer.

Her mind was still active and she kept herself updated on world affairs. Like the majority of Mosman's aged population, Mrs Falconer had been alarmed at the continuing attacks against elderly women. After Doris Cox was savagely bashed, she pondered whether to improve the security on her home but did nothing more than talk about it. Why should she — she already had a heavy black security screen fitted to the front entrance and all her doors had strong locks and bolts. As the murders continued her son John, who lived at Frenchs Forest on the upper north shore, had begged her to leave the house until the killer was caught, but she declined.

"If that's the way I'm going to die then so be it," she told her son. She was still as independent as ever.

Her knowledge of the granny killer case was not sufficient to stop her going on foot to the shopping centre and back — and doing it when she liked. Mrs Falconer went shopping almost daily but at no set time. It was a 200 metre walk along tree- and shrub-lined Muston Street, via Raglan Street, to the Mosman shopping centre — the foliage obscuring the view of pedestrians from the road.

On Thursday 23 November after a brief chat over the fence with her neighbour and good friend of 15 years, Maggie Hughes, Mrs Falconer set out sometime after 3 p.m. to Clancy's supermarket, where she was a "popular and regular" visitor. She left there and went and bought two bananas from grocer John Danieli. When last seen by a shopkeeper she was walking back towards her home along Military Road at 4.30 p.m.

After finishing work that day, John Glover drove to the Buena Vista Hotel at Mosman to check out the Scotch whiskey specials. He parked his car next to the hotel, opposite the police station. As he rounded the point of the building into Middle Head Road, he saw Muriel Falconer walking slowly on the other side of the street, burdened by her grey-striped shopping bag.

Glover went back around the building to his car. He put a pair of gloves in his pocket and the hammer under his shirt. He walked back around to the front of the Buena Vista and was just in time to see Mrs Falconer's brown-clad figure rounding the corner into Muston Street, a short block away. He had to hurry. As he rounded the corner, he could see her on the other side behind a row of native shrubs and plants. She went through her hedge-lined gate and he followed her in, with some sort of rage welling in his head.

Practically deaf and blind, Mrs Falconer had not noticed the man behind her.

He looked around. All was quiet and the row of shrubs along the street and the garden hedge afforded perfect shelter. The gloves went on his hands and the hammer was pulled from his belt as Mrs Falconer opened her security door.

She opened the main door and then bent down to pick up the groceries. Her frail body had straightened as much as it could when she felt a rubbered hand grasp her mouth. Almost immediately, the hands pushed her inside. The hammer came down on the back of her head and the groceries dropped from her hands, landing upright inside the door without spilling. Mrs Falconer collapsed to the beige carpet.

Glover put the hammer down. He stood over her body then lent down and began to pull her dress up over her bloodied head. He began to remove her pantyhose when she regained some semblance of consciousness. She called feebly for help and began to struggle. Glover left her and went back for the hammer. She had struggled to her knees and was on all fours when Glover hit her cruelly with a strong blow. He was in the process of wrapping the pantyhose around her neck when Mrs Falconer managed one last plea for help.

John Glover stood, walked back for the hammer and struck her again, for the last time. He pulled his nylon ligature tight around her neck, cutting deep into Mrs Falconer's throat.

He turned and shut the door. He searched her handbag but found nothing he wanted. He left it open and began to explore the dimly lit house, searching each room and finding $300 in a drawer. He put the hammer and gloves in a shopping bag and left.

He returned to his car and drove home. There, he changed into his casual clothes. He put his brown brogues in a wardrobe and disposed of his gloves in the kitchen bin. It was garbage night and the rubbish would have to be put out before going to bed. But before this, before he could sit down with a gin to watch the evening news, there was one last chore to be done.

He went out to his small tin garden shed which also doubled as a tool room. He removed the lid from one of two small plastic drums of hydrochloric acid that he used to obliterate any moss on the brick work of his home and garden. He dipped the head of the hammer into the acid then swirled it around until every last skerrick of blood and sinew was scorched out of existence.

Mrs Falconer usually opened her back door around ten o'clock each morning and could be seen pottering in her garden. But this day, Friday 24 November, the door had not budged when her neighbour, Mrs Hughes, left for work. She was not suspicious at first. A trained nurse, Mrs Hughes had been given a spare key to Mrs Falconer's house. It was for the reassurance value as much as anything — so that she could keep an eye on her friend.

A short time after arriving home from work that afternoon Mrs Hughes noticed that Mrs Falconer's back door was still shut. She decided to investigate.

At the front door to the house she noticed something peculiar — Mrs Falconer's key to the security screen was still in the lock. She pushed the screen to one side and used her own key to get in the front door. As she stepped through the door into darkness, she almost fell over a dark mass on the floor. She recoiled at the sight of the body of her friend. Mrs Falconer was semi-naked, her dress pushed up over her head to expose her buttocks and her legs, which had been spread apart. A pool of blood enveloped her head.

Mrs Hughes' nursing training told her instinctively to check all the vital signs but it was obvious that her friend was dead. Although horrified by what she had found, Mrs Hughes knew immediately her friend had been murdered. She telephoned Mosman police.

The first officer on the scene sealed the house immediately upon seeing the body.

Detective Sergeant Dennis O'Toole had left the task force office at Chatswood early after a relatively quiet day. He was just through the city traffic and was pointing the car north on the freeway for a weekend at home with the family when he got a call on the radio from Detective Senior Sergeant Ron Smith.

"We've got another one."

"Get nicked," O'Toole told him.

"No mate, I mean it. You've got to come back," Smith said, leaving no room for doubt in the tones he used.

The siren went on and the mobile flashing light was placed on the roof. O'Toole started searching for an exit so he could turn around and go back to Mosman. Dinner with the family would have to wait again.

Although news of a sixth murder instilled further alarm within the task force, detectives who arrived at the scene felt some relief. It was their first undisturbed crime scene since Lady Ashton was killed. Their public statements about crime scenes being destroyed in the previous murders seemed to be working.

Phil Flogel had just about made it to his home in the northern beaches suburb of Dee Why when his pager went off with a message to go to Mosman. He turned around and headed straight for the station where he was directed around the corner to the murder scene, 200 metres away.

Detectives were milling out in the street waiting for the Physical Evidence unit to go in. Crime scene protection guidelines meant that nobody could move until they had gone over the area. Too many scenes had been ruined in years past by assistant commissioners ordering their drivers to drop in on the spot of a high-profile case or a dozen highway patrolmen nosing around leaving their "dabs" on the walls and their size twelves in the dirt.

The officers stood around and talked softly among themselves. They knew there were footprints inside, they could see them from the door. They hoped that this woman, the fifth murdered and sixth attacked, had not crossed into the killer's corridor of death for nothing. There was a feeling that her death just might bring about the end of the killing spree.

The scene was so untainted no one dared turn the lights on inside the darkened house in case the killer had left a fingerprint on one of the switches. Portable lights were set up on the doorstep to illuminate the hallway. Mrs Falconer's body was photographed before anybody went in the door. Using flashlights, a path had been picked out skirting the footprints and the body.

The house was in immaculate condition. Antique vases and figurines sat thick atop beautiful old pieces of furniture. It was the house of a meticulous woman with a lifetime of memories surrounding her.

There was no sign of ransacking. There was a set of keys sitting on a side table in the hallway. A walking stick was inside the doorway in the umbrella holder. Two purses were open on the floor and some small coins scattered on a table. A grocery bag was full on the floor except for an upturned container of ice cream which had melted in a puddle.

A blood splatter was patterned on the wall nearest the body. "He used a weapon," Flogel thought out loud. There were splash marks on the victim's hands ... she had defended herself.

Flogel followed the shoe prints down the hallway. They went to the back of the house and stopped. He turned into a bedroom where a small wooden chest, like a valuables container, was open.

It seemed that the guy had not stayed long. He was probably nervous, Flogel thought.

They went back to the shoe prints. Police cameras were flashing away trying to bring out the contrast as best as possible. One print close to the body was singled out as the clearest. A carpet knife was produced and a large square was cut around the bloodied shoe print to be taken back to the office for more detailed photography and to be mounted as evidence. As far as Flogel could make out, the shoes had not left much detail.

The house was vacuumed and swept. Mrs Falconer had kept a spotless house and few fragments were picked up. So when a tiny piece of shale was found in the bag of the vacuum cleaner, it was taken very seriously.

The killer might have picked it up on the vacant block next door to Mrs Falconer's house, which appeared to be an excavation site. He might have stalked her from there.

The phone on the *Daily Telegraph* police rounds desk rang. The caller had a tip but wanted to remain anonymous.

He said he was an off-duty security guard and had been messing around with his radio scanner when he accidentally picked up a mobile telephone conversation. "I think there's been another murder at Mosman," the man said.

"What makes you say that?" asked the disbelieving but interested reporter.

"Well, I only picked up bits and pieces but I heard the name Mosman mentioned. It was a sergeant talking to an inspector. One of them said 'it looks like the granny killer' and the other one said 'Shit! if the press get hold of it they'll have a field day'."

Although lit by streetlights, Muston Street was virtually black when Kevin Ricketts from *The Australian* newspaper, *Telegraph* photographer Roy Haverkamp and reporter Les Kennedy arrived at 8 p.m. It was the night of the Miracle Mile (Sydney's biggest trotting event) and, with every available news car out at Harold Park Paceway to ferry urgent film back to the office, they had been forced to catch a taxi. The only sign that something was happening was a lone motorcycle cop leaning against his bike parked across Muston Street at the intersection with Raglan Street.

Perhaps it was their means of transport which confused the officer but the three walked straight past unchallenged. As they neared the house, torch lights could be seen flickering within. Standing outside on the road with task force detectives was Detective Inspector Mike Hagan and a bevy of uniformed high-ranking police — among them the State Operations Commander, Executive Chief Superintendent Joe Parrington.

"How the hell did you blokes get here?" a uniformed inspector shouted at them. "Umm ... we walked," said a surprised Ricketts.

"Oh really! Well you fellows just turn around and go back down there and tell that constable on the motorbike that I want to talk to him after this!" the inspector boomed.

Joe Parrington interjected: "Fellas, Les, we'll be making a statement in a couple of hours at Mosman police station." As the three were escorted back down the street by an officer they knew, without anything having been said, that the granny killer had struck again. Haverkamp knew he had to get the shots and, trembling, fired off three frames into the face of the angry cop.

Residents confirmed their suspicions over the next 30 minutes, telling them of the police canvass of homes that had begun earlier in the night.

Among those officers called out was plain-clothes Constable Megan Wilson. She was about to leave her home to go to a police social function when her phone rang.

Her commitment to the investigation was starting to wear thin on her boyfriend. "Don't answer it, don't answer it," he called out. It was too late. Dinner was off.

As the canvass wore on a postmortem was being conducted at the City Morgue.

At 10 p.m. journalists and camera crews had begun to gather at Mosman police station. It was a curious, almost tropical night, steamy and stirred with showers.

The Buena Vista, where 29 hours earlier Glover had intended to buy a bottle of whiskey before seeing Mrs Falconer, was packed to the gunwales. Drinkers spilled out on to the footpath, oblivious to the massive police presence in the next street. The focus of their attention was the battering which boxer Jeff Fenech was attempting to give Mexican Mario Martinez in Melbourne on his way to a crack at the world super lightweight crown. Shouts of "Git him, git him ... go on knock his block off ... smash him!" were drifting out into the balmy atmosphere and across the road to the police station to the west and the yellow police ribbon to the east.

A grim-faced Detective Inspector Hagan read a brief statement confirming the worst to the reporters who flocked around him at the back garage entrance to the station. By midnight, the task force knew that Mrs Falconer had died the day before. Her body had been lying there for at least 24 hours.

Her head wounds had a peculiar circular pattern to them ... the murder weapon was most likely a hammer. It was a breakthrough as big as any. For the first time, the task force knew what the blunt instrument was that they were looking for.

The pathologist also considered it a possibility that Mrs Falconer had been sexually interfered with but it was inconclusive. Some grey hairs were found around Mrs Falconer's hands, but they were long and probably her own.

Back at the Crime Scene laboratory late that night, Phil Flogel got to work on the bloody shoe print. It was a question of how to best bring out the contrast between the dried blood and the carpet.

The print was photographed over and over using different amounts of light and different exposures. Infrared light was used in varying amounts and then laser lights.

The results were sent away to a private company which specialised in computer enhancement. Differences in shade not distinguishable to the eye could be exaggerated and highlighted by computer.

The square of carpet was mounted behind perspex. It was a treasure — the only piece of physical evidence against the killer — and it would have to be kept secret. Any leak about its existence and the killer would surely destroy the shoes.

The next day, the elderly in Mosman became virtual prisoners in their own homes. The killer had returned to his trolling ground and police seemed powerless.

An elderly friend of Mrs Falconer was quoted by the *Sunday Telegraph* that Sunday as saying she felt under siege. "The neighbourhood is hiding behind locked doors. The killer is winning while he keeps us in the house. Fancy some lunatic creature putting you in that horrible position."

The young held no such concerns. A dozen children on push-bikes comprised the bulk of onlookers who gathered outside Mrs Falconer's home. Their carefree inquisitive nature masked the pandemonium among their elders that Saturday morning. The killer had struck right under the noses of police. Police foot patrols had been increased in the suburb in the previous three weeks after the Pahud–Cleveland murders, yet he had taken another life with blatant ease.

Detective Sergeant David Hughes and Phil Flogel from the Physical Evidence section had also returned to the scene by mid-morning with Detectives Paul Jacob and Kerry Larsen. The police cordon of Muston Street had been removed before dawn but a guard had been left outside the home to ensure the continued preservation of the crime scene.

On Flogel's mind was the piece of shale found on the carpet during the night. It meant there was a good chance the killer had been on the vacant block next door, a 1.5 metre deep excavation hole cut into the orange and yellow sandstone following the demolition of a house on the site.

The morning was clear and the day promised to be hot but the natural light provided ideal conditions for a search of the area. A couple of fresh shoe prints were glaringly obvious as detectives entered the vacant lot. They appeared similar to the prints found in the house. If the prints proved to be the same as those on the carpet, the quality would be better because they had been made in soft earth. Flogel and Hughes set about making plaster casts of the indentations.

There were no signs of forced entry to the house and it appeared as if nothing had been stolen. It was still uncertain how the killer had entered the house; the search for clues led police to scale the roof, checking to see if any tiles had been prised loose.

Mosman Mayor Barry O'Keefe was alarmed about what was happening to his suburb. He had been inundated with calls all morning from ratepayers, other aldermen and the media.

Alderman O'Keefe announced that the council's small band of rangers would patrol the main shopping thoroughfares and provide escorts to elderly women. But such a task was beyond the means of the council: it would require a small army of volunteers. A demographic survey of Mosman in the months following the murders of Mrs Mitchelhill and Lady Ashton found that more than 2200 women over the age of 65 lived within its boundaries.

That Saturday, half the task force was relocated to Mosman. A police caravan was stationed in the heart of the shopping centre to gather any information from passersby. More than 150 shoppers responded on the day, filling out forms with their names and addresses and detailing their suspicions.

The murder also brought with it a new influx of crank calls to the police hotline.

A ten member police motorcycle squad was dispatched to Mosman to act as roving sentinels. More than 60 beat police patrols from other northern suburbs were hastily seconded to the suburb for the duration of the investigation to reinforce Mosman police. Doorknocks of homes, shops and businesses as well as random questioning of residents were intensified.

Ten officers from the Police Tactical Response Group scoured Ashton Park that Saturday where Lady Ashton's possessions had been dumped three months earlier. But the search, based on the hope that the killer used the park again as a dumping ground, proved fruitless.

The next day, the *Sun-Herald* quoted Alderman O'Keefe as saying the killer was a "mad person" loose in a "very gentle, genteel, decent community". "The police say it is quite likely the person is somebody who is so frequently around that you don't see them, just as you don't notice taxis or familiar things."

His statement was so true. Mayor O'Keefe knew John Glover.

The same article quoted eminent forensic psychiatrist Dr William Barclay as saying the killer "could be the boy next door". "Psychopathic killers generally don't have a criminal record and are not known to the police but they do display interest in sadistic things," Dr Barclay said.

He too knew John Glover. Glover's wife Gay worked as Dr Barclay's secretary for a number of years and the pair had attended social functions given by the doctor.

Behind the scenes the task force mounted covert surveillance operations — the Mosman "lunatic" was back near the top of their list. A house was rented close to his home so that police could maintain a 24 hour watch. His phone was tapped, his house bugged and police listened night and day.

On 27 November, the New South Wales Government increased the reward for the killer's arrest to $250,000.

Flogel had been hard at it in the lab that day. When the photographs of the shoes were processed, they were as good as he had dared hope. They highlighted some good detail. He could see stitching around the outside of the sole, so it was obvious that it was a leather shoe. There was a tread pattern distinguishable on the heel so the shoes had not been worn too much. Part of the pattern was obscured by a foreign object. It seemed that the killer had stepped in gum. He had worn down the outside edge slightly, meaning that he walked with his weight on the outside of his feet. There was a good chance, therefore, that he walked with his toes splayed slightly outwards.

For the task force, the news was a godsend. Detectives were immediately dispatched to all the local shoe shops. With an impression of the shoe print in hand they could be seen discreetly checking the racks out the front, turning each new brand over and examining it. The managers of the shops were called out to help bring boxes down to show off the soles. The search lasted a few days but the shoe was not on sale locally.

Phil Flogel contacted the Victorian State Forensic laboratory at Macleod which had established a shoe print catalogue. Shoes made locally and imported were kept on register and categorised like fingerprints. Flogel sent down a copy of the print but the laboratory reported back that there was nothing like it on file.

He decided to go to Melbourne to search through the index manually. Flogel sifted through page after page of prints, thousands in all, yet came up empty-handed.

Four days after the discovery of Mrs Falconer's body, a packed public meeting at Mosman Council Chambers was told of plans drawn up by police, the council and community groups to safeguard the elderly. It was called Operation Grandame and was aimed at establishing a network of community-based "minders" for old people.

Mayor Barry O'Keefe appealed to the many elderly women who he said remained "fiercely independent" to co-operate with the scheme. He said Grandame would operate for three months — or less, "if the person or people responsible for these murders is caught".

The scheme required volunteers in different parts of Mosman to befriend and "adopt" elderly women. They would help with shopping, contact them at pre-arranged times each day and provide security and comfort. It also involved escorting the women on outings. The Mosman Returned Servicemen's Club was among the community groups to offer assistance. All applicants were heavily screened by police for past criminal records and issued with identity cards from Mosman Council.

Alderman O'Keefe's public condemnation of the murders and moves to mobilise the community evoked anger from one person. The rotund senior lawyer was interviewed the next day on a morning television show about the steps the council was taking to help the elderly.

That afternoon, his secretary at Mosman Council, Nerida McPherson, received a strange phone call. The male voice on the line had the demeanour of a "gentleman" and was softly spoken and polite at first.

"I would like to speak to Mr O'Keefe, please."

"He's not available at the moment," she said. "Do you want to leave a message and I'll get him to ring you?"

"No, I just want to speak to Barry O'Keefe."

"If you want to talk to Mr O'Keefe, I'll have to take your name."

"That doesn't matter."

She started to get annoyed with the caller. "If you want to talk to the Mayor you have to give me your name."

"You just tell him this ..."

"All right then."

"I've got a message for him." His tone changed. The voice remained calm, but low and grave. "Tell him to mind his own business ... If he doesn't mind his own business his wife will be next."

The line went dead.

Ms McPherson thought it was a prank from someone who had seen the television program that morning. "I really didn't think I was talking to the murderer," Ms McPherson recalled.

She remarked about it to someone nearby and they told her to ring the police. An officer later came and took a statement from her.

She detailed what the caller had said and gave them a description of the man from the sound of his voice. "It sounded like a local call. It was a clear line. It was definitely not a pay phone. There was no background noise. He could have been ringing from a house. He was fairly well spoken and sounded like a man in his fifties."

She rang Alderman O'Keefe, who took the matter seriously. The mayor stepped up security at his house and employed a security guard to patrol outside his home.

The same Tuesday, Sydney reporting legend Jack Darmody was on to a hot story. He had heard that police were seen taking an assortment of shoes into the Falconer home.

As Darmody set about standing the story up, the task force received the report on the casts taken on the building site. It was not the same shoe as the print in the house; however, police, alarmed that the press were about to blow their best lead, would use the excavation site print in a misinformation campaign. They took the punt that the killer might not get rid of his shoes if he believed their clue came from an area in which he had not walked.

The story splashed across the front of Wednesday afternoon's *Daily Mirror* was headlined "Footprint Found at Granny Murder House". The sub headline ran: "Police Know Killer's Height Weight and Shoe Size".

The exclusive story was a little less effusive than the head, but a disaster for the task force nevertheless.

A footprint in soft earth could help police solve the horrific murders of five elderly women on Sydney's north shore.

Police believe it is the nearest link they have to the cowardly killer who has terrorised the area since March.

They are confident they can assess weight, height and possibly the sex of the wearer and perhaps determine a trademark on the sole …

Executive Chief Superintendent Joe Parrington confirmed the find to Darmody and was quoted as saying: "There is no conclusive forensic evidence yet to say whether the killer is male or female but all available evidence indicates the killer is male."

Darmody had got it half right but had been thrown a dummy.

In the same edition of the *Mirror*, clinical psychiatrist Dr Tim Watson Munro made one of the most accurate profiles of the investigation. He predicted the killer came from a broken home and was palmed off on an elderly relative; may have been assaulted by a grandmother or aunt; and may have experienced the death of an elderly relative within the last year.

Dr Watson Munro said the killer was not able to take the aggression out on the elderly relative because there was still a bond of love. "Now the person has gone, the killer feels there is nothing standing in his way to exact revenge for his past experiences."

But Dr Watson Munro also predicted the killer would be young and of above average intelligence.

As it would later emerge, Glover did not buy a newspaper that day.

The pressure was beginning to show in Mosman. Relatives came to stay with their elderly mothers, others moved them out of the suburb, some even took them interstate. Sales of hand-held beeper alarms rocketed along with home intruder alarms. The army seconded a dozen soldiers a day from the 11th Terminal Regiment as escorts for elderly women and to help police patrol the streets.

Most residents were sympathetic to police and the difficulties they faced in catching the killer, but flak was still levelled their way. In its editorial on Thursday 3 November, the *Mosman Daily* attacked the police handling of the case.

Perhaps a greater visible police presence in Mosman might have saved the lives of the two women who were brutally murdered after the first savage killing last March.

It is hard to say, of course, but a more up-front police presence most certainly would have been a lot better than has been the case up until last Thursday's murder.

The authorities would do well to look at their overall performance in these investigations for some future guidance leading to, dare we say, an improved performance in combating more of these vicious killings.

The public face of John Glover viewed the horror besetting his neighbourhood with open concern and anger. While out on his rounds that week on the north shore he had been drawn into a conversation about the murders by a customer. "I tell you if I got my hands on him I'd cut his balls off!" he said.

While Glover would rarely be the first to raise the topic, there were times when he could not avoid it. Everyone in the club was talking about the granny killer. When the conversation required that he said something he would nod agreement. But the most he would say was: "They had better catch this bastard quickly ... let's hope they catch this bastard."

CHAPTER SIXTEEN
THE GREY-HAIRED MAN

S o, what are you up to mate? Do you live around here?" the young constable asked the scraggy young man wandering aimlessly along Muston Street.

He appeared vague and lost in thought. His scruffy appearance did not fit in.

"I've done nothin' wrong ... I'm just looking. Just want to see if I can smell it."

"Smell what?"

"Death," he replied.

The constable was taken aback but hauled the young man in for questioning.

"Not you again!" was the response from Detective Sergeant O'Toole on seeing the man. He had been pulled in for questioning once before after being found wandering in a back street of Mosman. He was patently disturbed but not the person they were looking for.

"Where do you live?" O'Toole had asked on the first occasion.

"Lidcombe."

"So why are you here?"

"Just want to see if I can smell death. It's a hobby of mine ... haven't smelt it here yet ..."

As the interview wore on, it emerged that the man usually passed his time closer to home at Sydney's largest cemetery, Rookwood, where he would lie on graves trying to communicate with the dead. He was sent packing back to Rookwood with a stern last warning: "Don't come back."

At the end of November, Detective Inspector Mike Hagan appealed to doctors, psychologists and psychiatrists for information. Someone in one of these professions may have already been treating the killer, but was inhibited by professional ethics from contacting police.

Hagan asked that they break ranks. Police would treat any information in the strictest of confidence, he said.

"Investigators are starting to be very pleased with the progress," Mosman District Commander Chief Superintendent Jim Rope told a doggedly persistent Miranda Devine from the *Daily Telegraph*.

"How far away from an arrest?" she inquired.

"If we tell [the media] then he [the killer] will know. We have to keep quite a degree of this inquiry under wraps. We can't muck it up by being too kind to the media," he said.

In reality they had no idea.

In the week following the Falconer murder plain-clothes officers, some on bicycles, roamed the deserted streets. Reporters also wandered around in search of news leads, in particular during the 3 p.m. to 5 p.m. "killing hour". Residents, police and reporters alike wondered if the madman would strike again. Media ears were glued to radio scanners listening for anything involving Homicide or the Crime Scene unit.

The competition in the media was intensifying parallel to the pressure on police. "We had to have a new front page every day," recalled *Daily Mirror* police roundsman Richard Lenarduzzi.

"It was the story that was gripping Sydney, it was *the* police rounds story. While the public was scared they couldn't get enough of it.

"We were desperate for a new line on the murders every day," said Lenarduzzi. "When they began to run out of things to say we would propose ideas to detectives and they would say: 'We cannot rule that out' — then we would have our front page."

Stories like "Does Killer Dress as a Granny?", "Family's Poem to Murderer" and "The Last 15 Minutes of Muriel's Life" were soon confronting readers.

The idea of a killer in drag, or a young person dressed like an old man to win the confidence of his victims, did evoke a response from the public. On 3 December police swooped on a young transvestite dressed in old women's clothes and walking near the Garrison retirement village at Spit Junction. He was cleared after several hours of questioning.

By the end of the first week in December, the pile of theories coming from the public continued to grow. Many of them were from people who stopped to chat with officers at the mobile station.

Mosman Alderman Dom Lopez suggested to police manning the mobile station that the killer could be a woman used to dealing with the elderly, maybe even someone who had worked as a volunteer for Meals on Wheels. The Council's community services branch was enraged when his suggestion hit the press. Several volunteers threatened to resign in protest over his accusation of such an honourable service.

"Everyone is a suspect, who's to know who it is?" Alderman Lopez replied. It might not have meant much to him then to know that his silver-haired drinking companion, John Glover, had years earlier helped Meals on Wheels with their deliveries to the homes of old women in the suburb.

An "old man" had also come to the attention of the task force during the canvass of Muston Street the day after Mrs Falconer's body was found. A young boy on a bicycle told Constable Wilson about an "old grey-haired man" whom he rode past a couple of times. "There is an old warb that hung around the area and we checked him out, the description fitted him," said Constable Wilson later.

John Glover fitted the description but so too did many men living in Mosman.

Sergeant Jim Green, a 51-year-old veteran street cop, thought he had come to a sleepy village when he was posted to Mosman police station as its patrol tactician. He began his career at one of Sydney's heaviest crime stations, Darlinghurst, moving on to North Sydney and then Manly. His job was intelligence analysis — looking at local crime trends and working out a response.

Before Sergeant Green went to Mosman his peers had joked that he was off to the "koala bear station", because it was close to the zoo and because koalas slept all day. It was regarded by most police as "a quiet little retirement village": a place where police go when they need a bit of rest and recreation before retirement. Within four months, he was looking at two murders and "the big boys" from the Homicide Squad were camped in the station.

At the time of the first murder the station's patrol strength was 36 — enough police to run three shifts, 24 hours a day, keeping a car on the road and someone in the station all the time. The number of officers increased slightly following the Cox attack but by late November the station was overflowing with police — three times the normal strength. At one stage there were more than 100 uniformed police officers walking the streets.

For one full week there was not one reported crime in Mosman. No crook in his right mind would go near the place. In other north shore patrols which had lost officers to Mosman, the crime rates doubled.

But still the granny killer slipped in under the net to kill Mrs Falconer and that disturbed Sergeant Green. It showed that beat police could not be everywhere.

"Mrs Falconer lived almost directly across the road from the police in Muston Street when police were everywhere. We had heaps of police, plain-clothes and uniformed, walking in back streets and just particularly looking for something out of the ordinary in relation to old people, observing old people walking around. It didn't make any difference to the killer."

Among those the Falconer murder affected was 75-year-old widow Mary Zanelli. She lived in Macpherson Street, Mosman, just around the corner from Glover's home, but following the murder of Lady Ashton had been taken under the protective wing of her son Graham and daughter Rosemary, who lived in Middle Head Road, only a short walk from Muston Street.

She put herself in the same bracket as the victims because they did things that she had done, playing bingo and walking to the bank. It gave her an eerie feeling. She knew it could have been her.

The murders forced her to change her habits. She would not go out after dark and she made sure she drove her car whenever possible.

She thought a "mob of hoodlums" was responsible. "We noticed a lot of them getting about, we used to say that they are from the army, they are from the navy. Every time there was a murder everyone I know was of the opinion that it was the young fry at the army or navy."

Although she took precautions, Mary Zanelli found herself walking back from the hairdresser's along Middle Head Road by herself a few weeks after Mrs Falconer's murder. She became aware that someone was looking at her as she walked past the last shop before Muston Street. She stopped and looked in the window until she saw a captain from the army approach.

"Righto, I'll go now because he's behind me," she thought as she scurried off, looking over her shoulder. She was still unnerved and cast a glance behind her as the soldier loomed up.

"Are you nervous of the granny killer?" he said bluntly.

She nodded and he escorted her home. It was a simple act of chivalry she would never forget.

Dr Rod Milton had watched the mounting murder toll with grave concern. He prepared a second report to the task force shortly after Mrs Falconer's murder, this time including information from an assault on an elderly woman called Mrs McKay on 25 April 1987. She had been followed by a man who grabbed her from behind while she was entering a lift. She described him as in his late teens, 170 centimetres tall, of slight build and with a fairly short haircut. It was consistent with Milton's impression of the murderer being young.

He again stressed to police that this killer was not mad and he was not a drug addict. He was too well organised. "I also thought that there was an unconscious or partly conscious wish on the part of the offender to be caught," Dr Milton recalled.

"The risks taken and just possibly the calls to the police station on 3 November were consistent with this."

The main thrust of the second report was twofold: that the huge risks taken by the offender, "in addition to his impulsive and extraordinary violence", indicated there was a strong chance he would attempt suicide; and that the offender would eventually "take direct action against someone close to him, namely a person in his own family".

Milton also discussed the possibility of issuing a public warning to this effect. "It was just too difficult to get it in the paper," the doctor recalled. He discussed with police how to frame a "little warning" in the paper which would say: "Is someone close to you doing odd things? Are they absent at these times? If so let us know because you may be at risk." But the correct phrasing was almost impossible and "we would have got a million calls".

By the end of November police were only too aware that the killer was slipping in and out of brutal murder scenes without anyone paying any attention. The obvious answer was that everybody was looking for the wrong sort of person.

Dennis O'Toole started tossing around the idea that the killer was a woman — maybe a man dressed as an old woman. It was difficult trying to get the point across at morning conference without copping a smart remark. He said he was just trying to emphasise the need to keep an open mind since the earlier, specific hunts seemed to have ended in failure.

But like the public, everyone in the task force had their own pet theories.

Three weeks after Mrs Falconer's death, the shoe angle had almost been exhausted as a line of active inquiry. The only option police had was to start going back over everything. Detective Sergeant Paul Tuxford and his offsider, plain-clothes Constable Melissa Post, were sent out to re-interview a neighbour of Mrs Falconer. The woman had seen a rough-looking young male in the street on the afternoon of Mrs Falconer's death but he had been found and cleared. Their intention was to see if she had remembered anything more about the afternoon in question.

"There was something else," she offered. "I remember I was walking up the lane because I had to go and get my hair done and I remember seeing a grey-haired man crossing the road in front of Muriel's house."

"What did he look like?" Tuxford asked.

"Like a doctor because he had a silvery grey suit on. He looked about 60 and very well-to-do. It's all a bit vague. I didn't pay much attention at the time."

They walked over the path that this grey-haired man had taken. It matched the direction of a person leaving the house heading to Military Road. Tuxford thought back to O'Toole's belief that the killer might have been a woman — someone no one would notice. No one would notice a silver-haired gent, he thought, not in Mosman.

Tuxford had been seconded to the task force from the Licensed Dealers section at Chatswood. He was used to dealing with pawnbrokers on the trail of stolen goods but this didn't seem that much different. The task force inquiries included checking with pawnbrokers throughout Sydney for items of jewellery stolen from the victims. They had yielded nothing.

Another neighbour of Mrs Falconer had seen a grey-haired man walking down Muston Street. An old chap, he had said hello in that neighbourly way that younger generations have lost.

Tuxford went back to the office and took what he had to Eva, the operator of the PIR (Persons of Interest Reports) computer that processed information coming from daily run-of-the-mill crimes. "I've got something of interest here and I wanted to know if we could just put a hair colour in and see what the computer turned up?" he asked her.

"Sure, but you're going to get a hell of a lot depending on how far back you go and what colour hair you want," she replied.

"Well, it's grey — there can't be too many of them can there?"

"We'll see. How far back do you want it?"

"Um, let's do six months."

She plugged the details in and they waited. Five minutes later the machine began printing out its findings, a series of summaries and reference numbers indicating how to access the full files on each case. Tuxford went to the files.

There was an incident at Balmoral Beach. A woman was minding her grand-daughter when an elderly grey-haired man had approached them and started up a friendly conversation. The woman looked away and did not see the man put his hand down the child's swimming costume. As the woman turned back she saw what she thought was the man pulling his hand from the costume and then walking off quickly. She had reported it to the police. Tuxford thought it was interesting but the next report really opened his eyes.

On 25 August 1989, a woman by the name of Effie Carnie had been punched and robbed of groceries and $90 outside her retirement village on Treatts Road, Lindfield.

The incidents were tied together by more than one common thread. Not only was the perpetrator in each case a grey-haired man, he was a stocky, well-dressed grey-haired man.

Tuxford re-read each case then got Eva to go back another six months. There was another incident on 11 January 1989 when Mrs Margaret Todhunter, 84, had been hit in the head while walking down a street in Cremorne. Her handbag containing $200 had been stolen. She described her attacker as portly with grey hair. Tuxford's eyes were opening wider and he was trying to read it all as fast as he could. He had a feeling in his guts that he was in the process of solving the murders.

Tuxford marched into Ron Smith and Geoff Wright's office and told them what he found, a hint of bragging in his voice. They seemed interested but not as interested as he thought that maybe they should have been. But they understood the potential importance of the find. They remembered the grey-haired man who had helped Enid Benckie to her door with the groceries on the day Mrs Pahud died.

They checked the files. There was another sighting of a grey-haired man by a solicitor, Prue Gregory, and another up at Belrose when Miss Cleveland was killed the following day.

Tuxford had a task force analyst put together a flow chart of the grey-haired man's known movements — each of the assaults plus the three sightings near the last three murder scenes — so he could more easily demonstrate to his colleagues the basis for his belief.

At the next morning's conference, the burly figure of Paul Tuxford rose at the first opportunity. "I've got him. I have the killer," he declared. "In this hand is a description of the killer, I know what he looks like," he said, holding the analyst's report with a cheesy grin on his face.

"Well, fine, what's his name and address?" came the slightly dismissive reply from the floor. Light-hearted bragging about good work was one of the few releases available to the detectives and having a dig at a colleague was another.

"Sorry mate, that's all I've got right now — but it's him."

Tuxford ran through the reasons why he thought he had him. The story was dampened somewhat by the fact that the witness who had seen the grey-haired man leave Mrs Falconer's house had also seen the rough-looking suspect. It led to a suspicion that maybe she was seeing things. After all, there had been a three week gap for her memory to play tricks.

O'Toole was interested though. He'd copped enough of a ribbing about his theory that it could be a woman. He had tried to make the point the killer was slipping in and out unnoticed.

"Of course the person we are looking for isn't what everybody imagines the murderer would look like. Whoever it is blends into the scene. Nobody sees him. What's going to be more camouflaged than a grey-haired man in Mosman?"

Brisbane police were asked to interview Mrs Todhunter. She had grown up in Mosman, gone to school there, married there and raised children there but had left for Queensland some years earlier.

She was found in the suburb of Toowong just before Christmas. It was more than a year since the attack but it was still vivid in her mind. It had ruined her holiday back in Sydney.

The police had to explain that they were still hunting her attacker and they thought they now knew who he was. They said nothing about the murder investigations and took a statement from her, more detailed than her original complaint.

She said she could remember his face vividly and agreed to have a Brisbane police artist do a sketch of him. It was mailed down to Sydney a week later.

When Paul Tuxford looked at the drawing, he stared hard, very conscious that he might be looking at the killer. The sketch showed a round-faced man with short white hair. He wanted this man, knew in his heart he had the killer and wanted to convince everyone else in the task force of the same thing but there was a sense of not wanting to jump to any conclusions. There had already been enough disappointments with other suspects.

The picture from Mrs Todhunter's description was not going to be published. There had already been too much time wasted and the credibility of the task force was on the line. As each new identity picture had been trumpeted by the media as "the face of a killer", it had only served to fuel cynicism — everyone could see each new face was different. There was a growing public perception that police didn't have a clue who they were looking for. Largely, the perception was right.

A circular was put out to all north shore stations asking for any incidents or reported incidents involving a grey-haired man. The sketch from Mrs Todhunter's description was included with the circular.

The circular was marked "secret". The task force had receded under a shroud of privacy. It was decided that the less the killer knew about the police case, the better.

Christmas Day came and went. Concessions were made for the officers with families. The unmarried men and women were all rostered on and then volunteers were called for from the ranks of the married. Two shifts worked through the holiday. It was just another working day.

O'Toole took the day off. He had hardly seen his family in nine months and the strains were showing.

"I honestly don't think they have ever got over it. My two youngest daughters were given a pretty free rein because my wife was home by herself most of the time. I think they still think they can get away with — I won't say murder — but a fair bit."

His involvement in the case had rubbed off on his four-year-old. She shocked him when she asked: "Daddy, where is the granny killer?"

Around Christmas, Joan Sinclair told John Glover they had to see less of each other. He took the news hard but she knew it could not go on. He was still married with kids and that was the bottom line. Joan was also concerned about his depression.

As a single woman living alone, she had become afraid for her own safety. She had electronic intruder alarms installed around her home following the murder of Mrs Falconer. Security floodlights were added to her garden, and a new wooden security gate was installed out the front. She asked neighbours not to tell anyone she lived alone, such was her fear. Within a few weeks of the devices being installed, neighbours were being driven mad by Joan's mischievous silky terrier triggering them off.

The routine investigations continued, with every knock on the door revealing another small story, another mystery. People were bewildered as to why they might have been nominated as a potential mass killer. The interviewee would be assured that he was just one of hundreds of suspects. In many cases the officers knocking on the door did not know who had nominated the suspect, or why. But the questions continued.

"Where were you on the afternoons of March 1, May 9, November 2, November 3, and November 23?" the detectives would ask. The dates were well memorised after being recited so many times a day, every day.

People would, naturally, respond that they could not remember. "Do you have any diaries, work records, or calendars that might remind you?"

As the person went off to find the material to jog their memories, the police would try to see the soles of their shoes. Like the dates, the shoe print from Mrs Falconer's house was firmly printed in their minds.

If the suspect could not produce an alibi, he remained on the list of suspects. This tended to discriminate against the less well organised.

People were ringing the task force telling them the names of anybody slightly out of the ordinary. A mentally ill man who might have lived quietly for years was finding himself a suspect.

A bus driver who had only just retired was singled out. He had worn a dress to work on the last day on his regular route. One of his early morning commuters, aided by the story in the paper, thought cross-dressing to be a sufficient warning that he could be the granny killer.

He was interviewed by Detective Constable Kim Barwick. She found him near death with emphysema, being nursed by his caring wife. She hardly bothered to disturb him or his wife.

By January the task force, which had started as so united a unit, was beginning to falter under the stress. Nerves were fraying and small problems started to create bigger arguments for the overworked investigators. "There was a bit of segregation between the task force and Mosman police. I think that information wasn't flowing all that well between the two. There was a bit of animosity," said Constable Wilson.

A rumour surfaced that on the night Mrs Falconer's body was discovered a senior officer had accidentally stepped in her blood and left a second footprint at the scene which confounded scientific police. The task force deny it to this day.

One afternoon in January, Megan Wilson was helping take calls on the public hotline. Among them was one from a nurse at Gosford on the Central Coast.

"I'm just ringing to see if you were aware that two elderly women had been murdered in their homes up here at Ettalong and Umina," the woman said. She was referring to the unsolved murders in 1984 and 1986 of Josie McDonald and Wanda Amudsen.

The woman thought they sounded similar to the north shore murders. Constable Wilson wrote the information down on a running sheet and it was entered into the computer.

Inspector Hagan considered it a viable lead and details were sought from Gosford Police. But the Central Coast murders bore one other similarity to the north shore attacks — there were no clues of any substance.

CHAPTER SEVENTEEN

SUICIDE

1 January 1990 was a hot summer's day and Daisy Roberts was propped up in bed fanning herself with a luncheon bib, waiting for her midday meal to arrive. The wide open doors leading to the hospital verandah were bringing in little breeze to relieve her discomfort. She was dying of cancer in the palliative care unit at Greenwich Hospital. It was the saddest of places.

Although terribly ill, Daisy remained lucid. Visitors were impressed by the way the 82-year-old faced death with an uncanny serenity.

Another woman, Miss Best, similarly beset with illness, was drawing out her last days in the same room. She was in a wheelchair with her back to Daisy and so did not notice when a man walked into the room from the main foyer of the hospital.

Daisy was watching him though, not out of any special interest but because not very much happened in room one. The man walked past the end of her bed, then out the double doors at the other end of the room onto the verandah, hardly pausing to glance at her.

A few minutes later she saw the man come back into the room. He entered from the foyer and again left via the verandah. She saw his clipboard and his blue jacket with an identification badge on it the same as hospital staff wore. She presumed the fellow was some sort of doctor or orderly.

A minute later he was back again, this time coming from the verandah. He walked past the foot of her bed and stood on her left-hand side, very close, looking at her. She was still waving the bib in front of her face, trying to create a gust.

"You seem to be losing your body heat," he said.

"Just a little," she said, still believing him to be a hospital worker.

The man reached out and put his right hand down Mrs Roberts' pink nightie. He held her left breast, asking if it hurt. He then moved his hand down to her stomach and placed his other hand on her back as he rubbed her stomach and edged down towards her genitals. The entire incident lasted maybe ten seconds and the man left, going back into the hallway. Miss Best had seen nothing, just the flash of a fat man walking by.

Sister Pauline Davis, a long-time employee of the hospital, was on duty that afternoon. She had been ill at ease over the safety of her patients since November when the granny murders had moved from Mosman, east of the hospital, to Lane Cove, a kilometre to the west. Not only that, but two of the attacks had now occurred around nursing homes. Hospitals like Greenwich specialising in care for the elderly might be next.

Sometime before one o'clock, she too had seen a man carrying a clipboard as she passed him in the foyer just around the corner from room one. Minutes later she had walked back to the hallway and as she passed the open door to room one she looked in and saw a man standing on the verandah outside the room.

He was looking in through the windows. She noticed he was wearing a blue spray jacket with white stripes.

She kept walking past the door, not paying much attention to the somewhat officious-looking middle-aged man. He was, after all, only standing on the verandah.

But soon after, nurse Jody Smith came in from her rounds. "Mrs Roberts just said something about a doctor or somebody feeling up under her nightie. She's not very happy about it," the nurse said.

Sister Davis rushed straight back out to room one but saw nothing unusual. Turning back towards the nurse's station, she saw the grey-haired man with the clipboard again.

This time he was in a telephone booth and she could hear him talking. As he left the booth she confronted him.

"Are you lost? Are you looking for someone?"

"The catering supervisor, her name escapes me," the man told her.

"I'm sorry, I don't know her name," she said politely. "Were you just in the ward, have you been into room one?"

"No, I've just come in. There was another man wandering about. I sent him upstairs."

Sister Davis left it at that and went in to see Mrs Roberts, whose room was just around the corner. She left the man heading towards the lifts, which were outside the telephone booth.

Mrs Roberts told Sister Davis what had happened and gave her a description of the perpetrator. He was tallish with fair straight hair and a solid build. He was about 35 with a blue jacket on, she said.

Sister Davis went upstairs where she saw the man with the clipboard again, walking into the kitchen this time. She knew she could not prove anything and just kept an eye on him.

After a few minutes on the ground floor Sister Davis walked to the front glass doors of the foyer. Through the doors she saw the man walking along the driveway and up a slight hill leading to River Road before he went out of sight towards the carpark.

Pauline Davis put in a report to matron and Mrs Roberts' family were informed. Mrs Roberts had been unhurt in the incident but she was deeply offended.

It was decided to call the police.

Plain-clothes Constable Pam Whittaker was on the verge of becoming a detective and could not wait for the 11 days to pass before the course began at the Academy in Goulburn. It was what she had wanted since she did her basic training six years earlier.

When she arrived for work at the Chatswood police station that night on the 5 p.m. shift, she was told that there had been some incident involving an old woman out at Greenwich Hospital. Her partner, Constable Alison Cremen, was not able to go with her. She had been called away on another job.

Sister Davis had gone home by the time Pam Whittaker arrived at the hospital. Mrs Roberts recounted to the constable what had happened. Pam Whittaker sat on a chair listening intently. Mrs Roberts was adamant she wanted to press charges if police could find the man.

"She was a lovely lady, really peaceful — and clear-minded — she certainly was frail physically but she didn't appear to be too traumatised. She wanted to tell me the facts. She kept to the facts," Pam Whittaker recalled of Mrs Roberts, who died not long after the incident.

Matron had in the meantime spoken to the catering officer, who gave a list of people who had visited her that day. The catering officer deduced from the descriptions that the man they were looking for sounded most like the fellow from Four'N Twenty pies. His name was John Glover.

This name was given to Constable Whittaker along with Sister Pauline Davis' home phone number. She got back to the office around 9 p.m. and rang Pauline Davis and they had a long conversation.

She got a phone number for Glover but decided it was too late to call. She reasoned that the connection to him was not strong enough to warrant ringing after 10 p.m.

The next day, exactly one year and one day after Margaret Todhunter was bashed from behind in a Mosman street, John Glover was contacted by police.

"I'm Constable Whittaker from Chatswood police station. Do you work for Four'N Twenty?"

"Yes," he replied without hesitation.

"I'm making inquiries into an alleged sexual assault which occurred at about 12 midday at Greenwich Hospital. Can you tell me anything about this?"

"I was at the hospital about that time for work but I don't know anything about an assault."

"I just thought I would like to talk to you further about this allegation — are you able to come to the police station?"

"No. My daughter's just got her HSC [Higher School Certificate] results and we are going out to celebrate."

Pam Whittaker tossed up in her mind whether to force the issue. He did sound like a family man and he did have the excuse ready — a good one too. It really didn't sound like he'd been caught out.

"Well it will have to be tomorrow then," she told him. Glover agreed without hesitation and they set the meeting down for 5 p.m. at Chatswood police station the next day.

To Pam Whittaker he did not sound like a man trying to hide something, but the fact he was obviously a family man had not changed her view of him as a suspect. "He certainly had a confident manner about him that didn't strike me as being guilty from the start. I certainly didn't think it couldn't be this man."

The next day, when the appointed hour came around, there was no sign of John Glover. By six o'clock, Pam Whittaker was getting suspicious. She pulled Glover's phone number out of her notebook and called him to see where he was. Gay picked up the phone.

"It's Pam Whittaker from Chatswood police here. Your husband had an appointment with me at five o'clock, I was wondering where he is."

Gay did not know about the appointment. She had more pressing things on her mind: "Look, he's just tried to commit suicide."

She put the family doctor on the phone. He explained that Glover had just been put in an ambulance and was on his way to Royal North Shore Hospital at St Leonards.

With all sorts of suspicions in her head, Pam Whittaker got in the car with her partner, Alison Cremen, and headed for the hospital. "He really doesn't want to come and see me, does he," she said to her partner with irony in her voice as they headed out. The two were friends and had been working together for a year or two. They looked like sisters, both with red hair and fair complexions.

It seemed to both of them that the suicide was closely linked to the inquiry. "But not knowing anything else about the man there may have been many other reasons why he tried to kill himself then," Pam Whittaker recalled.

They arrived at the hospital just after the ambulance but there was not too much they could do while the doctors were busy saving Glover's life.

A few minutes passed before a woman came in crying with a teenage girl hugging her arm. "Looks like the wife," said Alison Cremen. The pair left that area of the hospital and waited elsewhere. The wife was having a hard enough time as it was without them adding to her stresses.

They came back several hours later. Gay was standing over in one corner, distraught, clinging to her daughter and offering what comfort she could. The police officers decided not to approach her but spoke to Dr Dominic Rowe. He said that Glover was going to be all right. He had taken a mixture of valium and whiskey and had left a garbled note.

"Can we have it?" Constable Whittaker asked.

Dr Rowe was reluctant to hand it over. He had patient confidentiality to consider.

"I'm sorry, doctor, but the law says police have to investigate all suicide attempts," she explained, not entirely sure just how far her investigative powers overrode patient confidentiality.

Dr Rowe produced a copy of a Petersville Pastries superannuation form which had been used as note paper. The form said that Glover's family was to receive $69,697 on his death.

But it was the suicide note, scrawled in heavy black marker pen over the form, which the police were interested in. But it did not make very much sense.

NO MORE MORRIS
YEA TEAM
NO MORE GRANYS
GRANNIES
DET
BUON ANNO
GO FORWARD DON'T LOOK BACK
YO STAR, YO MARNEY, YO NED.

On the second page was written:

GAY DON'T TRY TO UNDERSTAND ESSIE STARTED IT
MARNEY SAVE SOME CHICKEN SKIN FOR ME
KELLIE TAKE OVER
SELL UP AND PISS OFF
LOVE YOU ALL
RSOB
SOME DAYS ARE DIAMONDS SOME DAYS ARE STONES GIRLS
SING ROSE OF TRALEE

There was a Star of David scrawled in one part.

Pam Whittaker turned to Dr Rowe: "Have you made any sense of the note from either the wife or Glover?"

"According to his wife, he's recently lost his two grandmothers," Dr Rowe answered, sounding as though he had discussed it at some length with Mrs Glover. The line about no more grannies was interpreted as John now being without his beloved grandmother figures.

While Constable Whittaker thought the circumstances cast Glover in a very bad light as far as Mrs Roberts' allegations were concerned, she accepted the explanation. She did not make a connection to the murders of the five elderly women.

Dr Rowe forbade the police from seeing Glover and told them to call back to find out when he would be well enough. "So from that day I knew Glover was in hospital, in the care of the hospital until they released him, and I think that's important," says Pam Whittaker of criticisms which have since been levelled at her for failing to act more swiftly. "As far as I knew he was not being released that night or the next morning. He wasn't to be on the streets. That was quite clear."

As soon as John was well enough, Gay had asked him about the allegation and he had steadfastly denied it. Sitting in hospital, he said it was a case of mistaken identity. She believed him.

He confirmed what she told Dr Rowe, that the meaning of "no more grannies" lay in the death of Essie and Freda. He explained that the Greenwich Hospital allegation, coming on top of problems he was having at work plus his impotence, had pushed him over the edge.

Gay realised her husband was going to need legal help. She contacted her former boss, Dr William Barclay, one of Australia's leading forensic psychiatrists who has dealt with criminal lawyers for years. He recommended solicitor Don Wakeling, who worked the courts out of a nondescript office in suburban West Ryde.

Wakeling took the case. It was just a minor matter the likes of which he sees many. It should have been simple enough.

Glover was put under the care of a psychiatrist, Professor Chris Tennant. At that time, the task force had put out a request through the media for psychiatrists who thought they might be treating the killer to come forward with the information.

"There was a mood among psychiatrists thinking, 'God — could it be this case? Could it be that case'?" said one prominent north shore psychiatrist of that time. "I had actually had two or three of my patients confess and I had to ring up and hand them on.

"One patient thought every time a police car went by it was telling him he was the granny killer and he had to confess. I had to pass it on even though nobody ever took it very seriously and the next week he had forgotten the whole thing."

Professor Tennant has refused to discuss the Glover case but whatever happened between him and his patient, he did not bring Glover to the attention of the task force. Why should he? He already had Constable Whittaker ringing each day trying to get in to see Glover and each day he would tell her "no, he's not ready". She had told him only that she had an appointment to see Mr Glover on an outstanding matter and Professor Tennant saw his role as the protector of his client.

Solicitor Don Wakeling, meanwhile, was also on the phone to Professor Tennant. "Whatever you do, don't let the cops speak to him unless I'm there," he told the doctor.

Wakeling was also trying to get through to Pam Whittaker to tell her the same thing. Each time he tried, she was not there and he had to leave a message. Each time it went unanswered.

It was the beginning of a long train of frustrations for the knockabout solicitor with a passing resemblance to Paul Hogan. He could not figure out why there was so much trouble over such a minor matter.

He kept phoning the police and asking when they were going to interview his client. It was a standard procedure.

He was expecting them to say "oh yeah, come around, no problems", but instead he would call for Pam Whittaker and someone else would answer. They would go away and come back and say "she's not here, I'll get her to ring you back". Wakeling never got his call.

By Thursday, almost a week since she first called Glover, Pam Whittaker was having her own frustrations. She denied she tried to avoid Wakeling.

Her problem was that she could not move without the permission of the hospital. Even if she were to barge in and demand to speak to Glover, all it would take would be one statement from the doctor in court saying "this patient wasn't fit to make a statement" and the whole case would be discredited, thrown out of court.

It is unclear why Professor Tennant was so reluctant to give his permission for five days after the suicide attempt. "Glover said after the suicide that he was suffering deep depression," said one staff member of the psychiatric wing at Royal North Shore. "But it was clear he was not depressed at all. He was at the piano being an entertainer for all the other patients. The nurses twigged he was not depressed."

Pam Whittaker was starting her detectives course on Monday and she had been rostered off on Friday, Saturday and Sunday. Thursday would be her last chance to see him. She had been getting the messages from Don Wakeling so she knew Glover probably was not going to talk to her, but she had another plan.

If she could convince him to let her take a Polaroid of him, she could take it back to the hospital and get Mrs Roberts and Pauline Davis to identify him. Mrs Roberts was too old and frail to be expected to face a line-up. The whole case would depend on a photograph.

On the Thursday, at last, Professor Tennant gave his permission for the interview. Polaroid in hand, Pam Whittaker arrived at the hospital alone. She knew she would have a better chance coercing a middle-aged man to co-operate if she went in by herself. A tall strawberry blonde, she was as attractive an investigator as anyone would meet.

"It seemed to have an effect," she recalled.

On arrival she was ushered into a small, sparsely furnished interview room and waited. Glover, wearing casual clothes, was ushered in and sat at one of several chairs. Pam sat behind the only desk in the room.

According to her official statement, Constable Whittaker introduced herself with all the proper police procedure. She asked for his full name, told him he was not obliged to answer any question et cetera, and asked him why he was at Greenwich Hospital.

"I'm a sales representative for Four'N Twenty Pies and I was there to see the catering officer," he told her. She was impressed by his calmness. He might have been on sedatives, she thought at first, until she remembered it was exactly the same way he acted when she spoke to him on the phone a week earlier. He just looked average to her.

"Were you carrying anything when you were in the hospital?"

"Just a board with my price list on it. I have been told by my solicitor not to answer any of your questions so I'm not answering any more."

"May I take two photographs of you for the purpose of continuing my inquiry? I want you to understand that you are not obliged to give me permission to take your photograph unless you wish to do so, but any photograph I take of you will be used in this inquiry and may be used in evidence against you. Do you understand that?"

"I understand. Well, that will be all right."

"Will you sign my notes to acknowledge our conversation and that you have given me permission to take two photographs of you?"

"No."

The reality, however, was somewhat different.

"When I interviewed Glover it wasn't exactly as it appears in the statement," Pam Whittaker now admits. She said a lot more, telling him: "Look, this silly old woman has made this complaint, I'm here because I have to talk to you before you can be cleared, now if you just let me take a quick picture that will be it."

Glover agreed. She had him.

She did not believe what she told him, but she wanted to let him think he had pulled the wool over her eyes — that she was just a stupid woman. "I knew I wasn't going to get any sort of statement out of him and I was right, so I had to go for what I could. I had to get the photographs."

The first that solicitor Don Wakeling knew about the interview was when Professor Tennant rang him. "Why weren't you here today when the police came and spoke to your client?"

Wakeling was angry. He'd left instructions that nobody was to talk to Glover unless he was there. As far as he was concerned they had tricked Glover into letting them take the photograph. It was probably going to make the defence case that much more difficult.

Constable Whittaker had by this stage thought that the photograph would be of interest to the task force. As far as she was aware, the teenage skateboarder was still the prime suspect but she thought they might want her material anyway.

In the meantime, she had to finish her investigation by that afternoon. She spent the lunch hour in the Westfield shopping centre with the Polaroid camera asking middle-aged grey-haired men to allow her to take their photographs. She needed anonymous faces in the folder when it was shown to Mrs Roberts and Sister Davis. The men were all surprisingly helpful, so long as they stayed anonymous. They certainly had no idea to whom they would eventually be compared.

She got photos of eight other men and took them straight out to Pauline Davis and Mrs Roberts. Sister Davis immediately identified Glover as the man. She had no doubts.

Mrs Roberts, propped up by pillows on her bed, pondered over the photographs for a while. She looked at each and then looked at them all again and then pointed: "He looks most like the man," she said, with her finger going straight to Glover.

It was late Thursday afternoon on 18 January. Pam Whittaker had her case. There was, however, no point in her continuing with it if the task force were going to take an interest in it.

She left work to have a long weekend before her detectives course started, well pleased that she had finished the job as far as she could take it. The next week she threw herself into the new challenge at the course.

According to Constable Whittaker, she rang Constable Cremen somewhere between 23 and 26 January to ask her to take the file over to the task force. This is where the picture blurs. Alison Cremen says that her friend did not ring her until the following Wednesday or Thursday, 1 or 2 February.

But as far as she too was aware, she was just dropping in a file about the case of a middle-aged pervert. The task force, as everybody knew, was looking for a young bloke.

When Constable Cremen walked the 100 metres from the Chatswood police station bungalow to the concrete office block housing the North Region Crime Squad on 6 February, her opinion was soon to change.

CHAPTER EIGHTEEN

LOOSE LIPS

ohn Glover was considered unfit to leave the hospital for 22 days. Shortly before his release, a family friend, Dr Peter Groom, bumped into Gay and John walking through the grounds. It was an awkward encounter.

"Hello, John. How are you?"

"I'll be better when this problem is over."

"What problem? It's not the breast cancer?"

"No, a few problems with the family," Glover said.

"Is everything all right?"

"No," he said solemnly and walked on.

Gay lingered. "It's no real problem, everything's okay. There's nothing to hide, don't worry about it," she said with what was almost a brave face.

Glover was discharged on Saturday 4 February and returned three times for further treatment. However, he was not a good patient. "He couldn't unlock his emotions. He couldn't get in touch with his own feelings," said one staff member.

Whatever was in Glover's head was staying there and no end of therapy was going to change it.

He was heavily medicated on anti-depressants and Gay was gentle with him, not wanting to trigger further bouts of depression. He assured her that there was nothing to the police allegation of molesting the old woman. He said they had the wrong man and she believed him. She made no connection to the murders, even after seeing the suicide note.

He had poured his heart out to her during the previous year about the problems he was having with management changes at work. She told him to change jobs but he thought he was too old to move. Combined with his impotence, it seemed a reasonable basis for depression.

She asked him about the line in the note "no more grannies" and he told her: "We're alone now," explaining that the generation before had all passed on.

Alison Cremen walked through the door of the task force office on the morning of 6 February. She went over to see Geoff Wright and Ron Smith in their office with the file on John Glover under her arm. She tossed it on the desk and showed them the photograph Pam Whittaker had taken.

Senior Sergeants Wright and Smith looked at each other. Their eyes were beyond bleary. They had been locked in their tiny office six days a week, 15 hours a day, reading every skerrick of information produced since the task force was formed three months and two days earlier.

But as they looked at each other, Constable Cremen could sense a sparkle returning to their eyes. Geoff Wright got up casually and went to a file, pulling out the Penri picture of Mrs Todhunter's attacker. "Look, Alison. Look at this."

As he held the photograph and the Penri side by side it was clear to all three that this fellow by the name of John Glover must have been the man who violently mugged Mrs Todhunter 13 months earlier.

Cremen told them everything she knew, from the molestation of Mrs Roberts to the suicide note to Glover's apparently respectable family life. She was excited. She spent the next hour talking to them and then two more hours filling in the running sheet. It was a good lead for the task force, she thought. They had at least found a weirdo who had something against old women.

O'Toole came back into the office later that afternoon. Wright showed him the note. The words "no more grannies" jumped out of the page at him. Wright threw the photograph onto the table. O'Toole was calm enough to notice that his pulse was beating hard. He had seen the face before and he knew where. Geoff Wright pulled out the artist's drawing of Mrs Todhunter's attacker. It was the same man.

He turned to Cremen with a frustrated look on his face and asked passively: "Where have you been hiding this? Why did it take so long?" She explained that she had been asked to bring it over by Pam Whittaker and had done so at the first opportunity.

He was impressed by the work the pair had done, particularly the other eight photos of elderly men. But 18 crucial days had been lost since Pam Whittaker first took the photograph.

Mike Hagan and selected members of the task force were briefed on the new lead. Ron Smith rang psychiatrist Dr Rod Milton and told him that there was a particular patient of Professor Chris Tennant whom they needed to investigate.

"We're a bit embarrassed by it all — can you see what you can do to find something out and make sure he realises the importance of the matter so he will talk to us?" Smith asked.

Milton rang his colleague. They spoke at length about the issue of confidentiality. Professor Tennant was hesitant at first but Milton emphasised the seriousness of the case and Tennant eventually agreed to break confidentiality. A time was set up for the following day for an interview with police.

As it turned out, Professor Tennant was friends with Dr Peter Groom, who knew Glover and knew that he had been having problems. When Dr Groom ran into Tennant in the corridor that afternoon, he asked Tennant what was wrong with John. Tennant told him a lot more than Gay had ever suspected.

"Look, they think this guy is involved in the granny killings," Tennant said. He asked Groom to sit in on the police interview, thinking he might be able to help.

"Oh yeah, typical cops — they want to interview everyone," Dr Groom replied. Then he thought about it. He thought about the brooding nature, he remembered the chip John seemed to have on his shoulder about old women. He agreed to go to the interview.

"It's possible I suppose," he thought as he walked off down the corridor.

Dennis O'Toole and Paul Mayger came in to the hospital the next day to interview Professor Tennant, who had been treating Glover for almost four weeks. Dr Groom was impressed by O'Toole's manner. He seemed "sharp as a tack, very bright".

Tennant told them what he had gleaned of Glover's background. Mr Glover had been impotent for years and his wife was tough and authoritarian. Mr Glover appeared unassertive and showed no manifest anger, Professor Tennant told them.

As Dr Groom listened, Professor Tennant mentioned the line in the suicide note about "no more grannies". It was the first time he had heard about the note. He was hanging on every word, quietly unsettled.

Then O'Toole asked about the line "Essie started it all", not knowing what it meant. Dr Groom sat fascinated and horrified. He knew John's relationship with Essie. It was all beginning to make too much sense.

After Professor Tennant finished giving the background, Dr Groom gave his piece: "This guy's the absolute straight-laced, rigid conservative type who hates radicals," he explained. "Essie, that's the mother-in-law, she hen-pecked him. There was this strange dynamic between him and her that seemed to turn him into a sort of a brooding, angry type. He'd tell you how much he hated all old women, how they were sending the neighbourhood to the dogs."

He was asked if he would be surprised by assaults against elderly women. Dr Groom *was* surprised — at first, "then it just all figured. It was like a jigsaw came together".

As much as he tried to disbelieve it, the whole incredible scenario was becoming less and less fantastic. This man he had known for years — this idiosyncratic but friendly family man, this upstanding member of the community — was the one who had put the community under a seven month siege. He shuddered at a most ominous thought: his mother, aged in her sixties, was still a close neighbour of Glover!

The meeting came to a close and the more Dr Groom thought of it, the more he slipped into "absolute shock". He wanted to know about his mother. Would she be all right?

He was assured that Glover, who had been released from hospital three days before, was being followed, that he would not be out of sight of police. He would not have the chance to kill any more — if he was, in fact, the killer.

All four men left the room thinking they knew who the killer was. O'Toole said they had just elevated him to the top of the list of suspects. Professor Tennant and Dr Groom were sworn to absolute secrecy. It could not get out. There was not a shred of evidence against Glover. The police needed time.

All they had was an equation that seemed to add up: the history of assaults; plus the job with no scrutiny; plus the anger and brooding nature; multiplied by the professed hatred of old women ... it seemed like it equalled the man they were looking for.

Dr Groom went home to his wife and broke his vow of silence almost immediately. It was too big a burden to carry by himself.

"I don't believe this but it's true," he told her. "They think John is the granny killer and I think they're right."

The couple remembered the last time they had seen John, when the murders were big news. His wife had mentioned that all the victims were "Mosman matrons". John had said in an almost sneering way, "yeah, they're all like that", as though the expression "Mosman matron" was an insult in itself.

They got the feeling that John thought of old women as vermin to be destroyed. The thoughts only made them feel worse. Would mother be alright? Only time would tell.

They had been telling her to look after herself even though the killer had been targeting women 20 years older than her. "Don't worry, it will never happen to me," was her ever so common reply.

That evening, there was a glow of confidence as the task force crew sat around for the informal brief over a beer, discussing what they'd found. Someone dubbed him "The Duke" for his Christian names John Wayne.

There was no celebration, they still knew next to nothing about this John Glover character and they were too tired to drink more than a few. But some dared to venture the opinion that they had the man. Others had been bitten before ... they were not game to jump to any conclusions.

One man who had no doubt they were on the right track was Detective Sergeant Paul Tuxford, who had first come up with the grey-haired man theory. He was frustrated that he was not working on Glover, whom he regarded as his, but he accepted that was the way things worked. He was back out doing the routine inquiries which still had to go on.

Tuxford knew Glover might be cleared so the investigation had to roll on. Even if Glover was cleared, he still thought it would turn out to be a grey-haired man. Tuxford's enthusiasm for his routine inquiries may not have been all it could have been: "But I knew, I just knew we had him."

The Central Criminal Index was contacted to find out if Glover had a record. Information came up from Melbourne. The man had been convicted of a Peeping Tom offence in 1965 and was cautioned for the same thing in 1959. He was convicted of an assault in 1967 and, in 1962, had "rendered two women unconscious", attacking them from behind. No more detail was given. What did it mean to render two women unconscious?

Scotland Yard was contacted to find out if Glover had criminal form in England. A list of petty thefts came back but there were no assaults.

Surveillance teams were called in on 8 February. They were briefed and told to start work on Glover from the next morning when he left for work.

O'Toole went to Lindfield to interview Mrs Euphemia Carnie, who had been punched by the grey-haired man in October outside her retirement village.

O'Toole opened the book of photographs in front of her. Mrs Carnie picked Glover immediately. It was a huge relief. For the first time in almost a year, things seemed to be going right, a lead was holding up.

He asked Mrs Carnie if she was sure about the picture, could she identify it with confidence. "Ooh no, I don't want to get anyone in trouble, he doesn't look like the type."

"Don't worry about getting anyone in trouble, Mrs Carnie. You look at these photographs and tell me if you can see the man who assaulted you."

"That's him but he looks too nice, I don't want to get anyone in trouble."

O'Toole explained to her the seriousness of the situation but she would not budge. John Glover looked too agreeable.

O'Toole packed up and left. He headed for the woman whose granddaughter had been molested at Balmoral Beach. She did not recognise Glover as the man.

O'Toole went to Mrs Benckie in Lane Cove, the woman whose groceries had been carried by a grey-haired man around the time her good friend Madge Pahud was killed. She was the really important one. If she could identify Glover as the grey-haired man, it would place him in the vicinity of one of the murders. It would give them an excuse to pull him in, maybe search his house for the shoes.

O'Toole introduced himself at the door, and explained what he was there for. She seemed a bit hostile.

"The man who carried my groceries was a gentleman," she explained straight away. "He was not a murderer."

"Sure, I appreciate that, but we would still like to find him," O'Toole explained, asking if he could come in to talk. "Maybe he saw someone else in the area."

They sat and O'Toole opened the book. Mrs Benckie flashed her eyes across it and looked up, saying, "No, not there."

"Please, could you have another look, just in case. This is the murder of your friend we're trying to solve."

She looked again, briefly. "No, he's not there. The man who carried my groceries was not a murderer. He was a gentleman."

O'Toole took the photos to the solicitor, Prue Gregory, who had walked around a grey-haired man at the time of the Pahud murder. She tried but could not identify him from the book of photographs. Neither could the neighbour of Mrs Falconer who had first brought the grey-haired man to the attention of Paul Tuxford.

O'Toole went to Four'N Twenty headquarters the next day. It was not going to be easy. He had to make sure that whomever he spoke to was not a close associate of Glover's and that they knew how to keep a secret.

O'Toole found a helpful employee who told him that Glover had come from Melbourne originally. He said that there was no way of checking where Glover would have been on any given day as all sales reps worked independently of the office.

Glover's territory stretched right across Sydney. He began work when he felt like it and he finished when he wanted. Glover could have been anywhere at any time in his company vehicle.

Detectives Paul Mayger and Barry Keeling were despatched to Brisbane to talk to Mrs Todhunter. They could not tell her about the murder investigation but explained that they had a photograph and if she could identify the man, they would have the case solved. She opened up the book of photographs with the pictures of nine grey-haired men.

"Oh my God," she exclaimed immediately, with her finger on one of the pictures. She paused and looked up at Mayger.

"I'm sorry, I shouldn't say that. I should look at the rest of them first, shouldn't I."

Mrs Todhunter carefully perused the other pictures but came back to the one that had first caught her eye. It was John Glover.

Her testimony alone would be enough to convict him of assault and robbery, but police were faced with the problem that they did not want to convict a bag-snatching thug. They were after a murderer. They were confident it was the same man but had no evidence. Detective Inspector Hagan, Senior Sergeants Wright and Smith and Detective Sergeant O'Toole had a meeting and talked long into the night.

If they arrested him and charged him with the assaults, he would be out on bail the next day. If he did not want to confess to murder, they would have nothing on him. If they searched his house, what would they find? He might have kept some of Mrs Mitchelhill's rings or Lady Ashton's gold watch. And maybe he had taken something else that they did not know about. They reasoned that the shoe had probably been destroyed after the publicity given to the print at Mrs Falconer's house.

If they searched his house, what if they found nothing? He might clam up, stay clean for a few years and then resume killing in a new location.

The decision was made — John Glover would be followed until some evidence was found, until they had "something to talk to him about".

While Glover was unaware of the police activity surrounding him, it was far from blissful ignorance. For the Glovers it was a harrowing time as John faced the allegations of molesting an old woman. Gay wanted John's name cleared as soon as possible and believed that it would be cleared. However, all their attempts to find out what was happening with the case were hitting a brick wall.

Solicitor Don Wakeling had been dealing with the police for 20 years and he had never had a similar experience. It seemed that nobody knew anything about the case and if anyone did know, they were never in the office. Calls were not returned. It did not make any sense because it was, after all, only a minor accusation when compared to other matters with which police are used to dealing.

Wakeling thought that if there was something afoot with his client he would be able to sniff it out. He had found police were usually pretty heavy-handed in such things. But this time he "never got a whiff". He simply thought he was dealing with incompetence on a grand scale.

Gay was indignant at how the police were giving them the run-around on what she considered a very serious allegation against her husband. John was "zonked out" on the prescription drugs for his depression and was not involved in pursuing the problem.

"Here we were trying to co-operate and they were running us around in circles — it was driving me crazy," Wakeling recalled. "I was on the verge of going to the Police Minister and local MPs to complain."

While the surveillance squad had Glover's future movements under control, it was realised towards the end of February that Glover's travels over the last year were only going to be traced by getting out and asking. Glover might have been attacking geriatric women all over the north shore. The task force had to find out.

Detectives were despatched to all the places where he might have been to sell his pies. Supermarkets, schools, hospitals and nursing homes were all going to have to be checked — especially the nursing homes.

Detective Paul Jacob was the first to make a strike. On 23 February, he and Murray Byrnes went back to Wesley Gardens at Belrose where Mrs Cleveland had been killed. They showed staff members the book of photographs. A sister picked him out and remembered an odd incident back in June. She pulled out her notes on the matter and told them it was 28 June.

It was the chap who had gone to the reception desk saying he had lost his good pen, the sister told the two policemen. While the receptionist had put out a message over the public address system, he had slipped off into the home and molested Mrs Marjorie Moseley.

The sister told the police that the man had at first been noticed because he had entered the building through the nursing care section. They usually told sales representatives, hawkers and visitors to enter through the front. He had put his head through the servery window and asked to see Rob Murrell, the catering manager.

The officers went off and found Murrell. He picked Glover's photo out as that of the fellow from Four'N Twenty.

"He was a pretty up-front sort of fellow, like any quick talking rep," recalled Murrell, a tough-looking Scot with red hair. He remembered telling Glover they did not need any pies, they made their own.

Jacob asked Murrell if he remembered Glover handing him anything. Murrell recalled a price list. He was surprised to find that he had kept it. Jacob took it away and had it tested. There were fingerprints on it.

Shortly afterwards, Detective Senior Constable Vivienne Crawford found staff at the Woolworths supermarket in Lane Cove who could identify Glover ... but not as being there on the day Mrs Pahud was killed 300 metres away.

Surveillance officers were following him and they observed him drinking heavily on occasions. They followed him into the club and several times struck up conversation with him. They even held his drink and watched his poker machine while he went off to the gents. They got to like him. He seemed like a nice old bloke. They thought their bosses had them barking up the wrong tree again and, if he was the killer, it could only have been to support his obviously hopeless gambling habit. Nevertheless, they noted that Glover practised what they called "counter-surveillance" techniques, jumping out of his car suddenly and looking back to see if he was being followed.

On 28 February, Detective Sergeant John May and Constable Stephen St John of the surveillance unit watched Glover park his station wagon at the Lane Cove shopping centre and wander around before returning to the car. He was followed to the nearby suburb of Wollstonecraft. He was in no hurry, slowing to a crawl at times and looking about. He parked in Milner Crescent, got out and walked into Shirley Road.

The two officers followed him on foot as he looked into a block of home units and at a group of old women. The "dogs" were getting edgy. Their hands were feeling for their guns and the radio was ready to call in the detectives on stand-by. Quickly, Glover seemed to change his mind. He jumped back in his car and drove off.

If Glover had approached an elderly woman with no reason, it would have given police the excuse they needed to talk to him and search for a weapon. As it stood, there was no justification for them even to do that.

On 6 March, Kim Barwick and David Paterson visited a nursing home in Lane Cove and found that the matron recognised Glover's photo immediately. She called in other staff who she knew had also seen Glover in action.

The cook was able to tell police that the man had introduced himself as a salesman from Four'N Twenty and calmly handed over a price list, despite the fact he had just molested 85-year-old Lillian Tracey and 69-year-old Jean McGilchrist. The matron explained that they had called the local Lane Cove police, who were given a description.

A few days later, Kim Barwick and David Paterson visited Wybenia nursing home in Neutral Bay. They asked if a Mrs Rolls had ever been a resident and gave the dates they thought she would have been there.

"She's definitely never been at this nursing home," Sister Ann Chan told them. "There's been a few homes closed down around here, she was probably in one of those," she explained. "Why do you want to know?"

Kim Barwick said she was not at liberty to say but asked if the home ordered pies from Four'N Twenty.

"No, definitely not."

"Do you get many salesmen coming through here?"

"We get a few, yes."

"Have there been any peculiar incidents, any strange people, in here in the last year or so?"

"Well yes, actually there has," said Sister Chan.

She told them how blind old Phylis McNeil had called out for help one day; how someone had fondled her breasts saying "It's all right, I'm a doctor"; and how the diversionary therapist had seen a grey-haired man leave the building and jump into a white station wagon. Matron theorised that Glover had come into the home via the fire stairs because the secretary at the front desk had not seen him come in.

A Constable Mayo at North Sydney had investigated the incident, Sister Chan told them.

The enthusiasm of the investigators was on the rise. After months of getting nowhere, suddenly, progress was being made.

There were 30 nursing homes on the lower north shore and they were just about all done. The work was attacked with vigour. Every shop and every home had the potential to turn up what was still needed — proof that John Glover was in the vicinity of one of the five murders on the day of the murder.

In mid-March the senior investigators had a round table meeting. Glover had been under surveillance for five weeks and they were no closer to pinning the murders on him. They had to decide how much longer they could go on tailing him.

After lengthy debate, it was decided to continue with the current policy for another three weeks, until the beginning of April. Everybody wanted action, but what else could they do?

In April they would sit down again and rethink the plan. They just might have to pull him in after all.

Detectives Kim Barwick and David Paterson walked into the James Milson Nursing Home at Kirribilli on Thursday 15 March. They approached the secretary, a middle-aged woman with glasses, and asked to see the matron. The secretary said in a cheery voice that the matron was tied up at the moment but if they cared to wait she would call her.

As she waited, Kim Barwick told the receptionist what a pleasant nursing home it was and the two got to chatting. The secretary had been there eight years and she thought it a fine establishment. The facilities were all that the patients ever needed, modern and comfortable.

The matron arrived and Detective Barwick explained that they were trying to find out if any strange incidents had occurred lately. The matron did not know of any and explaine she had only been there a short time.

"We're trying to find out if a particular pie salesman has been here," Kim explained. The matron looked blankly at her, but Kim Barwick could see the secretary was deep in thought on the other side of the desk, her mind racing.

"He's not from Four'N Twenty is he?" the secretary asked.

"Yes, he is," replied Kim, thrilled that somebody knew something more about him.

"His name's not John Glover, is it?"

"Yes it is," she replied, quietly ecstatic that he must have had extensive dealings with the home.

"It's my husband," the secretary said.

There was silence.

Gay Glover looked stunned, staring straight at Kim Barwick. The detective was equally shaken. The enormity of what had happened threw her completely off balance but she could see immediately that the investigation was in trouble. All the emphasis on secrecy that had been impressed on them since the day John Glover's name turned up was going out the window. The thousands of hours of slog were on the verge of being wasted. If John Glover knew he was being hunted, they might never catch him.

Barwick's mind was racing. The silence continued, becoming awkward, then torturous. The whole investigation might hinge on whatever she said in the next few seconds.

"What's all this about?" Matron asked, breaking the stalemate.

"My husband tried to commit suicide after the police wanted to talk to him about some incident at Greenwich Hospital," Gay explained. "We've been to the solicitor and he's never heard back from the police — it's just been a nightmare."

Matron was hearing it for the first time. Gay had kept it to herself.

The few extra seconds gave Kim Barwick time to think of a way out. Gay turned to her. "Why are you here? What's the problem?"

"I'm with the Sexual Assault Unit, it's part of my job to seek out sexual assaults and investigate them," she replied, pulse racing. "I'm making routine inquiries into a number of sexual assaults in nursing homes. John is just one of many suspects."

Gay was not entirely satisfied. She wanted to know why she was getting the run-around on the Greenwich Hospital business. She wanted to know what such a random inquiry had to do with that incident. She wanted to know when her husband was going to be told what the police were doing with the charges. Kim had to explain that she was not in charge of the matter. "It's in the hands of the local detectives, but I'll try and find out for you if you'd like. I'll try and get in touch with them."

Kim Barwick's mind was sprinting; she was trying to put herself in Gay's shoes, trying to work out what she would do. "Are you going to tell your husband?" she asked. Before Gay had time to answer Kim added: "The last time we had all this trouble he tried to commit suicide so maybe it's best if he doesn't find out."

Gay agreed. They made an arrangement to keep it secret and in exchange, Kim would find out what was happening with the charges.

Kim turned to leave. Gay stopped her: "This hasn't got anything to do with the north shore murders does it?"

"I'm just investigating these sexual assaults," Kim replied. It was a half truth, like the line about being in the Sexual Assault Unit. (She had transferred out to join Homicide only weeks earlier.)

Kim Barwick left the building and ran as soon as she was out of sight. Her mind was swirling with the significance of what had just happened. She ran as a release from the pressure. She needed someone to tell. Her heart was pounding so much she was amazed she had kept her composure.

She jumped in the car and headed straight back to Chatswood. She had to tell the boss, quick. She had to tell someone. The news was too big, too important, to hold to herself.

When she got back, the office was empty. Not a soul in sight.

Gay had not been able to hold back. When she saw her husband that night, she could not keep it to herself. She told him that police were still investigating him. He answered nonchalantly: "If the cops thought I had committed a crime, they would have done something by now."

That night, Glover took one of his daughters to a rock 'n' roll night at the Mosman Returned Servicemen's Club. Members recalled seeing him dancing with her and he appeared to be having a good time.

The next morning at 8 a.m., Kim Barwick had been in the office for only a few minutes when the phone rang. Gay was on the line to say that she had told her husband about the incident the day before. But she still wanted to find out what was happening with the charges against him. Kim promised Gay again to follow up on what was happening with them.

Constable Pam Whittaker had largely put the case of the molestation of Mrs Roberts out of her mind. She was almost through her detectives course and was enjoying it.

She had heard that John Glover had become of interest to the investigation, but did not expect to hear more about it because elite task forces tend to be insular at the best of times. She was surprised, then, when she picked up the phone at home to hear the voice of Dennis O'Toole.

He explained that her case had become the best lead yet and then he told her about what happened with Kim Barwick and Mrs Glover. He wanted to allay any suspicions Mrs Glover might have that Glover was a suspect for the murders.

"Can you ring Mrs Glover and tell her that you've been on your detectives course and that's why Kim Barwick was handling the case? We've got to calm her down."

"Sure, no worries," she told him.

Constable Whittaker called Mrs Glover and carried out her instructions. As she hung up she was confident that Gay had been calmed by her call.

Exactly what effect Pam Whittaker's call had on Mrs Glover is not known. Sources close to the family said that John was "very jovial that weekend". He seemed "very friendly and seemed to have come out of his depression."

Surveillance police were right behind him as he left home just before midday on Sunday. He drove to Neutral Bay. They watched as he stopped and sat in his car for some time before driving off. He headed north to a residential area of Lindfield, where he cruised briefly before heading home. A camera snapped his movements.

CHAPTER NINETEEN

GOTCHA

Monday 19 March 1991: an informant at Four'N Twenty rang the task force to tip them off that Glover was taking the day off work to see a solicitor.

9.10 a.m.: The "dogs" watched Glover reverse his blue station wagon, licence number WW 420, out of his twin garage. An unmarked car began tailing him from a discreet distance, following him as he drove the streets of Mosman. Surveillance police noticed a different John Glover to the one they had been studying for almost six weeks. He was wearing dark sunglasses despite the grey day and he was driving erratically. They followed as he stopped, started, slowed and sped up, not seeming to know where he was going, for almost an hour.

Unknown to Glover, police had placed an electronic tracking device on the vehicle six days earlier. They had hijacked the vehicle when he left it unattended while shopping with Gay at Mosman. It was found abandoned one hour later at Taronga Zoo wharf after an outraged Glover reported it stolen to police.

He stopped and entered the Liquorland bottle shop in Spit Junction and emerged carrying a wrapped bottle. He then left Mosman and drove down Spit Road towards the Spit Bridge. He was driving slower than the rest of the traffic. He suddenly turned left into Medusa Street, into the suburb of Beauty Point.

He followed the street to its end at a T intersection with Pindari Avenue where he parked. A surveillance car pulled in gently to the side of Medusa Street, well back from the intersection.

It was 10.26 a.m. The surveillance officers, Detective Sergeant John May and his team, watched Glover get out of the car carrying a black leather attache case. He combed his hair and adjusted his tie as he headed towards a gate in a house at the top of the intersection. It looked like a business call. They thought it must have been the solicitor's house.

He went through the dark hardwood gate of 14 Pindari Avenue and closed it behind him. He was out of sight behind the brick fence, which

Joan Sinclair's house at Beauty Point, the site
of John Glover's final murder.

was almost two metres high. John May got out of the car and hurried
towards the fence. He jumped up just in time to see the door close behind
John Glover.

The second surveillance car came up. May dispersed his men to the
four corners of the property.

The house was a large white single-storey dwelling sitting on a half-
acre block with a swimming pool and tennis court at the rear. A shingle
with the name "Pindari" painted on it adorned the front door.

Two officers hid in bushes at the back of the tennis court, hoping to
avoid the yapping Maltese terrier they could hear.

There was tension. Glover was acting strangely, they knew, but it was
too early for the killer to strike. They had five hours until "peak hour"
began at 3 p.m.

May radioed in what he had just seen, before taking up his post. The
house had been lifeless for about two and half hours when Paul Mayger
and Paul Jacob were despatched from Chatswood with orders to stay a
short distance away just in case something happened. They drove to a
spot around the corner and waited.

As the afternoon progressed, the two detectives sat there thinking and
talking about what might be going on. It became increasingly clear that
the house was not a solicitor's — legal fees would ensure that no
appointment could last that long.

Dennis O'Toole drove from Chatswood to the Mosman station to monitor the situation. Everyone was getting nervous.

The speculation became more pressing. Under emergency provisions in the Police Act, a check had been made with the Sydney Electricity authority. Joan Sinclair's name had come up. A further check on the Road Traffic Authority computer told them her age was sixty. She was not in the killer's prime target group of elderly strangers.

Back in the car, Paul Mayger speculated: "He must be in there with his girlfriend." The thought made both he and Jacob uneasy. They worried that maybe Glover had seen the police and escaped over the back fence — yet his car had not been touched and the surveillance team was adamant that no one had left.

"What's not to say he's not in bed with his girlfriend having a nice day in the sack," recalls Mayger of the discussion in the car at the time. "What right did we have to go in and say 'excuse me ma'am, are you alright? You're in there with a suspected murderer'".

At 3.30 p.m., a young woman came to the front gate with two young boys in tow. They went to the gate but could not get in. Police watched them standing there, the woman looking at her watch and wondering what to do. After a short while she took the kids next door and left them there. Shortly after, the next-door neighbour came out and also tried to get through the gate without success.

After four hours in the car, Mayger and Jacob were ordered back to the Mosman police station where they were to meet Dennis O'Toole and Murray Byrnes.

At 5.45 p.m., the next-door neighbour left a note on the gate telling Joan the boys were in with her. It was starting to get dark yet no lights came on. The dog was barking in the house and telephone calls were going unanswered.

But there was still concern about barging in. What if the pair were having an affair, had made a dent on the bottle of Scotch and fallen asleep in bed?

Back at Mosman, the decision was made to send uniformed police to the house. "There's a dog barking and the phone's ringing through, we've got some concerned neighbours. Go and check it out, will you," Dennis O'Toole told Constables Leon Bean and Dana Wakeling in assigning them to the task.

The two 21-year-olds did not ask questions. When someone as senior as O'Toole said jump, they jumped.

Wakeling and Bean went to the house of the neighbour, Mrs Mary Dick, who told them that Mrs Sinclair lived alone and that she was meant to be minding her two grandsons.

Constable Wakeling, with not quite three years in the force, was the senior partner. She did most of the talking. Mrs Dick struck Wakeling as a reserved woman who did not really like the idea of police involvement but she did offer the telephone number for one of Joan's sons. He was rung and asked if there was a spare key. He did not have one but, concerned, said he was coming over anyway.

The two young constables decided they would jump the high fence and see what was happening. It was about 6 p.m. and the light was fading as they went to the front door and got no answer. The curtains were drawn but there was enough of a gap for them to see a white Maltese terrier sitting on the lounge.

Moving down the side and around the back of the house, they came to a row of glass doors which formed a large back window. Peering in, they could see nothing at first. But, as their eyes adjusted to the darkness, a hammer became clearly defined on the tiles. It was sitting on a landing in an open-plan back room.

It was covered in blood.

Confused by the moment but knowing full well that something was afoot, Wakeling told Bean to stay while she jumped back over the fence to call the station. She knew one thing was certain — more senior people than herself were needed. She called O'Toole from Mrs Dick's telephone and contacted him on a direct line. "We've been on to the property, it's locked up, there's no lights on," she said with urgency in her voice. "We've looked through the back door and we saw a hammer on a landing with heavy bloodstains around it on the floor."

"Shit! Look, go straight back and secure the premises. We're on our way," is what O'Toole maintains he said.

Wakeling heard him say: "Go in. At whatever cost, get in the house."

Constable Wakeling went back and the pair tried the double back doors. They were locked but the pair pulled hard and the doors swung open with little difficulty. Mrs Sinclair had forgotten to bolt them.

Surprised by the piece of luck, the partners crept into the back room. The house was in complete darkness. They did not feel inclined to search for a light switch. It seemed that more important matters were at hand, because while they did not know exactly what was happening, they knew enough to know that a murderer could be in the house.

The outline of the hammer was clearly visible and they headed towards it up a small flight of stairs. Walking around the hammer, Wakeling turned to a door on the right. She jumped back a step. In the darkness was the body of a woman. She had almost trodden on it.

She could make out that there was a pile of clothing over the body's upper parts and that the woman was naked below the waist. Bean turned around and left; Wakeling followed without either of them touching the body. "It was obvious she was dead, there was no point staying and ruining what was there for Physical Evidence," said Wakeling.

Surveillance officer John May had been watching the whole scene evolve around him. He saw the two constables rushing out of the house and decided it was time to make his presence known. He introduced himself and told them the place had been under surveillance.

While all this was happening O'Toole, Murray Byrnes, Paul Jacob and Paul Mayger had been heading across from Mosman police station. They drove silently to the scene, about a kilometre away, with the heavy afternoon traffic on Spit Road slowing them and making the short trip seem long. They leapt from the vehicle at 6.08 p.m. and went straight through the gate which had hidden a full day's mystery from police.

Moving around the side of the house, they found John May and Constables Wakeling and Bean waiting. Dana Wakeling was distraught. Constable Bean explained what had just happened.

"She was lying on the floor naked from the waist down, with her clothes pulled up," Bean told O'Toole. "We came straight back out, we didn't see any sign of anyone else in there."

Sergeant May assured O'Toole no one had left the house. The killer was definitely inside. O'Toole got on the phone to Mike Hagan, who ordered them into the house and said he was on the way.

The four men — O'Toole, then Mayger, Byrnes and Jacob — moved slowly through the back door. There was still a half light in the sky but it was completely dark inside the house.

They knew that the man who had eluded them for so long was in there. But where? The house took on an eerie unreality. Questions filled their heads. Was the guy a fighter or would he cave in? He might have a kitchen knife. Would he come at them? Try and take one of them out? Maybe he had a gun.

The figures of the four men were silhouetted against the lighted doorway; they peered into darkness as they entered, guns at the ready. Their training told them they must stay out of doors and they moved in quickly. The narrow beam of O'Toole's torch pinpointed the bloodied hammer. He raised the beam up to the top of the landing. Filling the spot of light was the body of a woman on her stomach. Her dress was pulled up, her legs apart, the buttocks slightly raised.

O'Toole went over to the body of the woman he believed to be Joan Violet Sinclair in the vain hope that there was something he could do. She was cold.

He couldn't control the emotion welling in his guts. He had never felt it like this before. It was more than a dead body, it was a symbol of the senselessness, the waste. He had already seen the battered bodies of four innocent women cut up on the slab in the morgue. He was hardened to the barbarity of the act, close to brittle, but this was not just a murder. This was personal.

The landing presented them with two doorways leading into darkness. Paul Mayger and Paul Jacob had already gone left through a door into a hall. Murray Byrnes went right down a hallway. O'Toole followed him. They had no plan of the house. They did not know what could be behind each door. It was totally black save for the torch light.

Byrnes and O'Toole edged through what appeared to be an office, then passed through a kitchen and into the lounge room. Detective Mayger had turned left into another passage which appeared to lead to the bedrooms.

He was subconsciously recalling the fear of a similar night three years earlier when he had apprehended a knife man who had gone berserk in a big old boarding house in the Blue Mountains. This was worse. Glover was an unknown quantity.

Mayger's .38 six-shooter was in his right hand, pointing down by his side at the end of a straight arm. His torch, a long, heavy, black metal instrument that could double as a night stick, was in his left hand.

Hard on his left as he rounded the corner, he saw a narrow doorway. He fumbled for a light switch but could not find one. He pushed the double doors open with his torch. The right hand door hit something hard. The torch light showed that it was the end of the bath but Mayger's eyes were fixed firmly on two feet sticking out the end of the tub, so close he could touch them. He motioned his head sideways to indicate to Paul Jacob that somebody was in there. He edged in, cautious not to expose his body, just enough to assure himself that whoever owned the feet was not sitting up with a pointed gun.

He saw that the legs were horizontal. It seemed safe. He quickly shone the torch around, following with his whole body. He was looking at John Glover unconscious in the tub, the water lapping at his mouth.

There was relief and excitement in his voice. "Dennis, he's in here. He's in the bathroom." He felt for the light switch and found it as the others filed into the small room and assembled around the bath.

The chubby grey-haired man — who for the last year had been the target of all their energies and who for the last 42 days had been a name, a man in a photograph, the entire focus of their lives — was lying there unconscious, an empty bottle of Vat 69 beside him. Pathetic. Vomit and mucus obscured his face. Tepid water was encroaching on his lower lip.

All four of them would have liked to have let his head slip the few centimetres it would have taken to put his nose under. There was a conversation to that effect. For that fleeting moment their rage made it seem a real consideration. Then reality took over.

"I pulled his hair back and cleared the air passages," recalls O'Toole. "There's some suggestion that he reckoned he had a lump on the back of his head but I can't recall that at all." One wrist had shallow cuts across it but he was alive and breathing loudly.

Mayger recalled feeling an intense elation after all that had gone before. "I've never tried heroin but I'm sure it must have felt something like that. It was a high. After all the frustration, the long hours, the stress — I was sick of seeing all those dead bodies. I was sick of cancelling when friends were coming around for dinner, saying 'sorry, not tonight dear, I'm working' and breaking promises to the kids that I'd take them out on the weekend. 'Sorry, I've got to go to work.'"

But there was still plenty of work to do.

As they stood above the bath, O'Toole knew that they had solved only one murder. They had him for Mrs Sinclair but without a confession they had a long way to go before they had him on the five others.

"There would have always been a debate if he died — was he the granny murderer?" O'Toole explains. "He was obviously alive so we had to save him." O'Toole went out to the phone, glancing into the lounge room where Mrs Sinclair's dog was curled up on the lounge, oblivious to the action. He dialled for the ambulance. The bottom line was that O'Toole still needed this person he hated for taking a year of his family life and whose destruction of six women — six families — had been witnessed first hand by all four detectives.

Mike Hagan was still heading across from Chatswood when he got a message from O'Toole on the radio. Couching his words so the media scanners would not recognise it as anything interesting O'Toole told Hagan: "We've got him, he's overdosed, he's okay but we need assistance."

Hagan knew what he meant. Scientific would have to be called along with all the backup systems. It must be done secretly.

O'Toole's call to the ambulance made mention only of a suspected drug overdose, so when ambulance officer Michael Doyle arrived shortly after, he was surprised by all the fuss. It was only when he had to walk past the body of Mrs Sinclair that the gravity of the moment struck home. His partner attended to the victim as he moved into the bathroom.

He found Glover still in the bath and helped pull him from the almost cold water. He gave him an oxygen mask.

Glover's pulse was "quite strong" but his breathing was laboured. His body temperature was well below normal, having been sitting in the bath for almost seven hours.

Ambulance officer Doyle wrapped him in a thermal blanket to try to get his body temperature up. He tried speaking to the patient but got no response. "He was in a coma consistent with having taken a combination of alcohol and drugs."

Paramedics arrived and gave Glover an intravenous drip and put him on a heart monitor. He was taken to Royal North Shore Hospital, Jacob and Byrnes guarding him.

Sergeant David Forbes from the Physical Evidence unit found that Mrs Sinclair had two pairs of pantyhose tied around her neck with several knots at the back of her neck. He lifted a bloodstained yellow towel from her face only to find three other bloodied towels draped around her battered head.

He noted blood splashed on the TV screen in the study and blood splashes on the brick walls. Drag marks suggested the body had been pulled from the family room to the hall.

Meanwhile, Constables Wakeling and Bean had been given the job of securing the scene. They had to log the time each person entered and left and make sure that only authorised persons got near the house.

One of the first people to arrive was Mrs Sinclair's son, who had been contacted about the spare key. Wakeling had to tell him he was not allowed on the premises. She was not allowed to tell him what happened but had to say in veiled terms that his mother had been murdered. The details were not given. Later, the other son would arrive to pick up his two children and was given the same news.

CHAPTER TWENTY

AFTERMATH

ospital staff got in touch with Gay with the news that her husband had been admitted to Royal North Shore and that she had better come down and bring some clothes for him. Detective Kim Barwick had gone to the hospital and was sitting in a small room off to the side of the main entrance when Gay walked in with her eldest daughter, Kellie.

Gay saw Kim immediately. Her face dropped, deflated. Her worst fears were confirmed by the presence of the same police officer who had confronted her at the nursing home the previous Thursday. "Oh no, what's happened?" she asked as if she did not really want to know the answer. She was told she had better sit down.

"Your husband tried to commit suicide ... but also ..." Kim Barwick battled for words, "unfortunately, there was a dead woman found in the same house." She knew it was best in these situations to tell people the truth, but she wavered.

"It's not certain at this stage, but we think he could be responsible for her death."

Gay went into shock. She continued to talk and function but she was not all there. A blankness in her expression gave away her grief. It was the loss of a family member, the loss of the past 22 years of her life to a lie.

Kim Barwick was lost for words. This was beyond her experience in a job where grief counselling goes with the territory. The daughter was standing behind Gay and Kim did not want to say too much in front of her. The north shore murders were not mentioned. Mrs Glover went off to find a doctor.

A little later, Kim approached Mrs Glover again to ask if police could search her house. Mrs Glover agreed and police left with her shortly afterwards. She and Kellie sped back to the house. They wanted to beat the police there so they had time to tell Marney, who was asleep.

The three Glover women sat in a room while the police went through the house. They thought the police were considerate and apologetic. The police found them to be helpful, directing the half dozen officers to parts of the house they wanted to see, always keeping an eye on them.

Mrs Glover took them to a cupboard where there were about eight pairs of her husband's shoes. Kim Barwick peered in and began to pull them all out, but it was unnecessary. Her eyes had fixed on a brown pair of brogues sitting at the front. She turned one over — it was the shoe. She did not need to check. The pattern had been imprinted in her mind for months.

"I found the shoe, I've found the shoe, I've got the thing," she called to her colleagues in real jubilation, briefly forgetting the grief of the household. If it matched the print in the Falconer house — and she was sure it would — they had proof against him for a second murder.

The police left and Gay rang the family doctor, who stayed with them until 2 a.m. For Dr Groom, who knew the granny killer was living just metres away from his mother, it had been the most tense six weeks of his life. Despite the assurances police had given, he could not help but fret. The waiting came to an end at ten o'clock that Monday night. Professor Tennant rang to say that Glover had been found after attempting suicide.

"Oh, thank heaven it's over," he said, relieved and happy. Then, as Tennant outlined what details were available at the time, Dr Groom grew increasingly upset.

He realised his fretting had been justified. Glover had turned on someone he knew, someone with whom he was friendly and who police had no reason to think was going to become the next victim. Even worse, she was in the same age bracket as his mother.

He got on the phone to his mother and spilled out the whole nightmare that he had been through over the last six weeks. He then called the rest of the family, who also knew Glover. "Everyone was shocked, then a sense of 'well, it's not really all that surprising' seemed to come over us," he recalled.

O'Toole and Mayger followed Jacob and Byrne over to the hospital after finishing up at Mrs Sinclair's house, leaving Scientific to finish going over the scene. But it was clear Glover was going to be out to the world for some time so Mayger and O'Toole went back to Chatswood, leaving Murray Byrnes and Paul Jacob to guard him at the hospital.

At 2 a.m., they headed over to the house of one of Mrs Sinclair's sons, where the family had gathered. It was one of the most difficult things O'Toole had ever done. He had to tell them that police were outside while Mrs Sinclair was murdered.

He gave the reasons for their inaction: that there was no evidence against Glover for murder, he was only a strong suspect; that because he had seemed to know Mrs Sinclair it was presumed she was safe; and it was too early in the day for the sort of strike they were expecting. Mr Sinclair accepted the explanation, according to O'Toole.

Ross Sinclair told police he first met Glover 14 months earlier when his mother introduced him as a friend at her home. He said the relationship changed in January after his mother found out John had suffered a nervous breakdown and had been admitted to hospital. She had told Ross she no longer wanted to see John.

The two officers left the son's house and went back to his mother's place to check that it was secured. It was an eerie feeling going back through the rooms that, a few hours earlier, had seen so much violence and so much activity.

It was while walking the grim, lonely rooms of Joan Sinclair's house that Dennis O'Toole vowed he would get Glover for anything else he had done. Surely he had not become a serial murderer aged fifty-seven. There must have been more. He felt he owed it to the other families out there, whoever they were, to find out the true extent of John Glover's evil.

The *Daily Telegraph* had been on the street since midnight with a story that a man was under police guard in a northern Sydney hospital after a woman, aged in her sixties, had been murdered at Beauty Point in circumstances similar to those of the granny killer victims. It was the first public hint that the granny killer had been caught.

But even when press and television film crews began swarming outside the task force headquarters at Chatswood, Mosman police station and the murder scene in Pindari Road, senior police refused to confirm that the reign of terror was over. The staunch silence from police officers, many of whom had worked throughout the night, prompted complaints about freedom of speech.

Glover regained consciousness shortly after 4 a.m. Detective Sergeant Murray Byrnes was sitting next to the bed but had to wait until hospital staff had seen the patient before he could open his mouth.

Glover was seen by a doctor. A nurse propped him up with some pillows and gave him a cup of tea.

"How are you feeling, John?" Byrnes asked.

"Throat's a bit sore, but alright."

"Do you know who I am?"

"Police."

"I am Detective Byrnes."

"Do you know what's happened to my wife?"

"She was here last night with your daughter."

"Which daughter?" Glover asked.

"I don't know. Tall, dark hair."

Glover nodded. "What happens about jail? I am never going to see the sea again for 25 years. My sister doesn't know what I'm doing, the Greenwich thing."

Byrnes was surprised by Glover's matter-of-fact manner. He sensed he was about to open up. "Why do you pick on elderly women, John?"

"You probably noticed the photos in the paper. They all have an uncanny resemblance to my mother-in-law."

."Where is your mother-in-law?"

"She's dead."

"Did she used to live with you?"

"Yes."

"Did you have some sort of problem with her? Did she create problems with the family?"

"Oh yeah. In my first suicide I wrote a note mentioning Essie. She began it all."

"What do you mean?"

"Essie, I just wished she would hurry up and die. Even my wife said that."

"How do you think Essie influenced your behaviour?"

"I don't know. One side of me was alright. The other is dark and evil. I can't control it ... What happens about jail? They'll get me inside a week. Neddy Smith and Tom Domican have a contract out on me — $150,000."

"If you are concerned about your welfare, we can arrange to have you placed in protective custody."

"What about my family? There's no way they can stay in Mosman. They know too many people. It won't be long until it's out. The whole of Mosman will say 'Oh no, not John Glover'."

"Your main concern is for your family. You should not be worried about anybody else."

"I have done the deed. I should not be worried about my safety. I should be strung up."

"Is there anybody you want us to contact?"

"Only Barry Thiering. He used to live next door."

"Do you know how I can contact him?"

"Scots College. No, Cranbrook, he's the chaplain there ... I thought I could talk to him or he could talk to Gay. We both knew him very well. One of our friends died and he did the eulogy."

"John, where did you get the hammer from?"

"From home ... I didn't touch them sexually. My problem was as soon as it is over I just jump in the car and carry on as normal. Invariably I'd go to the club ... I was not aware of any blood on my clothing."

"What about Joan Sinclair?"

"She was not a casual friend. It is what you would call a bit of hanky panky."

"What, she was your girlfriend?"

"But Gay didn't know her. Her sons will come after me."

The conversation was curtailed by doctors who took Glover off for tests. Byrnes went straight to the phone to call Dennis O'Toole. Byrnes spoke quickly down the line. Glover had started saying some weird things. He looked like he was going to start confessing.

O'Toole rang the hospital. The doctor in charge of casualty said Glover was okay to talk to.

When the two officers left their office shortly afterwards to go back to the hospital they asked radio reporter Felicity Moffat, first on the scene that morning, how she knew about the story. "The look on your face," she told O'Toole. "The look on your face. You were beaming."

"I didn't think I had any expression," he replied, beaming as he jumped into the car and headed to Royal North Shore Hospital.

When Byrnes got off the phone from Dennis O'Toole, he resumed questioning: "How are you feeling?"

"Good. Before I had that anti-police thought. I have lost that now, I can talk all day ... Will there be any repercussions against my family?"

"That's something you will have to address for yourself. You will have to get some counselling."

"Psychiatric help or not, I will never see the sea again. You don't get bonds for multiple murder. I used to go to Long Bay Jail selling confectionery for Nestles [sic] 12 years ago."

Murray Byrnes questioned him about the note from his previous suicide attempt. Glover told him it was written "halfway through a bottle of grog" as a goodbye note.

He was asked about the words "no more Morris". "No more Morris Grant, my boss," Glover said.

"Underneath that the words 'Yeah team', what do you mean by that?"

"I was referring to my family."

"Under that again there appears to be the words 'no more grannies', what do you mean by that?"

"I was obviously referring to the problems I was having."

He was asked why "grannies" was written twice. He said it was because the first was illegible.

The word "DET" was going to refer to Detective Whittaker and the circles were to highlight the lump sum payable to the family in the event of his death. "Yo Star, Yo Marney, Yo Ned" were terms of endearment he used with his family. "Marney save some chicken skin for me" was because "My daughter Marney and I are both good pickers and we both vie for chicken skin before Gay cuts it up for our dinner."

He explained RSOB as meaning "rip shit or bust".

Dennis O'Toole and Paul Mayger arrived. They were shown into room G44. O'Toole introduced himself as being from the Homicide Squad, making inquiries into the death of Joan Sinclair. The sister on duty told O'Toole there was nothing wrong with the patient, he was not under medication, was talking coherently and was available for interview.

After Glover's last suicide attempt police had been made to wait eight days to interview him. For some unexplained reason the doctors now thought 17 hours was sufficient recovery time.

Glover told them he was not going to answer further questions unless his solicitor, Don Wakeling, was there.

"Whether or not you answer is up to you. There are still a number of questions I want to put to you."

"What time is it?" Glover asked, speaking clearly and confidently.

"Twenty-five past five."

"Half of me wants to do it and half of me doesn't."

"What do you mean by that, John?"

"I can't help myself. Half of me wants to do these things and half of me doesn't."

"What things, John?"

Glover stayed silent.

"Did it happen as soon as you got there or sometime later?"

"Not when I got there. Later."

"A hammer was found near Joan's body. What can you tell me about that?"

"I want to tell you when my solicitor gets here."

"What's his name?"

"Don Wakeling. My wife knows how to get him."

"There are a number of other matters I want to speak to you about, including the murders of a number of elderly women."

"I know that. I will tell you about them when my solicitor is here."

"You are under arrest and you will be charged with the murder of Joan Sinclair ..."

O'Toole went back to Chatswood and rang Gay. The two had never spoken. He explained who he was and that John was under police guard. "I'll come out and see you and explain it properly," O'Toole told her.

"No, tell me now. I want to know what's happening."

"Well you'd better sit down ... Your husband is going to be charged with murder ..." His words were measured and deliberate, for he was only too aware that another family was in the final throes of ruin. "I don't want to discuss it too much over the phone. I'll come and see you. I'll be out there shortly," he told her.

Gay did not want to believe him, but O'Toole assured her that Glover had said things only the killer would say.

O'Toole never made it out to Wyong Road. Things were moving too quickly back at the hospital. Kim Barwick and Physical Evidence were despatched back out to the house with a search warrant to do a more thorough check of the place. They found Gay was there with the family doctor, who had put her under sedation.

Solicitor Don Wakeling rose early that morning. He turned on the radio and listened while he got ready for work. The news bulletins were dominated by the arrest of a man at the scene of a murder similar to that of the granny killings. The bulletin said the man was in hospital after being injured fleeing the scene.

"Thank God they've got him," was his only reaction as he busied himself around his Top Ryde flat. He jumped into his car and set off for work, listening to a different radio station. When the next news bulletin came on, it said a middle-aged man had been found naked in a bath after overdosing on Scotch and pills at the scene of a woman's murder.

It dawned on Wakeling that John Glover, his client, had tried to go out the same way in January. John lived in Mosman. He had been accused of molesting an old woman.

Wakeling could see a long day ahead.

He arrived at the office just before 9 a.m. His partner and staff had not arrived, so he was alone when the phone rang. It was Gay Glover.

"Have you heard?" she asked in a flat voice.

"Yeah I've heard. Is it John?"

"Yes ... what can we do?" She was calm but distant. She sounded blank, like a robot.

"Look, don't worry, all sorts of things could have happened. Where is he?"

"He's at Royal North Shore."

"I'd better get straight down there and see what's going on." Wakeling's partner, Chris Nowacki, came in. "You know that bloke I've got who's been having trouble with the police," Wakeling said.

"Yes," his partner answered.

"They've arrested him, they think he's the granny killer."

They looked at each other, eyebrows raised. Wakeling said out of courtesy: "You're my partner, do you have any objections to us representing him?"

"We're lawyers, aren't we," Nowacki said without hesitation.

Wakeling rang the hospital and told a police officer that he was Glover's solicitor and he was to be present at any interviews. The officer told him Glover had already spoken to detectives and had started making admissions.

"Just hold on, I'm coming over."

By the time O'Toole got back to the hospital after ringing Gay, Glover's mood had changed. He had become surly and unco-operative. O'Toole sat down beside his bed and the other officers retreated.

They had a conversation, the contents of which O'Toole has never made public, but at the end of it John Glover was co-operative again. They had "come to an arrangement", O'Toole later explained.

Inspector Robert Worthington came in and asked Glover if he had anything to say for himself. "Yes, I'm pleased it's all over. I just want to tell them what happened." Worthington was struck by the normality of the accused.

O'Toole came back. "John, your solicitor should have been here some time ago. I have spoken to Gay and he [Wakeling] knows you are here. Have you any objections to commencing the interview prior to his arrival?"

Wakeling drove to Royal North Shore Hospital as quickly as he could in the morning traffic. As he weaved through the traffic he worried that his client might be mad: "One of these blokes who admits to all sorts of things he hasn't done." He thought his client might be determined to kill himself and go out in a blaze of glory at the same time.

The main entrance to the hospital was packed with media and camera crews filming anyone leaving or entering the main foyer.

Nobody knew who he was so he pushed his way through the crowd with ease.

He was moved through the layers of suspicious police guarding room G44. He saw Mike Hagan, whom he knew from a previous case. Hagan greeted him and introduced Wakeling around to the other officers.

Wakeling was taken into Glover's room. He was propped up in bed, looking like someone who had just come out of an operation. And there he was already having a statement taken.

"Okay, I'd just like to make it clear that my client will not be saying anything more unless I'm present. All right?"

The horse had already bolted.

In a statement read to the media, Assistant Commissioner Charlie Parsons said a man "was currently being interviewed in relation to a number of matters" and that was about all that the media got told all morning.

Pindari Street residents woke to a hive of press and police activity. Journalists were doorknocking homes and quizzing residents and joggers passing the Sinclair home, which was still under police guard. The overnight police crime operation had been conducted in such a low-key manner that most Beauty Point locals did not know of the murder until informed by media.

Mrs Sinclair's estranged husband Alan flew down from Brisbane to identify her body. "I went in this morning to do the ID and there was only a shell of a body," he was quoted as saying in the *Sydney Morning Herald*.

"The circumstances are quite horrendous. She was one of those rare creatures who was warm and wonderful to everybody and it's horrifying to think of the circumstances."

Mr Sinclair said his three sons had met Glover on several occasions in his wife's home. He rejected any suggestions that the relationship between Glover and his wife was a romantic liaison.

"It's 1990 ... from what I can gather I don't think there was any sort of liaison as such," said Mr Sinclair.

"All that's been said about my being an estranged husband ... divorce is really only a hiccup and of no consequence after knowing and loving a woman for 40 years."

Inside the hospital, Glover answered the police questions frankly but without emotion. Asked why he took the pills and then drank the Scotch, Glover replied: "To try to kill myself."

O'Toole: "Why?"

"I wish I knew."

"Why did you strike Joan with a hammer?"

"To kill her."

"Why did you want to kill her?"

"I don't know."

Glover gave the details of the Sinclair murder and admitted to committing the other five but on Wakeling's advice would not elaborate on the other murders while in the hospital.

He was transferred to the Sydney Police Centre at Surry Hills the next day. The details of the other murders unfolded over five days, one murder each day, in a series of marathon interviews.

Glover was at times deliberately frustrating with his answers. He was asked what he did after one of the murders.

"I went back to the car."

"What did you do then?"

"I opened the driver door."

"What then?"

"I got inside."

"Then what?"

"I put the key in the ignition ..."

Paul Mayger, who was given the job as typist, was ready to leap from behind the typewriter and throw it at him. Glover got the hint and opened up but would revert back to the tactic when the questions got too close to the bone.

During one long interview the smokers in the room, including Wakeling, stepped out into the corridor for a break. The typist, a hardened Homicide Squad detective, expressed disbelief at how calmly and willingly the gentle-looking Englishman in the next room was telling in such cold matter-of-fact detail how he murdered each woman. It was with a morbid fascination that they heard his story unfurl. His earlier blaming of Essie for "starting it all" had switched to his mother.

Standing in the corridor, dragging on a cigarette, one of the group composed a verse:

The gloved Glover kills another
and still he says it was my mother.

Two weeks later, Glover's name became public with his brief appearance at Glebe Local Court. No one needed telling when they walked into the Mosman Returned Servicemen's Club. It was the only topic of conversation and anecdotes were thick on the carpet about the quiet fellow whom almost everybody remembered but who few seemed to know.

One woman confided in a long-serving barman with whom she had become close friends that, following the death of her husband, Glover had shown a lot of interest in her. He had been caring and understanding over a period of weeks. While escorting her to her car one night he asked for her home phone number. She had given him a wrong number. It was not that she saw anything wrong with him. She had just not wanted to fall into a relationship so soon.

One of the local identities, Gwen, was saying that one night she sensed she was being followed home. She turned as she went through her gate and saw John Glover lurking in the background and he quickly turned away.

Irene Kurtesz could not believe the father of one of her piano students had been arrested. "Incredible. I got hit on my head to hear what he did."

The president of the Mosman Musical Society, Ian McCann, was kept busy on the telephone with members ringing to ask: "Is that our John Glover?" One of them, a woman in her early fifties, revealed to him that Glover had asked her out for a drink one night after rehearsals. "Thank God I didn't go."

Alderman Dominic Lopez was angered when he heard of the arrest. "He could have murdered my mother. Mum knew John because he spoke Italian. He would come around and sidle up to the ladies. 'Buon giorno signora, come'sta?' and all this. He use to talk to them in fluent Italian.

"When we found out that it was John [doing the murders] Mum said 'Gosh, that's the man who wanted to drive me home from the club'. She had been to bingo.

"I wouldn't mind betting that when he murdered Lady Ashton she was carrying a lot of money. Glover was a compulsive poker machine addict and he murdered for money. That's what I reckon. I mean, the bloke was a bloody crook. He was a thief and a murderer. He is as sane as you or me. I think he is just a born crook."

In the months that followed everyone who encountered him had a story to tell. Among those was Nerida McPherson, the Mayor's secretary.

Sometime after Glover's arrest the Town Clerk Vivian May had walked into her office. "I've just been speaking to the police," he said.

"Remember that phone call you took for Mr O'Keefe after Mrs Falconer's murder?"

She nodded.

"Well, the police say it was him, it was the killer."

The three Glover women went into seclusion after John Glover brought their world down around them. Gay had contacted Glover's sister Pat and she in turn had notified the rest of the family. It was the least she could do. They were all devastated. Clifford's by then former wife Leonie was informed by phone by Pat. It was likely to be on the news and they didn't want the children seeing it.

But for Leonie the news was an added burden. Even when the north shore killings were going on she had found herself wondering whether the killer was the same person who murdered her dear friend, Florence Broadhurst. Now she had a haunting fear that she had inadvertently introduced Florence to the killer.

Glover's own family members have become his ultimate victims. Mrs Glover bore the ignominy stoically. She took a day off work after the arrest but the next day, Wednesday, she was back on the job and the girls went back to school.

For a brief period the nuns at Loreto Convent took Gay and the girls under their wing to watch over them. A network of "safe houses" was set up and the Glover women began setting up the rest of their lives, having to first redefine everything that went before.

"She would never show whether she knew about his previous record, but immediately she just switched off, started talking about divorce," said a close friend of the family, who went on:

They tried to get Gay and the girls some treatment, some sort of counselling, but she would just say "oh no, it's alright, everything's fine".

She smoothed things down very quickly, dangerously quickly. She didn't want to know about it. She wanted to leave but couldn't sell the place because the market was down.

She took the girls overseas during the trial. The family was already Gay and the girls with John on the outside: Gay was just intent on brushing things aside: you wonder if she's alright but she has always been one who doesn't talk about nasty or difficult things.

We always knew they weren't getting on so well, but nothing special, just ordinary sort of stuff.

[After he was caught] you would run into her and ask her how everything was and she would say: "Everything is fine, Kellies's got her music and Marney's doing the HSC, everything is fine." You would feel there was no need to ask any more.

Gay has said she knew nothing about it and had suspected nothing. It's hard *to say what effect it had on Gay. They were probably sleeping at opposite ends of the house by that time.*

She was just getting on with her life and did her own thing, leaving him to do what he liked. It was as though they were already two separate parts of the family: there was Gay and the girls and there was John on the outside.

At the time of publication Mrs Glover had spoken publicly only once: in an interview with the *Australian Women's Weekly* in May 1992, to "set the record straight". There were rumours that she was paid a substantial sum for the "world exclusive" but the *Weekly* refused to confirm or deny this.

"I lived through the first year, obviously coping and doing a job and being a mother and being very down to earth, but you know, there are periods I can't even recollect. I think the brain goes into shutdown when there is too much to cope with," she told the *Women's Weekly*.

"I live a day at a time. The girls have seen me very sad, in tears. But we can sit down, talk, have a cup of coffee and find something funny. We are very strong people."

CHAPTER TWENTY-ONE

THE BAY

I shall never see the sea again," Glover said on the morning of his capture. He now lives on a grassy hill, a giant sand dune hardened to stone, overlooking the Pacific Ocean. But inside Long Bay correction complex the views are spartan. To the east lies the deep ocean and in the distance to the south and west, beyond the red roof tops, lie the shallow utilitarian waters of Botany Bay. It is a view seen only by low-security inmates working in the prison gardens behind the series of razor-wire outer fences.

It was at "the Long Bay Hilton" that Glover came to reside after five days of questioning by detectives. He was put into Ward C, the psychiatric wing of the maximum security prison hospital, for "assessment" and protection.

His fellow inmates included a man who had murdered his estranged wife by cutting her throat in a crowded Sydney street and a man who cut off the head, big toes and thumbs of an elderly man and hid the pieces around Sydney. "I'm not going to tell you where the head is, I'm not going to tell you where the head is," the man would suddenly blurt from time to time, interrupting Glover's conversations with his new associates — the prisoners whom he regarded as sane.

They included disgraced former New South Wales Chief Magistrate Murray Farquhar and former high-flying Sydney Detective Roger Rogerson. Both were in the hospital under special protection. Farquhar was on a charge of selling a stolen painting which was later dismissed, and Rogerson was awaiting his successful appeal against a wrongful conviction on a charge of conspiracy to pervert the course of justice.

Glover came to be good friends with Roger Rogerson. They did the crossword together in the mornings, played Scrabble and were partners on the hospital tennis and squash courts.

He was receiving only one regular visitor, a nun called Sister Toni who was a close family friend. Described by prison officers as "special", she also acted as a go-between for Gay.

During the first two years of his incarceration he saw Gay once and at Easter in 1991, one of the girls visited. It cut him to the bone to see them and to have them see him for what he was. He wondered if they would ever come back. They have not.

It was in the somewhat privileged surrounds of the hospital that Glover met a woman called Dawn, a 42-year-old mother of three, who became his friend, confidante and regular privileged visitor. "For several months following his arrest he was not given a book — he was given nothing," said Dawn. "It was just like all his friends and family had disappeared off the face of the earth."

The couple met in C Ward in May 1990, when Glover was undergoing medical evaluation while awaiting trial. Dawn had been working as a nurse in the general prison hospital for six months when she was transferred into the psychiatric ward. Her nursing duties included administering medication, but she was mainly responsible for talking to patients and counselling them.

She vividly recalls her first day in C Ward, a long room with depressing green, grey and cream decor and cells at either end — all commanded by an observation room in the centre. She did not know who Glover was. She knew him only as John and she thought him a likeable, charming sort of chap. Her first impression had been that he would make "a good Father Christmas in a big department store".

"No one said to me, 'That is the famous granny killer over there.' He did not tell me who he was," she said.

They played tennis. She found him "extremely handsome for his age". But he stood out because he was so clean and neat. She observed him wash his clothes at night and lay them out over a chair to make sure they were wrinkle free.

"His cell was so neat, like he was in the army. Even his bed was neatly made."

As she made a cup of tea on her second day in the ward she was told by another nurse of Glover's notoriety. "Oh, you're kidding!" she exclaimed. She walked straight over to him and put her cup of tea down on the table where he was sitting and said: "Did you do it?"

The question caught Glover by surprise. "I beg your pardon?" he said, affecting an upper-class English accent. "Did you do it?" she repeated.

Glover stared at her but gave no answer so she retreated. Three days later she asked him the same question and he said yes.

She did not mention it again until six months later. "In these situations if they want to tell you they will tell you. He very rarely would let anyone get to him. He would not trust anybody. It took a long time for him to trust me. Who knows, he mightn't still trust me."

Despite their rather abrupt introduction they soon struck up a friendship, sitting for hours, chatting and playing games like Scrabble and

Trivial Pursuit with other prisoners. "Sometimes I would play the guitar for the other prisoners and they would all sing," said Dawn.

John would talk to the guards and we would often play tennis. He taught me to play pool and we played in competitions against other prisoners.

I really don't know what attracted me. He just seemed to be the sort of person who shouldn't have been in there. He is an extremely intelligent person to talk to.

His prison mug shot published in the papers doesn't do him justice. They cut his hair. He has beautiful hair and eyes.

John would often talk about his family and what he did as a kid, everything except the murders.

Dawn was reading a political book one day when she noticed that he had an Agatha Christie novel. "Do you like murder mysteries?" she inquired, rather bemused. "Yeah, no worries," he replied, and they had a laugh.

He's not all bad. I know he has done some horrific things, but he is probably a lot saner than you and I in many respects.

I have sat with him day in and day out. I was with him for 18 months in the jail. Every shift I would be with him for eight hours, sometimes up to 16 hours when I had to work a double shift. I never felt scared or frightened around him. He has had no aggressive tendencies towards anyone since he has been there.

He was always protective of me towards the other prisoners.

But others have viewed Glover differently in jail. Forensic criminal psychiatrist Dr Rod Milton said Glover had revealed a "school boy bully" trait to his personality which was noted by prison doctors.

"He had a nasty habit of putting down the weaker, mentally ill patients. Of course, these were very sick people and he would put them down, call them mad."

A staff psychiatrist at the prison, Dr Joe Gluckstern, had been the only criminal psychiatrist to correctly predict that the killer was not a youth but an older man. He has since treated Glover and relations between the two have been strained.

Glover has felt that some medical staff and prison officers took a strong dislike to him from the start. Some regarded him as obnoxious. Some did not like him for the crimes and others for his north shore manners, he said.

No one, neither medical staff nor prison guards, could foresee the bond that formed between Dawn and Glover. The more she saw of him the more she became drawn to him and eventually she resigned from her job in order to continue seeing him.

"She must be mad," is what everybody has said upon learning of her existence. What drew her to the man almost 18 years her senior who killed at least six times and attacked unknown numbers of women?

Psychiatric opinion has it that women who fall for serious criminals within the confines of jail — and there are many — do so because it gives them control of a relationship. It is often the first time in their lives they have had the power to decide how much contact is made, when it is made and under what conditions. The prisoner is always glad to see them and they leave when they like. Dawn nodded and said "maybe" when told this.

Psychiatric opinion also has it that such relationships always fail upon the prisoner's release. The factors that made it work suddenly disappear. She disagreed.

She does not know if she is in love. She only knows "that we are really good friends and we like each other's company".

She says in a pleasant voice: "I can't ask anybody to try and understand it. I can't think what it is.

"John is like no one I have ever met in my life. I have travelled the world and I have done a lot of psychoanalysing of myself about it. I wrote down a list, reasons 'for' and 'against' it. There is nothing in it for me. John is not going to be let out, it is a pipe dream to think that."

Dawn maintains she was not sacked by the Department of Corrective Services as was claimed by members of the prison's Internal Security Unit.

One night as she arrived home from work she slipped and dislodged her knee stepping from her car. The injury could only be corrected with an operation and a six week convalescence — six weeks of absence from John which prompted her to begin corresponding with him. Unknown to the couple, Dawn's letters were being intercepted by the prison's Internal Security Unit. When she was fit enough to walk and make her first visit, the nursing superintendent was waiting for her. "Do you know what you are doing, Dawn, would you like time to think about this?" he said.

"I'm not going back to work," she replied.

"I really think you should think about this," he urged.

"I've thought about it, the ins and outs. How people may react and whether it's worth it to me, and I've made my decision." She quit.

She continued to see John, often taking up all three of his allotted one hour visits a week.

By then Glover had been transferred to the more austere special protection wing of the Metropolitan remand centre. His new exercise yard resembled a tiger cage at an antiquated zoo — cramped and exposed to the weather with concrete and iron bars. He complained of the overcrowding. There were three prisoners to a cell. Eventually, for his own safety, he was given a cell to himself.

All the while, Glover received visits from detectives going over his statements as the days ticked slowly closer to the start of his trial in mid-November 1991. The first sign that it was looming came with the arrival of the psychiatrists.

Professor Tennant had continued seeing Glover after his arrest but dropped the idea after a few visits. He decided Glover was not suitable for treatment. He had tried to give him therapy to get him in touch with his emotions but there was what psychiatrists call "no rapport" between them. He was beyond help. It is common in psychopathic people with no love, no remorse and no closeness to others.

The next psychiatrist to see Glover was Dr William Barclay for the defence. As soon as the eminent forensic psychiatrist laid eyes on the defendant, he disqualified himself. He realised he knew Glover from when Gay had been his secretary. Glover had attended functions at the centre where he worked. It was Bill Barclay who had recommended solicitor Don Wakeling to Gay and it was he who predicted to the *Sun-Herald* newspaper that the killer was going to turn out to be "the boy next door".

On 19 October, psychiatrist Dr John Shand visited Glover at the request of his defence lawyers. Dr Shand saw Glover twice — two long sessions in the Long Bay remand centre. As the doctor waited to see him for the first visit, he watched Glover through a one-way window. Glover was looking in the reflection of another window, "very carefully and assiduously combing his hair. He wanted to appear at his best". He noted that Glover placed a lot of stock in what was thought of him.

Dr Shand found him resistant to being examined. Glover sought to put limits on the nature of the consultation. He was willing to go into some detail of what he had done but he wanted to control the conversation. It was he who was going to do the talking rather than Dr Shand asking the questions and getting the information he needed.

Glover tried to play down the sensational and macabre nature of his actions and Dr Shand noted the way he particularly wanted to avoid any sexual implications. Shand would try to get Glover's description of what he did in a particular incident but his description would be vague at best.

"What did you do to the old women in the nursing homes?"

Glover was happy to describe how he gained their confidence by asking how they were, as a doctor might, before molesting them.

"Well, what did you actually do to them?" Shand asked.

"Oh, I just gave them a tickle."

It was as if to indicate that he was being playful and only faintly sexual. What he did not admit was that he put his hand right down and interfered with the genitals, not just the breasts.

Shand asked: "How do you think the women felt when you did these things to them?"

"Not much."

"Don't you think it must be a very frightening experience for helpless old ladies to have someone like you do these things to them?"

Glover wanted to appear co-operative. Without much conviction he answered: "I suppose you're right."

He minimised the seriousness of what he had done in the assaults and the "ghoulishness" of the murders. Dr Shand asked him what he did about cleaning the hammer after the murders.

"Oh, it didn't really need cleaning."

"How could that be so? You've smashed their skulls. There was blood everywhere?"

"It was so quick."

"That's nonsense."

Glover presented himself as an educated man who deplored the fact that he was not sufficiently in command of the Queen's English to express his thoughts; he often apologised for not expressing himself in a skilful enough manner. Dr Shand diagnosed him as narcissistically preoccupied. But it was Glover's objectivity, without emotion, which struck the doctor most. It was as though he were telling a story about someone else.

"That's how he was trying to defend himself: by saying part of him was standing off and watching this other bad John Glover doing all these things," said Shand.

Glover told Dr Shand he had no control, that he was suffering from split personality. "He was certainly angling towards the defence that he couldn't help what he was doing and that one side of him was a spectator to what the other was doing. The good and the bad John Glover. I think that assisted him in being able to be frank and somewhat detached in the way he was describing the difficult things he did."

Shand asked: "Was Gay in danger from bad John Glover?"

"I never ever thought of it in relation to her."

"Why not?"

"Because she's a marvellous woman, a great mother and I love her."

Dr Shand disagreed and thought Gay was in danger. "If he could kill Mrs Sinclair who he claimed to love a lot, his wife was certainly not out of the danger zone." Dr Shand asked Glover why he killed Joan Sinclair. Glover told him they had discussed having lunch and the question was whether they would go out or have it in her house. They decided not to go out and then he suddenly killed her. He said he had planned to commit suicide in her house. He explained possession of the hammer on the basis that he thought he might only have to use it if she got in the way and obstructed his suicide plan.

"That doesn't seem to make much sense," said Shand. "If you thought there was going to be difficulty committing suicide, why wouldn't you do it some other place where the same difficulty wouldn't apply?"

Glover again looked "puzzled and a bit nonplussed" but felt bound to agree with the logic Shand was putting to him. It was obvious Glover was desperate not to appear in too bad a light. He was trying to tell himself as much as anybody that "the homicide was not his primary goal but, rather, it was something which occurred for some other less ghastly reason".

He was lying to both of them, Shand thought. In the doctor's mind there was never any question of Glover's sanity. In the end, suicide was more acceptable to him than the indignity of being caught, tried, sent to jail and exposed as a murdering sadistic monster, the doctor thought.

He struck Dr Shand as being "genuinely concerned about not just his own image, but more of the sexual motivation ... he was concerned about how he would look as a sexual deviant and how this would reflect upon the family — the wife and kids".

Shand asked: "As far as your sexual activity was concerned you were impotent?"

"Yes."

"Well, what sexual outlet did you have?"

"Masturbation mostly."

"Well, that couldn't have been much chop if you were impotent."

Glover became vague about it — whether in fact he could do it properly and whether it gave him any satisfaction. He was wary about admitting to any masturbation; in fact he was prudish about it, amazingly enough. Dr Shand recalled: "What he did do was boast how attractive he was to women at the club, some of whom he referred to as predators — quite an extraordinary word to use. He made it quite clear there were any number of middle-aged women who were widows or unsatisfied with marriage and who were available for him at the club ... and Mrs Sinclair was one of those."

Dr Shand concluded that Glover was a sexual sadist. He had followed the documented paths to that end. It began in 1962 with the aggression against the two women he assaulted. By 1965 the voyeurism had taken him into sexual deviance.

Glover was reluctant to admit it but he was coerced into telling the doctor that he masturbated outside women's windows. "Goodness knows what his fantasies were at the time — but that's what voyeurs do. They usually peep and masturbate and so he admitted to not a great number of occasions of that kind."

The final phase of the sexual sadist diagnosis hinged on the straight-out sexual sadism of the murders — that Glover derived carnal gratification from the cruel and sexual nature of the acts he committed. Dr Shand's diagnosis depended on the gratification facet. If Glover got no sexual satisfaction or pleasure, his diagnosis would not apply.

"You need to know a lot more about what this guy's fantasies were all about. It's not just a matter of at the time of the murderous attack, did he have an erection or did he get some, you know, pelvic stirring or sexual excitement in a purely mental sense, it's also a question of how his fantasies at other times operated. I would be very surprised if at other times he had not had volumes of fantasies relating to what he finally put into action."

Glover never admitted to the fantasies. As the interviews went on, he continued to portray his actions as sudden, uncontrollable impulses where he was driven to murder while good John Glover watched.

Dr Shand thought Glover took it to an absurd point. On the second consultation he told Dr Shand that between the individual attacks and killings he had no recollection of having done it before, that each time was like the first.

"Oh Jesus," Shand thought to himself. It was totally inconsistent with the story that had been told before.

He said to him: "If that was the case, how do you explain the first overdose which you said was as a result of your remorse and horror at what you had done to five women?"

"Oh, um, I can see what you mean," Glover said.

Dr Rod Milton, who two years earlier had been working with police to identify the killer's personality, was called in by the prosecution to interview Glover. He saw him for five hours in the remand centre and could hardly hear himself talk with all the other visits going on around them. There was no table, just a bench along the side of the room.

Dr Milton put him through some basic tests. Glover was unable to remember a complex sentence even after a few tries. He was capable of interpreting proverbs "though not especially well". His general knowledge was satisfactory. His intellect overall was average or slightly better — possibly affected by his intake of alcohol, Milton thought, having been told of police surveillance observations about Glover's drinking. He thought Glover was capable of presenting himself as more intelligent than he really was. Glover spoke confidently about his business career, his life as a child and his service in the army. He told Milton he was hoping he would go to a mental hospital because it would be easier than in jail. He was less assured, becoming unsettled, when Dr Milton began to question him about the offences. He broke out in a sweat and was not keen to answer.

Milton experienced the same problem as Dr Shand with Glover's selective and limited answers. Milton had already spent many hours pouring over the crime scene reports and the police interviews. He felt that Glover was not going to give any answers more honest than what his deeds had already stated. Milton put a lot of stock in the belief that each crime scene was the enactment of a fantasy. In the crime scenes, Glover was making a statement more candid than anything he would ever admit. The strangulation with undergarments, the neat placement of shoes, the depersonalisation by covering the victims' heads and, most importantly, the incredible rage of the attacks — it all made a statement.

Because Glover killed women and robbed them and because of his history, Dr Milton started to think of him as a psychopath — a person with no conscience, who does not stick to the rules of society, who is prepared to do what he wants to get what he wants. The difference between that and the narcissistic personality is that the narcissist wants admiration. The narcissist is also very self-centred and that can lead to psychopathic traits. The big difference is that narcissistic personalities can maintain relationships and feel some social responsibility.

"You can take your choice with Glover," said Milton. "But I think his manipulativeness, his coldness, his willingness to just satisfy himself at anyone else's expense and his total lack of guilt I think is psychopathic."

Milton asked Glover about Gwen Mitchelhill: "She was walking down the street. This is where it becomes frustrating to me because as John Glover, sales manager of Four'N Twenty Pies, there seems to be another personality ... whatever comes out of me sees this person and wants to harm her. This personality, alter ego, whatever, like Mr Good Guy and Mr Bad Guy, picks up a hammer from under the seat of the car kept there for work purposes and follows her into her flat entrance. It comes to me that I recall it in detail because I was there but not as the perpetrator of the act, but as another part of me committing this act."

Asked how he felt: "It's as if I am watching someone through there committing this act. I'm saying that I really don't know the feeling of the person that is doing this dreadful thing."

Glover said he had tried to come to grips with his problem. "I have tried to reason with it, I know what happened, I saw it happen, it was quick, this other part of me finishes what it's doing. I'm back in the car and I'm John Glover, sales manager, going back home ... there's no way as a family man I could do such a thing."

Asked what his feelings were at the time of the murder, Glover did not answer. Instead he talked about not having much education and said this made it hard for him to describe his feelings.

"Which personality washed the hammer?" Milton asked.

"It must have been the alter ego. The alter ego must have returned at that time, I can barely recall doing anything with it [the hammer]."

Milton observed that he looked rather uncomfortable. "Who was the predominant personality on the way home from the murders?"

"John Glover Mr Nice Guy, but the other part came out briefly to take the hammer and try to clean it up."

"Tell me about the neat placement of the shoes and the walking sticks."

"I've thought about this quite a lot — again, I've not tried to evade the issues but I can't find any issues; it doesn't mean anything to me."

Asked why there was such a long delay between the murder of Lady Ashton and the attack on Doris Cox, Glover said: "Obviously the memories of it and the responsibility and the guilt ... but it seemed as if this other personality was carrying it — it wasn't me. I went about my life and work quite normally."

Glover said his second suicide attempt was "to stop this other side of me from doing anything else. If I had to go with it, then so be it."

Asked about sexual function, Glover said it did not worry his wife. She accepted it as one of the inevitable changes of age. However, he wondered about his impotence as a motivating factor, saying, "When you start to lose your manhood you start to clutch at anything." He did not think his alcohol intake was a problem: "My grandfather and Charlie Chaplin were both pisspots but they were both very horny at ninety-three."

"Did you get any satisfaction from the killing?" Milton asked.

"You mean was there any gratification? I knew there was something wrong happening but I was not in control. I was observing, I was fully cognisant of what was happening."

Having apologised for his language skills moments earlier he used a word like "cognisant".

Glover put his head on his hand to give the impression of experiencing emotion, according to Milton. "I just get this rush of remorse and start to feel for the relatives of the victims, for my own family, apart from it being an horrendous affair. I wish I could have stopped it from going on."

Asked about his stealing: "It was a Bohemian attitude — if I didn't have something that someone else had I just took it — as opposed to stealing for gain."

When Milton asked whether he had any emotional problems, he said: "Only the usual falling in and out of love as a teenager." On the army: "I thought I'd been put together. It's like potter's clay, you're off centre for years and years, then all of a sudden you centre the clay and start to make something out of it."

Asked what he felt while peeping: "It's hard to describe because I have got this duality — it starts to appear then. Normally, John Glover the happy working person, life and soul of the party, wouldn't hurt a fly; then his alter ego comes out, wants to hurt people. It wasn't hurting like striking with implements, it was humiliation ... By saying things like alter ego, humiliation et cetera I am not trying to dodge the responsibility for what I have done, I'm trying to clarify."

Glover told Milton about his dislike for Freda and the way she had used him, but said he continued to pay "due deference" to her because of his old-fashioned values of respecting one's elders. Asked about Essie, he said: "I couldn't stand the woman, my wife couldn't stand her either. We lived with them for a long time. Once again the old values came through and I paid due deference to her. I respected her for being my mother-in-law." Dr Milton said Glover tried unsuccessfully to convey sadness and deep concern for his victims and their families. He rejected the "good side, bad side" concept, saying Glover had too much to gain from presenting himself that way.

Milton concluded that Glover killed because he liked it. In searching for a description of Glover, Dr Milton recalled a conference he had been to a year earlier where a doctor from the United States, Dr Richard Walter, described the "anger retaliatory-type predator". It fitted Glover to a T, he thought.

When murdering, Milton concluded, Glover felt "gratification, anticipation, and anticipated pleasure and the pleasure of expressing anger". He felt this because of the grudge he bore against a particular type of woman — in this case old women.

If an anger retaliatory-type person sees a person in the particular category to which they have an aversion, they feel a rage welling inside them. If the opportunity arises, they will murder. If it is in a secluded place they will experiment with the body in a sexual way. They are usually too angry to get sexually erect.

All those things applied to John Glover, Dr Milton argued. His impotence prevented sexual arousal anyway, but it was obvious that there was a strong sexual element in what he was doing.

Dr Walter explained that this type of person does not plan their actions in great detail, but they have a whole repertoire of behaviours all ready to use. "Like soldiers going out on patrol, they don't exactly know what they are going to do, but they have in mind certain actions that they will operate."

"So this sort of person plans it, but the plans are fairly loose and they do take tremendous risks," said Milton. Milton theorised that the reason Glover did not give more detail about what he did was because "he continues to fantasise in his mind about the pleasure of what he did. It was a great pleasure for him to commit these things.

They are not acts in the strict sense of sadism, not quite the sense of seeing someone suffer because I think he killed quite quickly. So it wasn't so much the suffering that he enjoyed. It was the tremendous powerful feeling of killing and then the enjoyment of some sort of sexual experimentation. Almost like the way boys peep through the bathroom door at their mum having a shower. It gets that kind of feeling. One could imagine him doing some sort of experimentation, exploration or defilement of the body in a sexual way. Certainly the bodies are positioned that way and he covers the heads up to depersonalise them. Somehow he didn't want that person to be Mrs Sinclair, he wanted her to be something else.

Milton theorised that, while the anger went back to Glover's past, he wanted the victims to remain anonymous. "I think he just wanted to get on with the business of whatever sexual experimentation he was carrying out," Dr Milton explained.

But the anger did relate to his past. "The most likely things are incestuous feelings towards his mother and anger at the mother for making him feel jealous, and anger at the mother being sexually available to other men when he was an adolescent.

"The timing: when his parents broke up he was just entering adolescence. When she remarried one could anticipate that during that time of his early adolescence just as sexual development was going on, she was entertaining men at home or doing things like that which must have offended him a lot."

The last doctor to see Glover was Dr John Strum. He encountered the same difficulties as the others in getting Glover to give detailed accounts of his actions. But he interpreted it differently to the others.

Dr Strum found Glover to be a puzzle. On the one hand he was open and willing to help, but he had a "poverty of feelings". His memory was unclear and "there was a flatness of emotion, almost as though he was talking about someone else".

He was not like the psychopaths Strum had seen. At one point Glover became tearful "and very scared". But he was dismissive of the actual crimes he committed.

Strum discussed "badness". But John Glover could not see himself as bad because he had been good to his family. It left Strum scratching his head. Strum thought about the possibility of a split personality being present when Glover told him about good John Glover and bad John Glover. However, he dismissed the possibility as unlikely. He paid more attention to Glover's way of talking about a cutting off of feelings: "You see these old ladies and you become overwhelmed with rage and you have to hit them."

Glover told Dr Strum that there were other crimes he had committed for which he had not been charged, which occurred prior to the attack on Mrs Todhunter. Glover said he molested four old women in nursing homes prior to his first violent attack, on Mrs Todhunter.

Dr Strum was beginning to look at the problem in a way which was becoming increasingly common in the United States when dealing with serial killers. He was less inclined to challenge Glover on the inconsistencies and the memory lapses, viewing them to be part of the whole make-up of Glover.

He viewed Glover's history of violence as the phases in an illness. The attack on Mrs Todhunter was the point at which the illness progressed into a violent stage which carried through the murders. The illness had got out of hand to the point where he could not contain the hostility. The behaviour became more violent and more uncontrolled and more daring.

The attack on Mrs Sinclair and the attempted suicides were the beginning of the final, self-destructive phase of the illness. Dr Strum believed him when he said there was no sexual gratification and he did not get an erection from the attacks.

The defence had called in one other senior forensic psychiatrist, who was close to finding Glover insane but changed his mind at the last moment. So, after a month of having his brain analysed, and with a week to go before the trial, Glover told Dawn: "I wish we could just get on a boat and sail away."

Glover's state of unease about the pending trial worried Dawn. She privately feared he might attempt a third suicide.

"Why do they need the dramatics, why don't they just give me the sentence," Glover said. "They've got every man and his dog appearing. I wish they would get it over and done with," he said, depressed.

"If there was any time since his arrest when he would have taken his life, it was that time," Dawn said.

CHAPTER TWENTY-TWO

ON TRIAL

The trial opened before Justice James Wood in the Darlinghurst Supreme Court, Sydney, on Monday 18 November 1991.

Conspicuous by its absence outside the grand Victorian sandstone building was the screaming mob which had called for the lynching of so many other high profile killers in previous years. The mob had been uninterested in Glover from the start. While his killing spree had inspired terror, the murder of elderly people did not seem to evoke a corresponding degree of rage against the perpetrator. The return of capital punishment never raised its head as an issue.

One hundred and fifty prospective jurors were marshalled, taking up every available seat in the court. Justice Wood took the unusual step of having the charges against Glover read aloud, before asking for jury candidates wishing to abstain from selection to state their reason.

A dark-haired man, dressed in a navy blue suit, said he had been questioned by police over the murders. The excuse could have applied to thousands of north shore men but he was excused.

The jury settled at seven men and five women crossing age barriers and with no obvious pattern.

A sheepish looking Glover was brought before the court through an underground tunnel. It was the first time most people in the court had laid eyes on him, but nobody showed much expression. An old man at the back stood up for a better view then shook his head with a disbelieving look that seemed to say, "Him, the granny killer?"

Glover sat motionless in the red cedar dock. His head faced straight forward as it would for the next two weeks, his eyes occasionally glancing sidewards to take in the media box three metres to his right, the detectives box three metres to his left and the jury behind them.

The jury appeared reluctant at first to look at him. Detectives O'Toole, Mayger, Jacob and Byrnes, who each sat in the booth most days, had no such aversion.

In the public gallery was a large woman with a blonde wig sitting outlandishly on her head. No one in the room but Glover knew who she was, but he dared not look at her. It was Dawn, and they both feared she would be publicly exposed. By then she had found work at a private hospital and had arranged her shifts to allow her to be in the court for most of the trial.

Glover pleaded not guilty to all six counts of murder.

That night, the steel door to Glover's cell swung open with a loud clang followed by the sound of metal striking the cold concrete floor. There were sniggers and laughter in the darkness as the door slammed shut with an echoing bang, the sudden late night ruckus shaking Glover from his sleep with a jolt.

As his eyes adjusted in the dim light, a blurred object on the floor slowly took the shape of a hammer. It was a macabre joke by the prison guards but for an hour he lay there staring at the implement, too scared to reach out and touch it, frightened he was being set up for something. Then tiredness overwhelmed him and he dozed off back to sleep.

Two loud raps on the floor behind a large oak door signalled the entrance of Justice Wood each morning to Courtroom Five, cloaked in a purple gown with red sash, a squat woollen wig sitting squarely on his head.

It was a testing time for Glover the vain opportunist — having the past he sought to hide revealed publicly along with the horrors of his crimes. To those who observed or spoke to him in court during the trial, it was hard to reconcile John Glover, serial killer, with the personable grey-haired man sitting quietly in the dock. Dressed each day in one of two striped grey shirts, matched with blue jeans and tennis shoes, he looked more like a man one would find sitting at the local bowling club than a major criminal.

Crown Prosecutor Wendy Robinson, Queen's Counsel, was hardly a vindictive or even flamboyant Crown advocate. She was dispassionate and blunt in her pursuit of Glover, having brought the Crown case through from the beginning in the Lower Magistrates Court. Dressed in wig and black gown she stood before him again, accusing him and arguing his sanity before the jury. She described in calm detail how Glover strangled and bashed the life out of his frail and helpless victims.

Glover could not stand her. "How are you holding up?" he was asked by the police guard, Constable Richard Stephens, during a break in proceedings.

"She's a real hard one she is, she's a real hard one," Glover replied.

"What are you talking about?"

"The prosecutor."

Glover pointed to the walls of his cell and in an exasperated tone said: "I've been up that wall, and I have been up that wall and I've only got that one and that one to go. I'm getting there though, I'll crack sooner or later." Glover threw his hands in the air, sighed and ran his fingers through his hair and said: "I've had enough, she's driving me up the wall."

"Well," said the young constable, "remember the crimes you've committed. She is a female prosecutor and women have been murdered."

Constable Stephens, one year out of the Academy and seconded from Kings Cross police station, found Glover to be "a Santa Claus figure". It was the same description Dawn had used.

He escorted Glover to and from Long Bay and chatted with him in the century old underground holding cells. To the young constable Glover was big and jovial, with smile lines around his eyes and mouth. "You deal with other murderers and really they're just arseholes of people, but this guy was, if you didn't take into account what he did, you would say he was actually a nice old man."

"I suppose you're missing your family," the policeman said one day.

"Yeah, I don't think they'll like all this publicity."

"He would come in and he would get a little bit stressed if you asked him about the court, then after that he was okay. He was always very gentle, he would always politely place his hands out to get handcuffed."

Every morning during the trial Glover would be taken from his cell in the remand centre to a special holding yard at the jail, known as the bird cage, where the prison vans would wait before the 20 minute trip to the city. Glover was placed in a van with steel panelled isolation compartments because he was under protection due to fears that other prisoners might try to get him.

On one side of the truck there was room for ten "mainstream prisoners" and this area was always full. Glover shared the other half of the cabin with several other protection prisoners, all handcuffed.

On the morning of Friday 22 November 1991, the routine was broken when Glover was taken under special escort to Prince Henry Hospital for a CAT scan to determine if he had ever suffered any abnormal brain damage. His lawyers believed such damage could be used to account for his actions. The tests were kept secret from the jury at the time because the results may have proved crucial to their verdict but they found nothing unusual about his brain.

As Glover stepped from the van that day, his wrists handcuffed, the media were waiting in ambush. Photographer Geoff Henderson snuck in to the hospital grounds and snapped him with a long lens. As he was approached by prison guards, Henderson ditched the film into some bushes and cleared out, returning later to collect it. It was the first published picture of the granny killer and appeared that afternoon on the front page of the *Daily Telegraph Mirror*.

On the first weekend break of the trial Dawn visited him at Long Bay Jail. "I don't think anyone has ever been so glad to see me as he was that weekend." On previous visits Glover would walk up and kiss her on the cheek, but this time he was nervous and put his hand out to shake hers, all the time looking around for somebody watching. He was worried that someone might take a photograph of them kissing.

The week in court had left him uptight but the next week was going to be harder. The first week consisted mostly of cold analysis of what had happened and there was little dispute. The second week was going to tackle the question of *why* it happened. The psychiatrists would have their say and he might be called to make a statement.

Glover urged Dawn repeatedly during both her visits that weekend to end the relationship. "Give me a miss, don't come back," he said with a depressed tone in his voice. "I'm not getting out, I am going to be here for the rest of my life."

"Okay, if that's what you want," she said, her patience exhausted.

The next opportunity Glover had to make a phone call he was on the phone to Dawn apologising: "Dawn, I'm sorry ... I need you ..."

Glover had suddenly become a face in the jail. His picture in Friday's paper had been picked up by television and was seen by other prisoners. His 18 months of anonymity at the Bay were over.

As Glover stepped from the prison van at the rear of Darlinghurst Supreme Court on the following Monday morning he was recognised by the hardline prisoners from whom he was still segregated. They began shouting and jeering angrily from the van in which they were held.

They stomped their feet and banged their fists against the metal frame of the van, rocking it. "MURDERER, MURDERER!" they screamed with no hint of irony. "We're going to get you, we're going to kill you!" But Glover did not react.

"I think he was worried about it underneath but on the surface it was like water off a duck's back," said Constable Stephens, who had the job of calming the rabble.

That afternoon, the moment Glover had really been worried about came along. For six days reporters and members of the public, including the relatives of some of his victims sitting in the court, had watched, wondering if they would hear his story — hear him explain his deeds. His defence decided he would make an unsworn statement from the dock. He did not have to swear an oath and it meant the prosecution was not allowed to cross-examine him on it, but it carried less weight than sworn evidence from the witness box.

There was absolute silence when he spoke. Reporters scribbled furiously into their notebooks. They hung on every word.

"Your Honour, ladies and gentlemen of the jury ... I have been asked to make this statement from the dock as some form of evidence," Glover said nervously, beginning what was to be a 20 minute statement.

He said he knew the killings took place but "I don't know why they occurred". Glover said he was full of remorse for his victims and their families, as well as for his own family.

On several occasions he wept, visibly fighting to control his tears and maintain his composure. It happened after he spoke of his tortured life. His birth in England, the troubled divorce of his parents, life in the army, his move to Australia to start a new life.

He told of how he had served his two year contract as a tram conductor in Victoria (when in fact he had been sacked after three months). Then he brushed over his 1962 attacks on two women in Melbourne by saying: "No death occurred. I was put on probation."

"There was another matter which arose. I was accused of voyeurism, which was proved and I admitted anyway," Glover said.

"I mention these because I think they are relevant to the matters in hand." Then he paused, struggling to get the words out, the tears welling up in his eyes. "Explanations I can't give you," he said in a trembling voice. He began to sob. The tears overwhelmed him and he was given a few minutes to compose himself.

He resumed with bowed head: "My relations with women at that time — before, during and after — were quite normal, quite successful." He detailed his marriage and the move to Sydney but broke down once more when talking of the birth of his daughters and giving them good educations — everything he never had as a child. He was given a glass of water before continuing.

"My lifestyle in Mosman was superb ... lots of friends ... no worries ... I was well respected ... belonged to good clubs. But when it happened it was 'see someone and attack'. I felt detached, as if I was witnessing the thing and not actually doing it ... it's the only way I can explain it."

He said Joan Sinclair was a friend killed by the bad John Glover and in turn the good John Glover tried to kill the bad by attempting suicide. Then he turned his head and, looking at Detective Sergeant O'Toole in the police box, Glover said: "I wish to Christ you would have found me before."

Tears trickled down his cheeks. "The last 20 months I've had ample time for reflection and this may come out during the course of the trial, that it has been commented I have shown no remorse for these matters. That is absolute nonsense. What I've got locked up for, the victims, families, relatives and mine ... I am sorry [sobbing], I can't say any more."

For the first time during the trial Dawn was absent from the gallery after promising Glover she would not witness him bare his soul. "Don't come, because if I see you I will look at you and they [the press and spectators in the gallery] will wonder, wonder who I am looking at," Glover begged her. "I need to be able to concentrate. I have just got to fix my eyes on a point in the room and pretend I am not there."

On the seventh day of evidence, 26 November 1991, Glover celebrated his 59th birthday. He seemed to be in better spirits.

As usual, he was brought under guard into the court that morning before the jury and judge entered. In that brief interlude before proceedings began he chatted with lanky New Zealand-born journalist David Ikin.

"What a way to spend your 59th birthday," Glover said, a world-weary expression on his face.

"Will you be celebrating back at the jail tonight?" Ikin inquired, hanging on every word, not daring to pull out his pen for fear of the court sheriffs.

"Well, I expect some sort of prank on my return to Long Bay tonight — maybe the fellas will have short sheeted my bed, or put cornflakes in it, or stick a cockroach in my sandwich, something like that.

"I'm trying to make the most of life in jail. I'm in protection with an interesting bunch of guys. No names, but we've got ex-police, ex-politicians, the lot. It's an interesting little debating club.

"I also play a lot of chess and I'm also a crossword fanatic."

Glover expressed a desire to return to the prison hospital where he spent his first 15 months in custody. "There, they had outside caterers and if someone had a birthday the date would pop up on a computer and they would get a cake.

"It wasn't much but it was something. A thought at least."

Glover had taken to ringing Dawn, leaving messages on her answering machine when she was not home. "Dawn, it's day seven, it's eight o'clock ... I'm alright ... don't worry, it's going as expected ... I'm getting through," he would say before hanging up. Dawn would know if he had a bad day in court by the inflection in his voice.

Glover's plea of diminished responsibility meant the case was going to revolve around the psychiatric evidence. Dr Strum was called first, then Dr Shand and then Dr Milton — all differing in their views but all in agreement that Glover was sane in the eyes of the McNaghten rules that test a person's sanity in the eyes of the law.

Basically, the McNaghten legal test (devised in the late 19th century and still used in the UK and the US) is this. If a person can intellectually understand the difference between right and wrong and the consequences of his behaviour, then the person is legally sane.

While all three doctors said Glover was sane, Dr Strum argued for a fair degree of diminished responsibility owing to the illness which he diagnosed Glover as having. Dr Shand also said there was some degree of abnormality of mind from his "sexual sadism".

The prosecution was getting worried. Then Dr Milton got up and told the jury about what fun Glover was having all the while he was killing. Dr

Milton had changed part of his diagnosis, reclassifying Glover as a narcissist rather than a psychopath, but his main diagnosis, the "anger retaliatory", remained.

During Dr Milton's time in the witness stand Glover came to despise him. His evidence would decide his fate.

Perhaps Dr Milton's most telling statement was a warning about the common perception of insanity. "When I endeavoured to understand the motivation behind the killings, I was reminded that most people, when confronted with such outrageous violence resulting in tragedy for so many, are overwhelmed and tend to interpret the violence as the result of mental illness — it is difficult for them to conceive that a sane man could obtain satisfaction from repeatedly killing elderly women and defiling and humiliating them sexually." Milton argued that there are sane men who do all these things.

In his final submission, the defence counsel, Mr Leary, said that psychiatric evidence had shown Glover was suffering an abnormality of mind at the time of the killings.

"We're not saying this man is mad," Mr Leary said. The facts, he said, had established that Glover had diminished responsibility over his actions. "It would be less than normal if you didn't have some prejudices."

In her final submission, prosecutor Wendy Robinson told the jury that Glover "had organised himself in a premeditated fashion so he was able to strike again when the opportunity arose". Glover had always kept a hammer and gloves used in the killings in his car, and had given himself regular access to places where he might find suitable victims, she said. "From the time of the death of the first victim, the accused was constantly on the ready for a suitable opportunity to commit another killing."

On Friday 29 November 1991, Justice Wood addressed the jury. He told them they must bring to the case their "fair, unbiased minds".

Justice Wood said the prosecution claimed Glover was fully cognisant of what he had committed and that his actions bore an affinity with those of a serial killer. But he reminded the jurors that the defence had asked them to set aside any distaste they might feel about the crimes.

Glover sat with his head bowed, never raising it as Justice Wood recounted a detailed summary of evidence given during the two week trial. Every member of the jury had been given folders containing a chronology of each of the murders and another six assaults upon elderly women. Photographs of the victims in death were omitted as it would have emotively prejudiced Glover's defence.

Before sending the jury away to consider its verdict, Justice Wood told them: "You have to decide whether by reason of the mental state of the accused his responsibility for the crimes is reduced." The jury retired at 1.05 p.m.

CHAPTER TWENTY-THREE
PRISONER 13

riday 29 November 1991 was a beach weather day, hot and balmy with a clear blue sky greeting early risers. It was the type of summer's day that would tempt almost anyone to take the day off work to hit the surf.

For members of the 70 strong "granny killer" task force, it was *their* day in court.

From the outset, no matter how much Dawn told herself to put on a brave face, she knew it was Glover's day of public reckoning. A day that would determine whether he spent the rest of his life in jail and, if he did, whether he would spend it in a prison or a psychiatric institution.

She wondered how John would react, how she would handle the final scene in court. Her nerves made her stomach feel like it was tied in knots. She did not want to give herself away after all of this. Which wig to wear, the blonde or brunette?

But before she had a chance to walk out the front door of her inner western suburbs home, her nerves were to be placed further on edge by the detection of her relationship with John. There was an unexpected ring on her door bell. It was *Daily Telegraph Mirror* reporters Mark Jones and David Ikin.

"Dawn, can we have a few words with you about John?" It registered immediately that they were from the media. She was stunned. How the hell did they find out about her?

Her youngest son was standing near the closed door. She didn't know what to do, it was difficult to speak to them with him there. She refused to let them in. It was a strange scene. Questions were fired at her through the door and she replied from the other side, all the time hoping that they had not seen her. They told her Glover had already spoken to them. "What's he like?" Mark Jones called out from the other side of the door in his light cockney accent.

"Maybe the John Glover you write about isn't the John Glover I know," she retorted.

"Do you think your visits are helping him?"

"You'd really have to ask him that."

"Do you love him?"

"I don't think I can answer that because I don't know ... every person needs a friend. I'm just that person for John."

The visit had ruined her plans to go to court. She was worried she would be followed and photographed. Fearing the media would hound her throughout the day, Dawn rang the hospital and told her boss the reason why she had asked for the morning off. After abandoning her plans she managed to sneak out of the house and went to work.

It had taken the jury only two hours and 45 minutes of deliberation to decide Glover's fate — guilty on all six counts of murder. What had started as a bright and sunny day had turned grey as Justice Wood dispensed with any need to deliberate and turned to the task of sentencing the grandfatherly figure before him.

"This is a man, I'm afraid, of extreme cunning, of extreme dangerousness, who is prepared to attack whenever or wherever it pleases him," said Justice Wood in grave tones. "In any view, he has shown himself to be exceedingly dangerous and to protect the community he must remain for the rest of his natural life in jail."

By their verdict, said Justice Wood, the jury had rejected the defence proposal that Glover had suffered to such a degree as to constitute abnormality of mind, amounting to diminished responsibility.

"This is a case where the prisoner will never be released."

Glover was also sentenced by Justice Wood on three charges relating to other attacks on elderly women who survived, which he had admitted to at the beginning of the trial. They included four years for armed robbery with wounding, two years for robbery and three years for wounding with intent to do grievous bodily harm.

Glover, his shoulders hunched, showed no reaction to the sentence. As he waited for police to remove him from the court to the holding cell, he shed one solitary tear.

Reporters rushed to file copy and members of the task force shook hands in the detective's booth. They felt a sense of history. Kim Barwick had designed a commemorative tie featuring the scales of justice holding sway above a hammer perched atop a walking stick. The blue and red ties made their debut in court that day.

There were wide smiles when Detective Sergeant Dennis O'Toole walked from the court grounds into the mass of cameras and microphones. "I feel tremendous relief tonight. I am also greatly relieved for the relatives of the victims: they can now get on with their lives," he said.

The entire task force had been recommended for commendations. Within three months, Inspector Hagan was promoted to superintendent. The rest were still waiting for their awards at the time of writing.

Another person who beamed with relief as she left the court was Elaine Avis, the only daughter of Glover's third victim Margaret Pahud. "I came to court probably because I had my needs to see it happen. The police were fantastic all through, they worked terribly hard," she said. "The jury made the only decision they could have done."

Dawn was tending to an elderly patient — who had coincidentally lived at the Garrison retirement village when Glover attempted to murder Doris Cox there in 1989 — when the five o'clock news came on the radio. "A salesman charged with murders of six elderly women on Sydney's north shore has been sentenced to six life prison terms ..."

The news stunned her. She was speechless. Grief and sorrow welled up inside her.

"It all came to a head, it was such a weird feeling where you hope and hope that they will understand, that they'll be compassionate towards him, that he was a product of his childhood environment," she said. "One part of me said that they'll understand, but deep down I knew they wouldn't. I never thought that I would feel that way until that day. I can't explain how I was."

Tears began to stream down her face. The old patient could not understand what was wrong with her nurse.

Dawn could not work and sought condolence from a friend who told her it was not the end of the world. "You don't understand," Dawn sobbed, "they have given me a life sentence too."

Glover would stay in the holding cell of the court for five days. There was no room at the Bay and nobody really knew where to put him anyway.

"He was depressed. He would ring me, but was not allowed to say where he was. A policeman was with him all the time," said Dawn.

Her admission to her new employer about her relationship with Glover was soon being whispered about in the corridors by staff, some of whom had begun to give her a hard time. Soon she was told, "I think it might be better if you resigned." She left.

Dawn, a divorcée, has kept her surname private only because her youngest child, a son, is still at high school.

She resisted substantial cash offers from media outlets to tell her story, saying: "My friendship with John means more to me than money. I am not ashamed of the relationship that I have with John. If people don't like it then that is their problem."

Dawn has overheard people talking in shops about Glover's mystery woman and she "sort of laughs and walks away". "I heard people talking at my last job, a lot of them did not want to say it to my face."

One day she was confronted by an angry woman. "How could you, how could you even tolerate someone who has killed all of those defenceless women!"

Fed up, she turned around and said spitefully: "Well, actually I really think John did them a good turn." Sometime later she was able to laugh about how shocked the person must have been, but says: "I felt really bad after it."

Unlike most of Sydney, Dawn did not have much of an opinion about the murders when they were happening because she "lived on the other side of the harbour". A believer in euthanasia, she thought, "Thank God they were really old, they have seen everything.

"But I can't agree with murder, the way they died."

Dawn's relationship with John has brought her criticism from within her family. "My eldest son doesn't care about my visits to John. He calls him 'JJ Hammer' or says things like 'how's Hit With Hammer', as in the rap music star."

It was her daughter who was the most upset. Dawn's efforts to get to court each day had coincided with the birth of her daughter's first baby. She felt Dawn was spending too much time in court when she should have been tending to her as the birth drew nearer.

"Why is it that I can overlook the fact that he had killed six people and see the other side in him?" she asked a psychiatrist friend. "The reason why you can get on with him, Dawn, is because you met him after the fact," her friend said with concern in his voice. "He has never shown any aggression towards you or done anything to make you distrust him. For the same reasons, Dawn, you should be able to sever ties easily."

Another friend has got down on his hands and knees and begged her to stop seeing Glover. "Give him up Dawn, I don't want to see you get hurt," he has pleaded. She has ignored all such advice.

"The person who people saw in court is not the same person who I talk to every day. I believe that what happened to John was part of a split personality."

Dawn believes that John was under a great deal of pressure over the years from both his mother and mother-in-law. The fact that his mother-in-law constantly reminded him that he was from a background of no financial substance added to the pressures on his mind.

Her eyes become misty as she reflects back on the case.

I know that he committed the crimes, but I honestly do believe that there are extenuating circumstances. I thought he would get diminished responsibility.

I thought to myself that perhaps the only one they would get him on would be for the murder of Mrs Sinclair, because he had a hammer when he arranged to meet her. I talked to him about it and he said "I went there to get rid of myself"; he was thinking of his children and didn't want them to become involved if he took his life at his home. He thought Mrs Sinclair was the only friend whose home he could turn to take his own life discreetly, but he said, "There must have been a bad side to me then."

So who is Dawn's John Glover? Does she think he could have committed other murders?

"I know John has done really bad things, but I don't think the police really know much about John. From time to time he gets upset at media stories about him because he feels they may deter his daughters from coming to see him. He loves them so much and hopes that they will come one day to visit him."

One such report which made Glover furious was a *Daily Telegraph Mirror* story in January 1992, linking him to the unsolved 1977 murder of elderly socialite Florence Broadhurst.

"Did you do it John?" Dawn asked.

"No, I didn't do it. I only met her once and that was at the christening of one of my brother's children," he told her.

He could not recall meeting Florence at his brother Clifford's wedding. "I don't mind admitting to what I have done or what I know I have done, but not to anything else. They will have to go and find someone else to charge." Then in an exasperated voice he said: "I suppose they [the police] will come and talk to me."

"He has no reason to lie to me about that," says Dawn in his defence. Just because a murder sounds similar or he happened to live in the vicinity does not mean he carried out other murders, she says. "There is no reason for him to say 'I haven't done it'. He's not going to live six lifetimes."

To Dawn, Glover is a "very gentle man" who has since talked a young prisoner out of committing suicide, a man who has at last found peace in his troubled soul. She would trust Glover with her life. He said to her: "I don't think I can ever hurt anyone again." She believes him. "He has not shown any emotion to anybody other than me in the last two years."

"I really don't think that I would be scared to be out on the streets alone with him. The feelings I now have for him have stopped me from having any life outside the jail."

Following his conviction John Walter Glover, alias John Wayne Glover, was given the highest maximum security "A" rating by the New South Wales Corrective Services prisoner classification committee. He also became the second convicted felon in New South Wales to receive a true life sentence (never to be released) under new laws passed shortly before his arrest known as the Truth in Sentencing Act.

His official prison classification number is 13 — lifer thirteen.

He is now just an old "lifer" who dreams of faraway places, of bliss and peace in a tropical paradise. It is a dream that those in whom he has confided don't want to shatter. Without this hope the few people who still care for him fear he will not survive. He dreams the impossible — that one day people will forgive him for the lives he took, accept that he is cured and release him. Maybe in the dawning of the 21st century ...

Dawn has continued to visit Glover at least twice, but usually three times, a week. They are contact visits with no barriers between them. On sunny days they sit in a small neatly kept garden in the Long Bay remand centre, a guard always close at hand. As they chat, the children visiting other inmates play around them, many wives and mothers of other prisoners often stopping to talk to the friendly looking grandfatherly figure with striking snow-coloured hair.

Between visits, John rings Dawn at her home when the privilege of a phone call allows it.

By the time of publication Glover will be in Goulburn Jail in the newly built maximum security multi-purpose prison for prisoners who need protecting from others. He will be able to cook his own meals but there will be no tennis courts or views of the sea.

CHAPTER TWENTY·FOUR
BRICK WALLS

D ennis O'Toole had been talking to John Glover for weeks after his
arrest. He felt they were building some kind of rapport. Glover,
sitting on the other side of the table in the Long Bay psychiatric
hospital, thought the same.

O'Toole sensed it was time to make the move, time to pop the
question. "John ... I want to ask you about some other murders."

"Which ones?" Glover retorted.

O'Toole was pleased, if a little startled, that there had been no
attempt to deny guilt. O'Toole was keen to talk to Glover about the death
of at least four old women in Melbourne more than 30 years earlier and
about the death of his mother, Freda, whose body was cremated two days
after her death.

But O'Toole particularly wanted to ask Glover about two women,
Josephine Veronica McDonald and Wanda Amudsen. The two had a lot
in common in the twilight of their lives.

They were practically neighbours for ten years in the sleepy New
South Wales central coast retirement community of Ettalong. They were
both regulars at the Ettalong War Memorial Club, a five-storey grey-tiled
complex which dominated the otherwise rustic Ettalong shopping centre.
Both women were widows and they both attended weekly bingo games
and luncheons for pensioners.

Wanda had retired to nearby Umina, across Broken Bay from Sydney's
northern beaches, in 1971. Following her husband's death in 1976, she
continued to live in their neat white fibro cottage, 15 minutes' walk from
the club in Memorial Avenue.

"Josie" McDonald lived two streets from the club. She too had fled
Sydney, settling in Ettalong in 1974. Seventy per cent of the 20,000
people living in Ettalong and Umina were retirees who could delight in
the magnificent views of Broken Bay and Barrenjoey Head five kilometres
away. The same view from the Sydney side of the bay was for millionaires
only but in Ettalong it was working-class country.

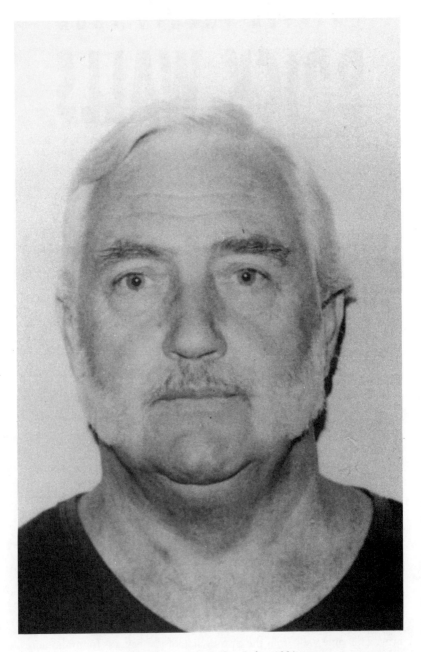

John Glover in Long Bay Jail in 1991.

In such a community it was surprising that Josie McDonald and Wanda Amudsen never met when their lives had so much in common. Josie's death in 1984 ensured they would never encounter each other but, in death, their names became intertwined.

On the late winter's afternoon of 28 August 1984, Josie McDonald, 73, sat down at the Ettalong Hotel for her once-weekly tipple with a group of elderly widowed friends. They would sit, some sipping shandy — beer with a dash of lemonade — in the palm tree-lined concrete beer garden facing the ocean at the rear. No one ever saw Josie drunk and she was always spotless.

The following night, Josie went to the club again, dressed smartly in a black and white spotted dress. Under one arm she carried a black handbag. She was in good spirits. Around 10 p.m., she left the club smiling, with extra cash in her purse after winning some money on a poker machine. It was a clear night. The sky beamed with stars and spring was only two days away. She decided to walk.

At 7.30 a.m. the next day a neighbour on his way out on an errand noticed Mrs McDonald's front door slightly ajar. The morning newspapers were sitting on the verandah. It was odd, but he thought nothing of it until he returned home at 1.30 p.m. and, on seeing the door still open, went to see if Josie was alright.

"Knock, knock, hullo," he called. "Hello ... Josie, are you alright?"

Pushing the door gently open he peered down the hallway and stared in disbelief. On the floor, two metres away, lay Josie.

She was naked but for a pink pullover which had been bunched up around her shoulders and over her face with her pink bra. Her pantyhose and panties were draped across her neck which showed signs of severe bruising. There was severe bruising and bleeding around her vaginal area.

A later examination of the scene by police found no sign of a struggle or forced entry to the home. A postmortem carried out at Gosford mortuary put the official cause of death down to strangulation by the pantyhose. The postmortem also found injuries to the vaginal, anal and facial areas of the body. Mrs McDonald had been struck a heavy blow to the face which caused a depressed fracture of a cheekbone.

Josie McDonald was only 140 cm tall so detectives deduced she was smaller than her killer. They believed the killer possibly picked her up or had followed her from the club, barging his way into her home when she opened the door.

In the week following her murder, amid local and national newspaper publicity, six other elderly women came forward to Woy Woy police with reports that they had been beaten, raped and sexually assaulted by a man who attacked them in their homes. The attacks, described as savage and sexually sadistic, had taken place in the Ettalong, Erina and Woy Woy areas over a three month period leading up to Mrs McDonald's murder.

Investigating Detective Sergeant Bill Smith of Woy Woy police said the women had been too frightened and embarrassed to report the attacks. Many of them, after being grossly humiliated by the ordeal, feared their identities would be revealed if they became involved in court cases and so refused to take matters further.

"The attacks have been very savage and often obscene," said Detective Smith. Many of the women never recovered from the trauma and died soon after the attacks.

Detective Smith said police believed that up to a dozen women may have encountered the man and appealed for them to come forward. Two weeks after Josie's murder a blurred picture began to emerge of the killer-rapist — a man aged somewhere between his late-20s and mid-40s.

On each occasion, the victims, all aged above 65, were followed from a club or hotel after enjoying a few drinks. Five of the women, like Mrs McDonald, had been attacked after leaving the Ettalong War Memorial Club. In each of those attacks the women, unaware that they were being followed, were set upon from behind as they opened the front doors to their homes. It was a well-rehearsed pattern.

The sixth attack occurred after the victim had been drinking at a Woy Woy Hotel. The woman was taken by a man in a car to the Woy Woy garbage tip where she was raped and assaulted before she managed to escape and run for help.

On each occasion the attacker physically assaulted and threatened to kill the women. From sketchy details given by the women, police tried to compile an identikit of the attacker, but never released it because he struck with such suddenness and violence that his victims were never given enough time to see him. Some of the victims were so traumatised that they could not remember what their attacker looked like.

Despite so many victims, police still found it impossible to gather enough information from the public to build a profile on the rapist.

Public hysteria in the wake of the attacks was to be echoed five years later in the Sydney harbourside suburb of Mosman at the height of the granny serial killings. According to the local newspaper, the *Central Coast Express*, one community club's attendances dropped so dramatically that it was forced to reschedule all its functions for pensioners to daylight hours. As with the north shore serial murders years later, a bus shuttle service for elderly women was introduced to and from their homes.

Police appeals for information from the public yielded no new leads on the attacker. The trail had gone cold. Frustrated, Detective Smith warned publicly that the man would continue to attack elderly women, even kill again, if he was not stopped.

"Bluzzz, Bluzzz, Bluzzz," shrilled the small telephone switchboard at Woy Woy police station.

"I'm a bit concerned about Mrs Amudsen," the nervous sounding young woman at the other end of the phone told the constable. "I haven't seen her in her garden for a couple of days. I think someone should check to see if she is all right."

Wanda Amudsen was an independent, 83-year-old grandmother who lived only eight blocks from Josie McDonald at Umina. Like most elderly residents living alone on the peninsula, it had taken her over a year to forget about the fear induced by the McDonald murder. At last though, life seemed to have returned to normal.

She began to feel lucky again to have escaped the city with all its crime. Just so long as she could see plenty of her four grandchildren, she was happy with her garden and with following her favourite football team. Mrs Amudsen also had two other passions: bingo and the odd dabble on the pokies.

But on the afternoon of Friday 21 November 1986, terror revisited the peninsula. News of it started at 5.25 p.m. with the rather innocuous phone call by a woman expressing concern for Mrs Amudsen. The woman said her name was Mrs Harrison, and that she was a neighbour of Mrs Amudsen.

Two uniformed officers were despatched in a patrol car to Mrs Amudsen's modest two-bedroom fibro cottage. There, in the hallway near the entrance to the bathroom, they found the figure of a woman in a pool of blood.

There was something strange about the scene — the killer had taken sheets and pillows from a nearby bedroom and piled them over her head. As the constables peeled back the material, they were greeted by the sight of the bludgeoned head of Mrs Amudsen. In the kitchen they found preparations for an evening meal.

News of the murder sent shock waves through the tiny community. Terrified elderly people began locking themselves inside their homes.

Locals openly blamed the two murders on "townies" — strangers and tourists from the city who flocked to the Central Coast during holidays. They also cast suspicion on the peninsula's youth, blaming the violence on the increasing rate of drug-related crime in the area — similar feelings to those voiced in Mosman during the granny killer's 12 month spree.

Mrs Amudsen's son, Hilton, drove from Sydney to Umina on the night of the discovery after being notified by police. They wanted to know what was missing and he looked around but everything seemed in place. There was even money still lying around and $110 in a tin in a wardrobe was left intact.

But slowly a bizarre inventory of missing items came to notice. The house had been partially ransacked and bedroom drawers were left open. Only odd things were taken, as though the killer had stolen for souvenir value alone.

There was a blue and grey china clown worth about $100, which Mrs Amudsen had bought during a holiday in Hong Kong. It was missing from the lounge room along with polyester curtains, which had been taken from three rooms.

Also gone were family photographs and a framed picture of Mrs Amudsen's little granddaughter. Mr Amudsen told police of 16 photographs of relatives in the back yard of his mother's home which were gone from a box. Mrs Amudsen's wedding rings remained in open view on her dressing table.

Also missing from the house was the removable plastic bucket from a kitchen tidy bin. The flip-top lid was found inside the house but the bin was located the next day in an old 44 gallon drum at the back of a nearby house.

Detectives speculated that it was used to carry stolen property from the house. The name and address given to police by the caller who alerted them to Mrs Amudsen also proved to be false.

It was the fact that Josie McDonald, like Mrs Amudsen, visited the Ettalong War Memorial Club once a week which brought Homicide detectives from Sydney to the scene within 24 hours.

From canvasses of the area police established that Mrs Amudsen was last seen alive at 11.30 a.m. on Wednesday 19 November, two days earlier. At that time she had attended a senior citizens lunch at the club and had left on her own.

Robbery was ruled out early on. The attack was too bizarre, too ferocious.

The adjacent cottages had been vacant for some time except for one house owned by a semi-retired man who kept an eye on Mrs Amudsen. He neither saw nor heard anything.

Police fingerprint expert Detective Sergeant Bruce McLaughlin was called to the scene on the night Mrs Amudsen was found. "It was a strange one, just different. With Josie it was rape and strangle, but Wanda was sort of just bashed and stuff was put over her face to cover her up and odd things like curtains were missing. We thought, gee this is strange, why would they take personal type stuff. We were even starting to suspect the families and that ...

"We thought with Wanda Amudsen, that it might have been something like a hammer hit her, you know ..."

McLaughlin found two lots of fingerprints — one on the lid of the toilet seat and one near the body near the bathroom door. There was a small drop of blood on the seat where it was believed she was sitting watching television.

A postmortem found that Wanda Amudsen had been dead for 48 hours before her body was discovered. Her injuries revealed tremendous ferocity and rage on the part of the killer.

It found that she had died from five heavy blows to the back of her head — inflicted by a hammer similar to that used in the north shore murders. The pile of pillows and linen heaped over her body covering her head was not unlike Glover's signature in the Sinclair, Cleveland and Falconer murders of pulling clothing over the victims' heads — an action which forensic psychiatrists interpret as the killer trying to depersonalise their victim. "One blow would have been enough to knock her to the ground, but she was hit four or five times, so it appears the killer kept hitting her even when she was on the ground," an officer said.

Added to this was the puzzle of the mystery woman caller. Detectives asked themselves: was she a participant, or did she accidentally stumble upon the murder after it happened and steal items from the house?

Earlier in the investigation they believed the woman, dubbed Miss X, may have killed Mrs Amudsen accidentally during a bungled burglary and then fled, later calling police out of concern. But the autopsy result blew this theory out of the water. The savage nature of the blows was consistent with a male having struck her.

In a strange twist, Miss X, aged between 20 and 22, her hair dark and in a shaggy unkempt bob, used Mrs Amudsen's bank book to withdraw money the day after she was murdered — the day before Mrs Amudsen's body was discovered. It was only a small amount of cash and the withdrawal slip appeared to have been signed by Mrs Amudsen. Police hypothesised that the woman may have found the pre-signed withdrawal slip and bank book dumped in the street by Mrs Amudsen's killer.

On 19 December 1986, police released a photofit picture of a man with a ruddy face and nose similar to Glover, but with dark hair. The man was wanted for assault and rape several days earlier upon a 73-year-old disabled woman at her Umina home.

The woman had returned home after a meeting and was confronted by a man in her lounge room who punched her in the face and knocked her to the ground before raping her. She described the man as 178 cm tall and aged between 35 and 45, and said he was well tanned and appeared overweight.

No new information was forthcoming from the lead. In late July 1988, police re-opened investigations into the murders of both women after an elderly woman came forward and informed them she had been attacked a year earlier, but had not reported it to police out of embarrassment.

A special task force based at Woy Woy was formed, setting up a telephone hotline and appealing for information into the past attacks. Police were certain there were more old women out there too frightened to come forward.

But police closed the hotline empty-handed after a few weeks. They had plenty of new information on crime in the area but nothing further on the murders.

In early November 1989, following the murder of Muriel Falconer — the fifth murder in the north shore granny killer series — Gosford police were asked to forward details of both murders to the task force. It was around this period that the task force switched their suspicions from a youth to a middle-aged man.

Mrs Falconer's murder bore all the combined characteristics of the McDonald and Amudsen murders. As with Mrs McDonald she was attacked at her front door by a killer who barged his way into her home as she opened the door to enter. Like both Central Coast victims she was found dead in the hallway.

As with Mrs McDonald her legs were splayed and clothes were pushed up to her chest, her pantyhose had been removed and she had been strangled. Like Mrs Amudsen she had been battered several times about the head with a carpenter's hammer by her killer, who then covered her face to depersonalise his victim.

Some officers said there could not be a connection with the north shore murders because Mrs McDonald had been raped. But Glover, by his own admission, had become sexually impotent since that time.

John Glover was a regular visitor to the Central Coast. He opened up Four'N Twenty's first route on the Central Coast in the year of Mrs McDonald's murder and ceased going up there in the year of Mrs Amudsen's slaying. He would drop in to see his mother Freda, sister Patricia and half-brother Clifford, who had all settled there in 1973.

When Dennis O'Toole first asked John Glover about the Central Coast shortly after his arrest, Glover replied: "I've never been there."

Forensic psychiatrists Dr John Shand and Dr Rod Milton, who both examined Glover, agree that he is almost certain to have attacked more women than he has admitted. They also agree that, in the light of evidence about the nature of both Central Coast murders and the attacks in which women survived, Glover was capable of the crimes.

Dr Milton is now of the opinion that Glover was the Central Coast murderer. "They, like the Falconer murder, are very well-rehearsed attacks. What he did to the women at the crime scenes are the secrets of his dreams," he said in his soft voice.

"Only he knows the full extent of his past crimes. He keeps them like photos in his mind as part of his ongoing stimulation. If he reveals them to anyone it would not be stimulating to him any more."

At the time of writing, and in the wake of Glover's conviction in November 1991 for the murders of six elderly women on Sydney's north shore, Homicide detectives were confident of Glover's involvement in the Central Coast murders. However, they expressed some doubt as to whether they would be able to land a conviction.

Dennis O'Toole has spent more hours talking to Glover since his arrest than anyone apart from Dawn. He is convinced of his involvement but says there are problems with reinvestigating Josie McDonald's murder. Vital exhibits such as sperm found splattered on and around her body and pants have disappeared, as have other crucial exhibits. The fingerprints have never been traced but are believed to belong to the anonymous female caller.

Glover's arrest and immediate confession to being a serial killer was viewed by other State Homicide Squads around Australia as more than just a unique case study. Like their New South Wales counterparts, they wondered if he had committed other murders, maybe even in their own States, which were still unsolved.

The Victoria Homicide Squad viewed him as a major catch. Since his arrest they have devoted hundreds of hours to retracing Glover's life and movements during his 12 years' residence in that State.

Their attention was drawn to the night of 3 June 1957. A group of teenage boys was playing in a park at the corner of Dandenong Road and Chapel Street in East St Kilda when one of them went to the toilet.

He walked into the women's by mistake and came running out. "There's a lot of blood on the floor," 15-year-old Ian Swannack shouted to his mates. They cautiously edged their way up the hedge-lined passageway back into the toilets. They could see a rivulet of blood running several metres from the door. Peering around the corner they saw more blood under the door and, in the pool, was the leg of a woman.

Swannack found two constables nearby who raced over and forced the door. Inside was the battered body of a woman.

Detective Sergeant W. Mooney and Detective Gordon Timmins of the Homicide Squad were on duty that night and arrived at the scene to find the cold Melbourne night had not congealed the flow of blood. It had by now flowed from the toilet and down five metres to the footpath. The red stream was broken only by the footprints of the people who had been first on the scene, destroying any evidence there.

The body of the elderly woman was wedged into a sitting position, jammed tightly between the side of the toilet and the cubicle wall. She had been battered about the head. Her neck had a number of specific, deep bruises, indicating strangulation.

But the thing which horrified the policemen most was the blood — the sheer volume of it. The body was white from the massive loss. It wasn't quite clear at first what had caused it but when they realised, they almost wished they hadn't found out.

A soft drink bottle had been driven into the woman's vagina, splitting through the thin wall of the bowel.

In most murders, the amount of blood loss is limited by the fact that the heart stops pumping. In this case, the woman was upright and the blood had simply drained away. Her body had been emptied.

Gordon Timmins began taking notes. There was no identification on the woman. Her blue floral dress had been pulled up over her waistline. It was untorn. Her red shoes were off and placed near her body. Only her right glove was on and her straw hat was wedged between her head and the wall. Her underpants were nowhere to be seen.

The next morning, the heavies in the Homicide Squad were called in. The first breakthrough came the next morning when the woman's handbag and shopping bag were found by a council worker in a railway cutting 100 metres from the toilet block.

The body was identified as Elsie Boyes, 68, a pensioner who lived in Windsor. She was a well-educated woman, the wife of a solicitor, who had a taste for drink. Each Monday, Friday and Saturday she would leave her husband and go drinking with a loose circle of friends who were mostly serious alcoholics. The drinking sessions would frequently move between pubs, wine bars and the tram shelter on the corner of Dandenong Road and Chapel Street.

Police believed the killer must have fled into nearby Alma Park, where he rifled the bags before throwing them down the embankment of the railway cutting that sliced the park in two.

Witnesses began to come forward. A woman passing by in a taxi had seen a man follow an elderly woman across Dandenong Road to the side of the toilet block. She was positive it was Mrs Boyes from the description of her clothes. She saw the woman go up the hedge-lined path into the toilets but did not see the man follow and she was unable to give a description.

A motorist, Ronald Tapp, said he saw a man following an elderly woman in the gardens between the shelter and the toilet. He saw the man grab her by the coat and pull her back as the woman shouted at him. "There was another woman in the shelter — small and thin in a red shortie coat," Tapp told police.

"This woman called out to the man 'leave her alone' and the man answered in a foreign language which I took to be Italian. As I drove off I thought I heard a woman scream."

That information launched a massive search for an Italian man and "the woman in the red shortie coat". She was found weeks later after police doorknocked every house in the area. She had feared for her safety and said she couldn't help the investigation anyway. As it turned out, she was right.

The man was never located and his connection with the murder never verified.

What has attracted police to this case in connection with Glover is almost purely circumstantial — that he was living three kilometres away in Hawthorn and the modus operandi was similar to his. The placement of the shoes, the brutal beating the killer inflicted on the woman before strangling her, and the petty theft of the handbag all bear resemblance to Glover's murders.

The presence of the Mediterranean man, however, would tend to make him the most likely suspect — but Glover was known to use Italian words with Dom Lopez and his mother at the Mosman Returned Servicemen's Club years later.

There is a weird series of coincidences which bear no direct relation to the murders but are, nevertheless, cause for wonder. Over the next seven years, Glover had two girlfriends who lived within ten minutes' walk of the murder scene. When he got married on 1 June 1968, it was two days short of the eleventh anniversary of the murder. The house into which the newlywed Glovers moved was at 21 Prentice Street East St Kilda, a 500 metre walk to the toilet block.

Other than to confirm that they have reopened this case in relation to Glover, the Victorian Homicide Squad has since imposed a degree of secrecy around their investigation. However, they have also examined Glover's movements in relation to the 1963 murder of Irene Kiddle, a 61-year-old Australian champion bridge player. She was found stabbed to death in a motiveless attack in a laneway at Windsor. A ladder was found propped against a window of a nearby unit, leading detectives to believe that Irene Kiddle may have disturbed a Peeping Tom. Because Glover's known method of attacking does not involve knives, detectives have all but ruled out a link.

Two other cases are also being examined by the Victorian Police. They are the stabbing murder of Emmie May Anderson, 78, in Clarenden Street, East Melbourne on 29 October 1961, and the 9 April 1968 murder of Christina Yankos, 62. Mrs Yankos was strangled with her dressing gown cord in a motiveless attack in her Albert Park home.

Despite Detective Sergeant O'Toole's enthusiasm for pinning more unsolved murders on Glover, he was not given the time required. So when Miranda Devine of the *Telegraph Mirror* contacted Detective Inspector Hagan with information that Glover had known the murdered Sydney socialite, Florence Broadhurst, it came as a shock.

Ms Devine was the first reporter to talk to any of Glover's relatives. She had been on their trail for some weeks when she spoke to Clifford's former wife Leonie. During the interview Leonie told of her haunting fear that she was somehow responsible for her friend's death, having introduced Florence to Glover.

Police had not talked to any of Glover's brothers and sisters at that stage. Glover's sister Pat, who has been affected deeply and has not spoken to him since his arrest, has since told O'Toole of her suspicion that her mother may have died by his hands. Due to the passage of time and the fact that Freda's body was cremated, both cases are likely to remain unsolved. Pat has also told police of Glover returning home late at night in Wolverhampton with blood on his clothes.

To date, the West Midlands Police have shown no interest in retracing his movements during his 24 years in their county. Only the Lincolnshire constabulary have examined Glover's period in their county and have found nothing more than theft.

Prison informants are alleged to have told police that Glover has boasted: "I've done things the cops don't even know about." But Glover says: "If I had done these things, what have I got to lose admitting to them? I'm not going anywhere here. I might as well say I'd done them, if I'd done them, but I haven't done them."

It is convenient, and even comforting, to blame Glover for these unsolved murders because if John Glover was not the perpetrator of the Central Coast attacks and the Boyes and Broadhurst murders, it means there are other John Glovers out there, unknown, unwatched, perhaps ready to strike again.

POSTSCRIPT

Much was said after the conviction of John Glover about the uniqueness of his crimes. He was the first known serial murderer of old women, it was said by police, psychiatrists and the media at the time.

There are, however, plenty of parallels between Glover and others of his ilk. His background bears comparison to others in a few striking ways but his crimes also have specific correlations.

The United States provides the examples.

• *Maryland 1961*: a jazz musician, Melvin D. Rees Jr, suspected of a string of murders, ambushed a family in their car. He bashed to death a young girl and shot the father in the head. The mother was found with her dress pulled up over her head and strangled with her own stockings.

• *New York 1974*: Calvin Jackson admitted to raping and then strangling 11 elderly women in their city apartments.

• *Atlanta, Georgia 1981*: 11 elderly black women were murdered in a short period and the crimes have remained unsolved.

But there is one particular serial killer who stands out with frightening clarity when looking for parallels to Glover. In 1977, the township of Columbus, Georgia, in the United States was in the grip of serial murderer Carlton Gary. He struck in Wynnton, one of the town's oldest and grandest suburbs.

Gary broke into elderly women's homes and raped them before strangling them with their own stockings. The bed sheets were usually pulled up over their heads.

He was caught and convicted but has maintained to this day, still on death row, that he did not kill the women: he watched while some other person did it all.

He was a black man who never knew his father; his mother was always on the move each time she met another man. Gary hated the white matrons of Columbus because it was for people like them that his beloved aunt and grandmother had worked as house servants, with long hours and little pay.

The above examples were compiled by an American psychologist, Dr Joel Norris, in his study Serial Killers (Doubleday, New York 1988). He devoted much research to Gary. As for the victims, Norris wrote, it was

Not that they weren't kindly churchgoing, charitable women; they were that and more. They were the epitome of what a Southern lady should be, but the antithesis of what Carlton Gary's mother actually had been. They simply looked right through Gary and other black males as if they weren't there at all. Thus when, after 20 years, Carlton Gary emerged as a full-blown serial killer, he struck from behind a mask of invisibility, ripping away at the very sex of the women who dominated his childhood but who looked right through him and strangling them with their own articles of clothing.

At the time of the killings, Carlton Gary was providing emotional support for his beloved aunt Alma. He would regularly visit her and walk with her in the grounds of her nursing home.

There is a fundamental similarity that unites all serial killers, according to Dr Norris. "The murder ... is a ritual re-enactment of the disastrous experiences of the killer's childhood. Only, this time, the killer tries to reverse the roles occupied in his childhood experiences. In this way he can almost magically cancel out his earlier suffering and re-establish his own power and identity."

John Glover's subconscious had been grappling since childhood with the treatment he received from his mother, the confusion at her behaviour and specifically the trauma of the photographs. The image of Freda, naked on her stomach, had been planted in his mind; it was the focal point about which all other thoughts of her would revolve. As Dr Rod Milton would later correctly hypothesise, it was the "picture in his head" about which he had subconsciously fantasised.

As for sanity, Dr Norris says it is very rare for a serial killer to fail the McNaghten legal sanity test. Most have been found sane by the courts because they seem to be fully aware of the nature of the charges against them and usually admit their guilt.

The reason their murder sprees can last so long is by virtue of their ability to act rationally within society. Does that make them sane? Norris argues: "They are treated as though they were within the range of normal human existence, yet had willingly become deviant. This is not the case. Serial murderers are non-personality types who eventually come alive only during the episodic cycle of murder."

Dr Norris claims that the similarities between serial killers — too numerous to cite here — indicate the sameness found in symptoms of a disease rather than coincidence. His findings correlate most closely with the diagnosis of Dr Strum in the Glover trial, who argued that Glover's criminal history was the symptom of the disease at work.

Among the common threads identified by Norris is an absence of "a sense of self which is the result of consistently negative parenting or non-parenting, and an almost hair-trigger violent response to external stimuli with no regard for the physical or social consequences". Recall John Glover's treatment of the cat burglar.

The FBI has calculated that there are at least 500 serial killers currently at large and unidentified in the United States. In the last 20 years, the US (with five per cent of world population) has produced 120 of the world's 160 identified serial killers. Norris fears the continued export of American culture will see the balance evened up.

Since the late 1970s Australia has witnessed the emergence of lone serial killers and serial "killing pairs". They include the following cases.

• Michael George Laurance, 36, a labourer from Griffith in New South Wales. He drowned three boys in a bath tub between 1984 and 1986 after luring them to his home, where he tied them up and raped them over a period of time. It emerged during his trial that he had molested more than 200 boys since the age of 15. He has since taunted police with claims of four more murders, but will not reveal the names.

• The "top-end killer", German-born tourist Joseph Schwab, 26. He shot dead five people during a ten day killing spree across remote northern Australia in June 1987. Dressed in camouflage, Schwab died in a shoot-out with police at a desert camp sight in Western Australia.

• Western Australian husband and wife killing pair, David and Catherine Birnie. Between October and November 1986 the couple abducted and murdered three women and a teenage girl, burying their bodies in remote bush graves. The women were held captive at the couple's Perth home for days where they were drugged, raped and photographed bound to a bed. A fifth intended victim managed to escape and raise the alarm. They are suspected of having murdered four other missing Perth women. The couple were also friends with Queenslander Barrie Watts, 34, who was convicted over the 1987 murder of 12-year-old schoolgirl Sian King.

• The "Truro murderers", James Miller and Christopher Worrell. Between 1976 and 1977 they embarked upon a spree of abduction, rape and murder, claiming the lives of seven young women (the majority hitchhikers) in Adelaide, South Australia. Six of the bodies were found buried in shallow graves in remote farming country at Truro in 1979. When arrested for the murders Miller claimed that Worrell, who died in a car accident in February 1977, was the killer. He showed police six graves, claiming that Worrell forced him to help dispose of the bodies.

• The "Tynong serial killer". To date this person has eluded all efforts by the Victorian Homicide Squad to catch him. The killer is believed responsible for the murders of four women and two teenage girls between 1980 and 1982. Four of the bodies were found close together off a bush track near Cannibal Creek at Tynong North and two off a lonely bush road at Frankston. One of the victims was the elderly aunt of the Victorian Police Commissioner. Police believe the killer has the demeanour of a priest or grandfather — someone who looks trustworthy. In 1989 an anonymous letter was sent to the mother of one of the victims, which police believe came from the killer. The writer boasted of four other cases of murder carried out in South Australia and New South Wales in which police have not located the bodies.

• "Mr Cruel" — at the time of writing the Victorian Homicide Squad fear that a paedophile dubbed "Mr Cruel" is emerging as a full-blown serial killer of young girls. He has been linked to the abduction of five girls since 1985. The first three were released alive, but since April 1991, his pattern has changed with the abduction and murder of Karmein Chan, 13, from her home. In June 1991 six-year-old Sheree Beasley was snatched while shopping with her mother at Rosebud. Her decomposed body was discovered three months later on the Mornington Peninsula. Police hunting Mr Cruel say he displays a knowledge of forensics and has gone to great lengths to ensure that he does not leave a trace of evidence on his surviving victims.